ANIMALS IN THE THIRD REICH

ALSO BY BORIA SAX

The Mythical Zoo: Animals in Myth, Legend, and Literature

Imaginary Animals: Monstrous, Wondrous, and Human

Stealing Fire: Memoir of a Boyhood in the Shadow of Atomic Espionage

The Raven and the Sun: Poems and Stories

*City of Ravens: The Extraordinary History of London, Its Tower,
And Its Famous Ravens*

Peculiar Flight

The Fantastic, Ordinary World of Lutz Rathenow (editor and translator)

Crow

*The Mythical Zoo: An A-Z of Animals in World Myth,
Legend, and Literature*

The Serpent and the Swan: Animal Brides in Literature and Folklore

*The Parliament of Animals: Legends and Anecdotes
From Books of Natural History*

The Frog King: On Fairy Tales, Fables and Anecdotes of Animals

Rheinland Market

I Am That Snowflake

The Romantic Heritage of Marxism: A Study of East German Love Poetry

Contacts/Kontakte: Poems and Writings of Lutz Rathenow
(editor and translator)

When the Glaciers Melted

MAXNotes Literature Guides:
Thomas Mann's Death in Venice
The Romance of Sir Gawain and the Green Knight
William Faulkner's The Sound and the Fury

ANIMALS
IN THE
THIRD REICH

by
BORIA SAX

With a Foreword by Klaus P. Fischer

YOGH &
THORN
PROVIDENCE, RI

Yogh & Thorn Books are published by
THE POET'S PRESS
279-1/2 Thayer Street
Providence, RI 02906

This is the 204th book from The Poet's Press

For my Mother, Susan Peters

*With loving memory especially of the times in Chicago
when I would stay up past my bedtime
and we would talk into the night.*

Then Nature approached me, calling me by name; and he bade me take heed, and gather wisdom from all the wonders of the world. And I dreamt that he led me out onto a mountain called Middle-Earth, so that I might learn from all kinds of creatures to love my Creator. And I saw the sun and the sea, and the sandy shores, and the places where birds and beasts go forth with their mates — wild snakes in the woods, and wonderful birds whose feathers were decked with many colors. And I could also see man and his mate, in poverty and in plenty, in peace and war; and I saw how men lived in happiness and misery both at once, and how they took money, and refused mercy.

— Langland, *Piers the Ploughman* (translated by J. F. Goodridge)

CONTENTS

LIST OF ILLUSTRATIONS

FOREWORD

by Klaus P. Fischer

The triumph of Nazism in the 1930s was not solely or even predominantly the result of a certain form of political extremism {Fascism} but rather the widespread acceptance, especially in intellectual circles, of a perverted form of biological-racial thinking. Its genealogical tree can be traced back to the distortions of Darwinian biology by German racialists who grafted a metaphysical world view onto Darwinian science that undermined the universalist doctrines of the Enlightenment and replaced them with highly-charged words, slogans, and images celebrating "struggle for existence," "survival of the fittest," competition, natural selection, the virtues of predators, contempt for the weak, and tribal exclusivity. Sometimes referred to as "völkisch ideology," it was a polluted intellectual stream that had absorbed the muddy waters of centuries of hatreds, prejudices, stereotypes, superstitious beliefs, and distorted perceptions of reality.

Anyone who wants to understand the rise of Nazism and the subsequent horrors it unleashed, especially the Holocaust, must understand the aberrant ideas embodied in this völkisch world view. This can be done either by looking at its overall philosophical framework or by focusing on its specific details and manifestations. Boria Sax's work *Animals in the Third Reich* attempts to solve the Nazi puzzle by looking at the individual pieces and using them as clues. This is a very worthwhile approach because the whole can often be explained by examining the relationship of the parts. A somewhat similar method, using Cartesian reductive analysis, was offered some time ago by William Sheridan Allen in his book *The Nazi Seizure of Power*, in which the puzzle of Hitler's rise to power was examined from the experience of a single German town between 1930 and 1935. In a different form, this is how Boria Sax analyzes the Nazi frame of mind. What appears at first sight to be a micro approach — the treatment of animals in the Third Reich — actually provides insight into the larger forces that made the Nazi horrors possible.

Animals in the Third Reich is not just a book about Nazis or animals, but also a revealing insight into the rest of us mortals who have increasingly blurred the boundary between humans and animals in a way that betrays both as sentient beings. In the course of this fascinating study, Boria Sax has managed to uncover some very important connections between how the Nazis perceived and treated animals and how they treated people, especially those people — Jews, Gypsies, homosexuals, the mentally ill — that they considered to be biologically inferior. Thinking about people as belonging to different animal species, including "inferior" kinds of animal species, compelled the Nazis to construct a new *scala naturae* of "superior" and "inferior" beings. As Sax has put it, just as Stalin "murdered in the name of the downtrodden, the Nazis murdered in the name of nature, invoking animals and landscapes."

In their obsession to create a biocracy, a racial-biological community of superior Aryans, the Nazis spared no expense in endowing chairs of racial science, founding racial institutes, and hiring famous scientists to help underwrite their racial delusions. Of particular importance is Sax's extensive documentation relating to Konrad Lorenz, the Nobel laureate, who willingly and enthusiastically promoted the cause of racism and Judeophobia — a sobering illustration that delusions are sometimes fueled by the very best minds holding professional chairs in the world's premier universities.

It was a mark of Nazi evil that animals in the Third Reich were treated with a far greater degree of kindness than the "biological enemies" the Nazis had targeted for discrimination, incarceration, and extermination. Some of the strictest laws protecting animals were passed during the Third Reich, laws that regulated the treatment of animals in minute detail: how to provide for them, protect them, transport them, breed them, and slaughter them. Boria Sax shows how all this sheds lurid light on the sort of obsessive, dehumanized, and racist mentality that was needed to carry out the Holocaust. The book warns us in no uncertain terms that we must not allow such racial-biological thinking to flourish and to infect our political life, even if this is done under the benevolent guise of making life so much healthier and happier for all of us.

March 2000

INTRODUCTION
TO THE SECOND EDITION

Not many younger people can appreciate quite how obsessed my own generation, the baby-boomers, was with the Nazis and the Holocaust. Even as it terrified us, this preoccupation often provided a paradoxical feeling of stability and comfort. When overwhelmed by cultural, social, and technological upheavals, we looked to the Nazis to provide an image of evil that was absolute and unequivocal.

In the decades following World War II, a question that constantly seemed to hover in the background, to surface in political rhetoric or moody reflections was, "Are we like the Nazis?" The true answer, which we would not often dare to acknowledge, is surprisingly simple: "Yes, we all are." Nazis looked, talked, and felt much as we do; they could be bland or brilliant, detached or sentimental, witty or dull, hunters or vegans, in fact just about all of the things that anybody else could be.

But what could one make of the circumstance that the Nazis not only expressed intense concern about the suffering of animals, but also backed it up by passing extensive legislation for the protection of animals? When I began writing about this paradox, I imagined concluding my book by banishing all confusion with some resounding moral at the end. My incisive analysis would cut through society's rationalizations, reveal our partial complicity in Nazi crimes, and then tell how we might regain our moral purity. That was my daydream, but things didn't work out that way. I tried all sorts of morals, but none of them seemed to fit my narrative very well.

Much of the mythologizing of the Holocaust comes back to the conception, popularized in large part by Eli Wiesel, of Hitler and the Nazis as representing absolute evil. To be sure, Hitler was among the great villains in history, and Nazism was among the most destructive of doctrines. But to absolutize an evil is to displace it from the realm of history to that of ideas and myths. Once Hitler ceases to be comprehensible in terms of chronological events, further mythologizing of him becomes much easier. One can, for example, maintain, as some of his admirers do, that Hitler escaped to a secret Nazi base beneath three miles of ice in Antarctica, where he and his followers are using their advanced "vril technology" to manufacture flying saucers.

In many ways, I now incline to the position of Peter Nowak in his book, *The Holocaust in American Life*, that the Holocaust itself has no lesson for us beyond the sort of moralizing that will seem disappointingly bland. The conclusion was very controversial when his book first came out in 2000, though many younger scholars simply take it for granted now. Nowak's thesis only means that the tale of Nazi Germany is like the rest of history, which offers hardly anything in the way of simple lessons. Nevertheless, it is not always easy to feel satisfied with the intricate, though ever tentative and incomplete, links of societal causes and effects.

Simply raising the theme of animals in the Third Reich means that our narrative is no longer only an account of what human beings have done to one another, but also about our relations with the natural world. If, viewed against the magnitude and terror of historical events, our personal lives appear almost trivial, the lives of animals may seem more so, and even to raise the subject can at first seem either insensitive or pedantic. At the same time, this new dimension places the events in an even vaster perspective still, one in which even the greatest battles and horrendous crimes can begin to fade into insignificance. This is the standpoint of evolutionary time, in which humankind itself may be no more than a relatively brief episode. Perhaps the focus on animals may help us to find a more harmonious balance between the personal, historic, and cosmic levels, on which, simultaneously we conduct our lives.

Since I first wrote *Animals in the Third Reich*, my account of Nazi animal protection has been widely accepted in scholarly communities, and with less resistance than anticipated. The book has been published in Japanese and Czech translation and received an 'outstanding academic title' award from the journal *Choice*. In preparing the original text for republication, I have confined myself to a very few small corrections and some rephrasing. The present volume, however, also incorporates an appendix entitled "Nazi Totemism," originally an article in *Zooanthropology* (#1), which discusses subsequent research on animals in Nazi Germany. In addition, it offers a new theory about the combination of solicitude towards animals and brutality toward people that ran through the Nazi movement. I leave it to the reader to decide whether my views have changed.

Boria Sax
February 2013

ACKNOWLEDGMENTS

Parts of this book have been published as an article entitled "What is a Jewish Dog? Konrad Z. Lorenz and the Cult of Wildness" in the journal *Society and Animals*, vol.5, #1 (1997). Another section was published under the title "Evolution: Why the Fuss?" in *ISAZ Newsletter*, #10 (1995). An article entitled "The Holocaust as Blood Sacrifice" which incorporates material from a few chapters of this book has been published in *Anthrozoös*, vol. 13, #1 (2000). Dr. Arnold Arluke first suggested that I write this book. Dr. M. Donald McGavin provided me with medical information on kosher slaughter. Belinda Davis supplied her excellent, though still unpublished, material on "the great pig murder" during World War I. Dr. Claudia Koonz provided me with an illustration for the chapter on apes. Dr. Fritz Martin Brumme and Dr. Helmut Meyer supplied me with several valuable materials on veterinary medicine in the Third Reich. Piotr Daszkiewicz provided me with information on the "false aurochs" of Hermann Göring. Dr. James Serpell directed me to materials on the social organization of wolves. Dr. Peter Klopfer read individual sections and later a draft of the entire manuscript, making useful criticisms. Paul De Angeles provided useful advice, and I would also like to thank him for his graciousness and patience. Dr. Jonathan R. Burt also suggested some corrections and made several valuable comments. My wife, Linda Sax, helped with the editing and proofreading and made several stylistic suggestions. Richard Balkin, my agent, worked faithfully and well to find a publisher. George Justus Lawler, Evander Lomke and others at Continuum Publishing took much care with the manuscript. The United States Holocaust Memorial Museum was helpful in supplying archival material and illustrations. Other illustrations in this book are taken from *Picture Book of Devils, Demons and Witches*, edited by Ernst and Johanna Lehner (New York: Dover Books, 1971), *Jews in Christian Art: An Illustrated History* by Heinz Schreckenberg (New York: Continuum, 1996), and *Art of the Third Reich* by Peter Adam (New York: Harry N. Abrams, 1995). Biblical quotations are from *The Jerusalem Bible*. Unless otherwise indicated, translations in this book are my own.

PROLOGUE

CHAPTER I
WHY ANIMALS?

> I knew full well that what I was seeing now was the essence of human
> history. Today the Poles tormented the Jews; yesterday the Russians and
> Germans had tormented the Poles. Every history book was a tale of murder,
> torture, and injustice; every newspaper was drenched in blood.
> — Isaac Bashevis Singer, *Love and Exile*
> (on being harassed by anti-Semitic hooligans in Poland)

BESIDE ME IS a well-worn copy of *Im Wald und auf der Heide: Ein Buch
vom deutschen Wald und deutschen Wild* {In the Forest and on the
Heath: A Book of the German Forests and German Animals} by
Hermann Löns, a popular author among the Nazis. The text consists
primarily of descriptions of German landscapes, and is accompanied by
138 black-and-white photographs. It is written in an austere style with few
metaphors or other literary adornments. The photographs are what first
caught my attention and moved me to buy the book. In a typical Germanic
way, they show only overcast skies and asymmetrical trees. Nevertheless,
they are full of lovingly recorded detail such as close-ups of a mother bird
feeding her young. It describes these somewhat forbidding landscapes
vividly, but usually from the perspective of hunters. Occasionally, the text
begins to revel in brutality.

I learned from the inscriptions in the front cover that the book was
given to a young man named Joachim Bulwachter by the Schott family on
the occasion of his Bar Mitzvah. An ideal gift for such an occasion, no
doubt — except for a few things! The book bears no date of publication,
but the notes by the photographer are dated 1932, and my copy comes from
the fourth printing; it probably came out a few years after Hitler's rise to
power.

The celebration of the German woods and animals, inspiring in itself,
was a usual feature of the "blood and soil" literature that anticipated many
themes of the Nazi movement. When, if ever, did Joachim Bulwachter and
the Schott family feel a sense of irony about this gift? I do not know. Since
I bought the book in America, however, I imagine that Joachim did not
die in a concentration camp but managed to emigrate in time. My guess
is that he valued the book enough to bring it with him.

Every historical event loses its visceral immediacy over the decades,
and the Holocaust is certainly no exception. The expression of pain and
anger is becoming increasingly ritualized in ceremonial speeches on formal
occasions. Many universities have Holocaust Studies departments, and
many special libraries are entirely devoted to the Holocaust. No other

<3>

historical era of such brevity is the subject of an entire discipline. Why do we devote so much time to these studies, to such an extent they sometimes seem to eclipse the millennia of Jewish and German history before? Surely it is because many people presume that events so horrible must necessarily have some commensurate lesson. But the sheer mass of scholarship necessitates increasing specialization, making a comprehensive picture ever more elusive. As even minor officials become the subjects of biographies, the field becomes more fragmented. The historian Yehuda Bauer has complained that academic treatment tends to turn the Holocaust "into a vast sea of footnotes and rationalistic analysis, a subject for academic careers, doctoral theses and suchlike, avoiding the abyss that was the Holocaust . . ." (p. 44).

Scholarship of the Holocaust is by now fairly conventionalized, and it does not easily come to grips with events as bizarre and as brutal as those of the Third Reich. The leader of this regime imagined himself a wolf as he screamed to adoring crowds. His most powerful deputy was a prissy little man who claimed to be the reincarnation of an ancient Saxon king and tried to breed human beings like chickens. At times, one can wonder how such lunatics could, say, negotiate a trip to the market, let alone run a vast empire. This historical episode seems to lead us into a distorted world where the usual expectations no longer apply.

Or do they? We are sufficiently far from the Nazi period to see that the regime was preposterous and insane, but we are not yet able to analyze the pathology with much confidence. There is no single distinctive feature or even group of features that sharply separates the Nazi society from the "civilized" world. Today we still have everything from the crudest prejudice to highly sophisticated theories of racial superiority, from an aesthetic of violence to medicalization of all ethical problems. Nevertheless, we keep asking, "How was that possible?"

One of the strangest debates to be carried on in academia is the question of whether or not the Holocaust is "unique."[1] Seldom is so much intensity and so much highly technical argument bestowed on an issue that is so vaguely defined. A lot of different reasons are offered for the uniqueness of the Holocaust: it was exceptionally systematic; it was perpetrated by a Western nation; it was directed against a religion. I do not at all deny that the debate has been productive. What, after all, would scholarship be without passion, especially on such a subject? Elusive though the question of "uniqueness" may be, it taps into elemental feelings that practitioners often try to exclude from scholarship. Quite a few have openly expressed frustration with the limitations of their discipline. Dan Diner, for example, has called Auschwitz "a black box of explanation,"

---

[1] For some of the debates see: Nolte et al., passim; Shandley, passim; and Rosenbaum, passim.

<4>

adding that it may only acquire meaning "outside of history" (Maier, 92). But the explanations offered by history are always partial and generally tentative. The historical record of every period is full of gaps, and we expect historians to disagree radically in their moral judgments. No event is ever entirely explained. Auschwitz has been explicated more extensively and probably better than most. The problem is that the explanations of it are very unsatisfying. What scholars such as Diner are up against is not the historical uniqueness of Auschwitz but the inevitable limits of an academic discipline which is unable to provide all that its practitioners demand. History can illuminate patterns and provide causal explanations; it is questionable whether it can ever truly supply "meaning." The vast scale of the suffering and destruction perpetrated by the Nazis makes the usual sort of historical explanation appear trivial. The passion generated by the subject pushes the studies beyond the inevitable limitations of any formal discipline.

Whether we choose to call the Holocaust "unique," most of the Nazi crimes unfortunately were not. History, once portrayed in our school texts as a sort of glamorous pageant, appears increasingly to be in the famous words of Voltaire, "little else than a picture of human crimes and misfortunes." The debates about the uniqueness of the Holocaust and related questions can often become a macabre competition as participants toss back and forth figures of hundred-thousands, millions, and even tens of millions murdered in one historical era or another, from Caesar's conquest of Gaul to the terror of the Khmer Rouge. The challenge of the Nazi period often impels researchers to the furthest confines of the academic discipline of history, beyond which lie theology, metaphysics, and uncharted areas.

The Nazi movement originally drew much of its power from mythic symbols, and it retains a mythic ambience in popular and even scholarly culture. In one study, Alvin Rosenfeld argued that "Not so much for its numbers . . . , although they were enormous, or for its political motives, which seem negligible, but for its nihilistic passions and the mythic and almost metaphysical nature of its design does the Nazi *Endlösung* stand out from other crimes of the century" (18). But there is no reason why this nihilistic fury should mark the limit of our understanding. In any area of study, when familiar approaches are unable to make much progress that is an indication that it is time for a paradigm shift. To analyze the motivations of the Nazis, we must examine their movement not only as history but also as myth.

<5>

The Importance of Animals

Günter Grass, as a young German writer at the end of World War II, faced the problem of how to confront the Nazi period. This was far too vast and important to ignore. Its horrors called for the most unequivocal moral condemnation, yet such an approach was not aesthetically promising. Sophisticated literature relies on nuance, not on polemic or melodrama. Grass attempted to solve this problem by telling the story of Nazi Germany through highly alienated characters who may not have been innocent but were at least exempted from knowing participation in the institutions of the Third Reich. In his first novel, *The Tin Drum* (*Die Blechtrommel*), the dwarf Oscar Manzereth was such a figure. In fictional works that Grass set in the Nazi period, the focus was never on either centers of power or concentration camps but rather on the chaotic lives of human beings on the fringes of historical events. By telling about the period partly through alienated people Grass created psychic distance. This alienation enabled his characters to survive and even to have adventures in the shadow of the concentration camps. It is not altogether different from the alienation which enables us to write scholarly studies of the Holocaust. Literature has always been used to confront problems obliquely when intellectual, emotional, or practical constraints prevent us from addressing them in a more direct way; it is a means of stepping back from events and gaining objectivity. In composing his later works, Grass realized that animals were ideal symbols of alienation; he told about the Nazi era through stories of dogs or rats.

The discussion of the Nazi era in this book centers not on people, whether Germans, Christians, Jews, Communists, Poles, Russians, or Americans; it centers on animals. This subject of animals in Nazi Germany has understandably been overshadowed by the human tragedy. There are, however, illuminating parallels and analogies between treatment of the animals and that of human beings.

When these analogies extend to the Holocaust, this could impress some people as "trivialization." My comparison between factory farms and death camps is not intended to suggest that these institutions are equivalent in every respect, and they are certainly not in moral standing. Comparisons between historical phenomena are always metaphors, neither more nor less. They are to be learned from where they prove applicable and disregarded when they are not. One result of the taboo against comparisons to the Holocaust is that it gives analogies when they are made {and they are made constantly} an excessive rhetorical force. A taboo against comparisons can, furthermore, prevent us from applying any lessons drawn from the Holocaust to contemporary problems.

The reluctance to compare other events with the Holocaust is less a matter of historical analysis than of religion. Elie Wiesel has called the

<6>

Holocaust "equal to the revelation at Sinai" in religious significance (Novick, 201). Leon Wieseltier has called survivors' accounts of the Holocaust "the American Jewish equivalent of saints and relics" (200). The innumerable monuments to the victims of the Holocaust recall early medieval churches filled with the relics and pictures of martyrs. As the Holocaust is sacralized, comparisons are perceived as blasphemy. This response is related to the traditional Jewish prohibition against "graven images." It is less a fear of social consequences than of the numinous power of certain symbolic expressions.

My primary objection to the prohibition against comparisons is that it makes an unreasonable demand. Even Yahweh, the deity so sublime that he cannot properly be named, is constantly approached through metaphors in the Old Testament. Thus in the psalms, he is called a "shepherd," a "lamp," a "rock," and so on. These images are not a trivialization of God, and so it is not clear why comparisons, even mundane ones, necessarily trivialize the Holocaust. The Bible uses a similarly wide range of metaphors for destruction of both Israel and of other kingdoms.

The Hebrews, unlike some other peoples of the ancient world such as the Egyptians, did not accord animals great power but neither did they regard them as trivial. The prophets constantly used imagery drawn from animals to describe the sorrows and aspirations of the Hebrew people. Consider, for example, the words of Joel in a time of severe famine:

What mourning from the beasts!
The herds of cattle wander bewildered
because they have no pasture.
Even the flocks of sheep must bear their punishment.

To you, Yahweh, I cry:
fire has devoured the pastures on the hearth,
flame has burned up
every tree in the orchard.
Even the wild beasts wait anxiously for you,
for the watercourses have run dry,
and fire has devoured the pastures on the heath (Joel 1:18-20).

What is "Human"?

This book is an examination of the ways in which metaphors drawn from animals and the natural world were abused in Nazi Germany. The ways in which we define "humanity" in ethical and philosophic terms need not correspond closely to the accepted biological definitions. We grant human beings certain dignity and rights which are not usually accorded

<7>

to animals. In this sense, "human" status has often been in practice a matter of race, nationality, gender, class, and many other factors. In the first century B. C. E. the Roman scholar Pliny the Elder observed in his *Natural History* that for people of another race, ". . . a foreigner is hardly a member of the human species!" (book 7, chap. 7). An emerging discipline known as "Anthrozoology" consists largely of studying the ways in which we use comparisons to mark these boundaries between human beings and other creatures.

For those who wish to pursue such study further, it is now carried in such publications as *Society and Animals*, *Anthrozoös* and the *ISAZ Newsletter*. Perhaps the most systematic study of these boundaries is *Humans and Other Animals* by Barbara Noske, which surveys the way people understand the border line between animals and human beings in anthropology, biology, sociology, agriculture, and a wide range of other human activities. Corbey and Mason have written, the ". . . seemingly endless construction and reconstruction of the boundaries of the Self and Other also passes by way of an animal idiom . . ." (91). Western conceptions of the divide between people and animals sometimes excluded the inhabitants of India or Africa from full human status. The idea that Negroes are close to apes, for example, was frequently used to justify the slave trade. Around the middle of the twentieth century, the psychologist Karl Menninger wrote:

> I take it to be implicitly observed that . . . attitudes, both conscious and unconscious, stem from an unconscious displacement from a human object toward whom they cannot be expressed. . . . Many persons, for example, who are very fond of certain pets, become dimly or even clearly aware of the erotic element involved, and here I mean the physically exciting element. But few, I am sure . . . become aware except through psychoanalysis of the fact that the animals represent a sister, mother, father, or other relative. Similarly, cruelty to animals may be characterized by the perpetrators as uncontrollable rage, justified sport, necessary evil, or even sadistic perversion, but this much insight never extends to recognition that the real objects of his mistreatment are human figures toward whom such behavior could not be expressed (44).

This analysis is from an orthodox Freudian perspective that may seem dated today, but it clearly contains a partial truth. Sometimes treatment of animals, whether kindness or cruelty, is a displacement of feelings about human beings. But why should the displacement move in only one direction? Animals of their own accord can sometimes inspire feelings in us such as intense fear, affection, or resentment, and these reactions may then be displaced on human beings.

<8>

Jean-Pierre Digard writes that since the advent of domestication, "In every case, one sees that animals have served human beings as means of orientation, by defining the appropriate place of men and women in the universe. Human hierarchies, however elaborate, vary according to the historical epoch or legal system and correspond to the types of relations with domesticated animals" (71). Keith Thomas has pointed out in his study of early modern Britain: "At home animal domestication furnished many of the techniques for dealing with delinquency: bridles for scolding women; cages, chains and straw for madmen; halters for wives sold at auction in the market. . . . Domestication thus became the archetypal pattern for other kinds of social subordination." He goes on to argue that domestication also provided the context for slavery, with its markets, brandings, and continual labor (44-45).

In Paris around the end of the Middle Ages, a Christian man and his Jewish mistress were convicted of "bestiality," sex between people and animals, and both were burned alive. The same legal principle was applied not only to Jews but also to Turks and Saracens "in as much as such persons in the eye of the law and our holy faith differ in no wise from beasts" (Evans, 153).

Writing of the medieval persecutions of heretics, witches, and Jews, René Girard has pointed out "the gradual disappearance of the borderline between animal and man in those who are marked as victims" (*Scapegoat*, 48). The inquisitors believed that sorcerers were shape-shifters, who could run about in the form of animals. Close association with a pet, whether dog, cat, or bird, was considered grounds for suspicion of witchcraft. So was any deformity, such as a foot that might suggest the cloven hoof of a goat. In his study of propaganda images, Sam Keen remarks, "That we regularly use a repertoire of animal, reptile, and insect images to dehumanize our enemies shows the extent to which modern technological societies are rooted in a metaphysic of war against nature" (134). Such imagery of war is universal, but it was possibly used by the Nazis even more than by their contemporaries. Their enemies were regularly depicted in posters and propaganda as monkeys, leeches, rats, pigs, snakes, and a wide range of other creatures.

This sort of rhetoric often mirrors or anticipates military reality. In World War I it became common for both sides to compare their enemies to beetles, ants, locusts, and other pests. At the same time technologies developed for fighting insect pests were frequently transferred to the battlefield, while poisons developed for use against enemies were often turned on bugs. Thus Zyklon B was initially developed as a powerful insecticide used to fumigate army barracks (Breitman, 202-204). When its extreme potency was observed, it was first tested on Russian prisoners of war (Russell, 1513), then later used for mass killings of Jews, Gypsies, the

<9>

handicapped, and others. In a parallel way insecticides such as DDT were a byproduct of military technologies (Russell, 1507).

The rhetoric and policies of the Nazis constantly blurred the roles of animals and human beings. Höss, the commander of Auschwitz, said of Russians prisoners of war, "They were no longer men. . . . They'd turned into beasts who thought only about eating" (Todorov, 160). Kurt Franz, a commander of the Treblinka death camp, would order his dog to attack prisoners using the words "Man, bite the dog" (Friedlander, 239). The Nazis herded human beings, branded them with numbers, neutered them, and slaughtered them industrially, as people had traditionally done with animals. This blurring of boundaries, however, also applied in many ways to those who were considered genetically relatively pure. In the Lebensborn hostels of the Nazi state, in which young Aryan women were impregnated by SS men to increase the population,[2] girls were sometimes referred to as "cows" to be mated with a "stud-bull." Himmler demanded reports on the milk production of nursing mothers and gave prizes to those who established records (Engelmann, 199-200). The depersonalization demanded of victims in concentration camps was also demanded of guards and officers. They were expected to show complete and unquestioning obedience (Todorov, 165-169). As Konrad Lorenz, who was a Nazi party member, put it, "For us, race and ethnicity are everything, the individual human being as good as nothing" ("Nochmals," 32). This common depersonalization did not bring anything like equality. Other distinctions took the place of the traditional divide between animals and human beings, particularly those between different ethnic and racial groups. While one might still be a half-breed or "Mischling" {a word also used for hybrid animals}, it became impossible to be both a German and a Jew.

These categories, as I will show later, were extended to animals. A "Jewish" dog might be shot, but a "Germanic" dog would be treated with honor. When a group of farmers in a small community pooled their money to buy a bull for their cows, the government authorities decided that their bull was "Jewish" and would not be allowed to reproduce. Bella Fromm, who reported this in 1936, remarked that she was "overcome to discover there was such a thing as a non-Aryan cow" (Fromm, 192).

This book describes the complex, and often paradoxical, attitudes of the Nazis toward animals. To do this, I compare several perspectives on the treatment of animals in the Third Reich, including those of zoologists, public officials, veterinarians, soldiers, students, painters, sculptors, novelists, pet-owners, and the general public. Nazis, just like other people,

---

[2] The activities of the Lebensborn hostels were kept strictly secret during the Nazi period, and there is still controversy about them today. The hostels did provide sexual partners for young women in order to breed Aryan children, though not as often as was rumored. For a summary of the goals, activities, and organizational structures of Lebensborn, see Bäumer, pp. 103-08.

<10>

could be either kind or cruel to animals, either intimate or detached. The Nazis identified with nature as a harsh and implacable power. The obedience they demanded of others and themselves was the subordination of behavior to nature. It was obedience to the force known as "instinct." In their nihilistic perspective the important distinction was not between "humans" and "animals," at least in any traditional way. It was between victor and vanquished, between master and slave. The underlying paradigm was, as I will show, that of predator and prey.

The ways in which we distinguish, morally as well as biologically, between animals and human beings have fluctuated constantly from one historical era to the next. There is no reason to believe that this shifting is about to stop. The traditional divide between animals and human beings is challenged intellectually by Darwin's theory of evolution. Furthermore, new capacities such as transplanting organs or even genetic material from animals to people threaten to blur the distinction more than ever. We live in an era when the sharp boundaries by which people once divided reality have grown unclear: between people and animals, living beings and objects, men and women, heroes and villains, the Holocaust and normal life. Some understand this as a sign of cultural decline, a descent from order into chaos. For others, it is a liberation from our mental prisons. I prefer not to attempt a final judgment on this blurring of categories, though I have shared both the panic and the exhilaration that can accompany the process. I do not see it as a permanent state but as a reshuffling of basic divisions as we pass from one historical era to the next. The process is perhaps nowhere more apparent than in our confused and contradictory attitudes toward and animals, adored as pets and brutalized as meat.

Harold Herzog, a professor of psychology writing in response to an article on Nazi animal protection by Arnold Arluke and me, observed in *The American Scholar*, ". . . Nazi animal protection is the ultimate paradox . . . for it may be the central metaphor haunting all our relations with other species. Is a vegetarian Hitler any more paradoxical than the pain physiologist who administers electrical shocks to devocalized beagles in the quest for a better analgesia during the day but who is met at the door by his faithful cocker spaniel when he returns home from his laboratory? Or the animal rights/vegetarian cat owner?" (348). This paradox reminds us of the inconsistencies in the treatment of both human beings and animals in our own society. Nazi Germany can thus serve as a mirror for us, revealing the intricate multiplicity of standards by which we judge both animals and people. In probing Nazi Germany, we may discover much about ourselves.

<11>

PART I

ANIMALS
AND THE INTELLECTUAL ORIGINS
OF NATIONAL SOCIALISM

CHAPTER 2
PREDATOR AND PREY

How can wolf and lamb agree — ?
Just so with sinner and devout.
What peace can there be between hyena and dog?
And what peace between rich man and poor?
Wild donkeys are the prey of dessert lions;
so too, the poor are the quarry of the rich.

— *Ecclesiastes* (13: 17-19)

AFTER COMPLETING THE work of Creation, the Biblical Yahweh says, "To all wild beasts, all birds of heaven and all living reptiles on the earth I give the foliage of plants for food" (Genesis 1:30-1), strongly suggesting that animals and human beings did not initially eat meat. Isaiah describes the Kingdom of God as a place where lion and lamb will feed together (11:6-8). Predatory mammals and birds are considered unclean in the Old Testament (Leviticus 11:1-19). Jewish tradition views domestication, particularly of herbivorous animals, as a return to the peaceful state of subordination to Adam that came before the Fall. This attitude is a legacy of the origins of the Hebrew people as herders, for whom large predators such as lions or wolves were a continuous threat. According to Jewish tradition, animals and human beings were vegetarian until the Flood, at which time Yahweh allowed predation as a concession to weakness of the flesh. After the Flood human beings, or at least Jews, are only prohibited from eating flesh with blood in it (Genesis 9:1-5). The ideal of a world without predation was carried over into Christianity. It was a zoological version of universal conversion. Just as all pagans might someday embrace the cross, all carnivores might someday eat grass in the "peaceable kingdom."

The Christian Eucharist substitutes vegetable products for meat. Bread is eaten as flesh while the wine is drunk as blood. The whole ceremony betrays an ambiguous attitude toward the dietary restrictions of the Jews which was characteristic of early Christianity. Most Christians, including Catholics and Lutherans, believe the transubstantiation of the Eucharist is literal rather than symbolic. The Eucharist violates kosher practice by the drinking of blood. On the other hand, the Eucharist, apart from its mystic transformation, is still a vegetarian meal. Some passages of the *New Testament* contain explicit repudiations of Jewish dietary laws. A vision recounted by Peter in *Acts* seems to celebrate the new freedom with an orgiastic culinary abandon:

<15>

I . . . saw all sorts of animals and wild beasts — everything
possible that could walk, crawl or fly. Then I heard a voice that
said to me, "Now, Peter, kill and eat!" Certainly not, Lord;
nothing profane or unclean has ever crossed my lips. And a
second time the voice spoke from heaven, "What God has made
clean, you have no right to call profane" (11: 5-10).

Apart from some monastic orders, Christianity continued the eating
of meat, but it had little ceremony to sanction or consecrate this food. The
prayer with which the hunter once asked forgiveness of his game became
the giving of thanks to God before a meal. This meant that Christians in
general had no means of dealing with their uneasiness at the killing and
consumption of other creatures. Their discomfort could only fester, and
the ideal of a world without predation continued to be important in
Christian culture.

Pagan and Christian Symbolism

What we know as "Western civilization" has been a series of uneasy
compromises between two competing systems of animal symbolism with
predators glorified in one and demonized in the other. Large predators
such as wolves and lions are models, rivals, and sometimes personal threats
to human beings, and they evoke a strange combination of admiration and
terror. Eliade has written that in ancient Eurasia and the East,

> . . . the invasions and conquests of the Indo-Europeans and the
> Turko-Mongols will be undertaken under the sign of the
> supreme hunter, the carnivore. The members of the Indo-
> European military confraternities {Männerbünde} and the
> nomadic horsemen of Central Asia behaved toward the
> sedentary populations that they attacked like carnivores
> hunting, strangling, and devouring the herbivores of the steppe
> and the farmer's cattle (*Stone Age*, 36).

The indigenous warrior cultures of Europe and the Near East adopted
fierce animals, usually predators, as emblems, in admiration of their power
and courage — the wolf, lion, boar, falcon, and eagle. The Hebrews were
a notable exception. Even the Biblical kings of Israel, in contrast with those
of Egypt and Mesopotamia, are not celebrated as mighty hunters. The
Bible repeatedly forbids eating flesh that has been torn by predators (e.g.,
Exodus 22:31; Leviticus 7:24). This prevents use of hunting dogs, a nearly
universal part of the chase. Many Orthodox Jews will not eat meat from
the hunt at all.

<16>

This totemic symbolism of competing religions also reflected social class since Christianity had begun primarily among slaves. Since the end of the Neolithic period, when large animals became rare, hunting big game was a privilege of the royalty and nobility. Up to the start of the modern period, hunting large animals was forbidden to the peasantry, often under penalty of mutilation or even death. Common people were allowed to possess neither the weapons nor dogs used in hunting. Eating of meat was a luxury that most people could rarely afford. When captives including Christian slaves were fed to lions or other beasts of prey at Roman circuses for public amusement, the gory spectacle used predation to symbolically affirm the privilege of caste.

Occasionally some of the patriarchs of Israel were identified with predators, for example the lion as a symbol of Judah. The warrior symbolism also influenced Christianity. The lion and eagle were used as symbols of evangelists. Both religions, however, tended to prefer animals that were raised as food, usually herbivorous, and often domesticated — the fish, lamb, ox, and dove. The customs of the various social strata merged further as the Roman Emperor Constantine began to embrace Christianity in the year 312. As Europe was gradually Christianized, the use of predators as symbols was retained by aristocratic houses in the regalia of battle. In the Crusades, Christianity became increasingly a religion of warriors. This trend culminated during the High Middle Ages when the military tradition was fused with Christian devotion in the cult of chivalry and courtly love. Knights were expected to show the virtues of loyalty and fierceness on the battlefield, while being gentle and courteous at home. Their violent and erotic impulses were, as the Arthurian romances show, only precariously controlled by knightly codes.

A similar tension between the pagan and Judeo-Christian systems of animal symbolism has continued to this day. Those animals that were favored in heraldry and as national symbols have always tended to be large, wild, carnivorous, and purely bred. The wolf, eagle, and lion were favorites. These still evoke images of archaic warrior societies. Benjamin Franklin gently poked fun at these fantasies, already anachronistic in his time, when he suggested adopting the turkey rather than the eagle as a national symbol. In the aristocratic animal parks of the Middle Ages through the early nineteenth century, large carnivores were especially popular and people delighted in bloody spectacles. Early public zoos also appealed to a taste for horror by stressing and exaggerating the savagery of their animals. Feeding the great cats was a popular event. Around the end of the eighteenth century, visitors who could not afford the price of admission to the Tower Menagerie in London might instead bring along a dog or cat to be used as food for the large predators (Blunt, 16-17). In 1806 an advertisement stated that the duke of Cumberland, on visiting a British

<17>

menagerie, "could scarce express his gratification at being so highly delighted with the great Bengal tyger devouring a whole bullock's head, horns and all!" (Ritvo, 224). The bars on the cages of animals were not there exclusively for safety but also as a symbolic acknowledgment of the ferocity of the animals.

With the rise of more democratic forms of government in the eighteenth and nineteenth centuries, predators were increasingly stigmatized as cruel. Princes had ruled under the emblems of predators, and now predators were blamed for the rapacity of royal houses. The dream of an idyllic past without the eating of flesh was given secular form by thinkers like Georges Luis Compte de Buffon, who believed that predation was a corruption of nature (Sax, "Predators," 61-64). Oliver Goldsmith in his enormously popular *History of Animated Nature* condemned all carnivores as "cowardly by nature," while stating that "The greatest animals are made for an inoffensive life, to range the plains and forest without injuring others ..." (170-171).

For many philosophers and theologians up through at least the middle of the nineteenth century, the propensity of animals to eat one another was an essential flaw in the universe itself. This was true particularly of those who espoused a method known as "natural theology," which endeavored to reveal a divine plan in the construction of the world, thus demonstrating the benevolence of the Creator. William Paley, one of the foremost spokesmen for this school, wrote in his highly influential *Natural Theology*, first published in 1802:

> ...the subject ... of animals *devouring* one another, forms the chief, if not the only instance, in the works of the Deity, of an economy stamped by marks of design, in which the character of utility can be called in question. The case of *venomous* animals is of much inferior consequence to the case of prey, and, in some degree is also included under it. To both cases it is probable that many more reasons belong than those of which we are in possession (331).

Others felt even more helpless before the phenomenon. "Why has Nature established a system so cruel?" asked William Smellie. "Why did she render it necessary that one animal could not live without the destruction of another?" His only answer was that "No being, except the Supreme, can unfold this mystery" (222). For such thinkers, the mere existence of carnivorous animals was even more troubling than war or human cruelty. Human guilt was something that they knew how to deal with, however imperfectly. It might at least be either reformed or else balanced through justice, whether human or divine. Yet carnivorous animals suggested

<18>

something far more distressing, a defect that could be neither compensated for nor eradicated. They were the fundamental flaw in an otherwise benign universe.

It was inevitable that less theologically-minded people would see the extermination of predators as a way of improving the world. This thinking reached its culmination in the latter nineteenth and early twentieth centuries when the campaign to eradicate predators such as the wolf from the United States became, rather than merely a matter of saving livestock, a moral crusade to destroy the forces of evil. Wolves were often portrayed as slouched over in a sinister manner with a malicious gleam in their eyes. Theodore Roosevelt described a puma shot in a tree as "the big horse-killing cat, destroyer of the deer, the lord of stealthy murder, facing his doom with a heart both craven and cruel" (Worster, 260). But as predators were driven to near extinction, many people began to see them as victims, even as heroic adversaries of civilization.

Nietzsche and the Wild Predator

Writing at the end of the nineteenth century, Nietzsche divided moral systems into those of slaves and masters. He believed that the slaves advocated pity, compassion, and altruism. The masters, by contrast, celebrated sensual enjoyment and exuberant egotism, while viewing weakness with contempt. Nietzsche believed that the morality of slaves was a creed of sickness and the morality of masters was one of health. In Judaism and even more in Christianity, the weak had triumphed over the strong.

In the natural world the creed of the masters corresponded to the ways of wild predators, while the morality of slaves was appropriate to the life of domesticated animals and prey. Nietzsche longed for what he viewed as the primeval vitality of predators and gloried in their perceived cruelty. In *The Genealogy of Morals*, originally published in 1886, he wrote of the early warrior societies:

> . . . we are the first to admit that anyone who knew these "good" ones {the warrior elites} only as enemies would find them evil enemies indeed. For these same men . . . who are so resourceful in consideration, tenderness, loyalty, pride, and friendship . . . once they step outside their circle become little better than uncaged beasts of prey. Once abroad in the wilderness, they revel in the freedom from social constraint and compensate for their long confinement in the quietude of their community. They revert to the innocence of wild animals: we can imagine them returning from an orgy of murder, arson, rape, and torture, jubilant and at peace with themselves as though they

<19>

had committed a fraternity prank — convinced, moreover, that the poets for a long time to come will have something to sing about and to praise. Deep within these noble races there lurks the beast of prey, intent on spoil and conquest. This hidden urge has to be satisfied from time to time, the beast let loose in the wilderness. This goes for the Roman, Arabian, German, and Japanese nobility as for the Homeric heroes and the Scandinavian Vikings (174-175).

He believed that the "Teutonic blond beast" still inspired terror in Europeans, though he added that the racial connection to the ancient Germans had been lost (175). "One might be justified," Nietzsche continued, "in fearing the wild beast lurking within all noble races and in being on one's guard against it, but who would not a thousand times prefer fear when it is accompanied by admiration to security accompanied by the loathsome sight of perversion, dwarfishness, degeneracy? And is that not our predicament today?" (176).

The frequent allusions to beasts of prey and wild animals were highly abstract, as might have been expected from a person who had probably never seen a large predator outside of a zoo. Nietzsche did not even find it necessary to specify which beast of prey he referred to, assuming an essential similarity among wolves, bears, lions, eagles, and others. The imagery is only understandable within the context of nineteenth-century thought, which placed people and animals in a continuum of savagery to civilization. Never questioning the appropriateness of these categories, Nietzsche simply reversed their most conventional valuation, celebrating savagery and scorning the decadence of civilization.

In his final work, *The Will to Power*, Nietzsche made the identification of civilization of human beings and domestication of animals even more explicit. Like many of his contemporaries, he interpreted the theory of Darwin as one of inevitable evolutionary progress, an idea which he rejected as sentimental. In his view evolution was purposeless and chaotic. The more complex or "higher" forms were actually more prone to decay than others, and to retain their superiority required an effort of will. Rather than an extension of biological progress, civilization, particularly the Judeo-Christian tradition, was an expression of decline:

The domestication (the "culture")[1] of man does not go deep —
Where it does go deep it at once becomes degeneration (type:
the Christian). The "savage" (or, in moral terms, the evil man) is
a return to nature — and in a certain sense his recovery, his *cure*
from "culture" — (fragment # 684).

[1] Parenthetical notes in this quotation are all Nietzsche's.

<20>

Closeness to the natural world conferred superiority but no evolutionary advantage; the strong had to be defended against the guile and cunning of the weak.

Nietzsche had known nature through his delicate constitution as an assortment of terrible pains and prohibitions. He had also known it in the spectacular vistas of his walks along Alpine paths. He transmuted these experiences into symbolic comments on the panorama of human history. His encounters with nature had sometimes been fearful or ecstatic, yet never intimate, and his vulnerability made him identify with symbols of power.

The Cult of Savagery

As predators ceased to be a part of daily life for Europeans, their symbolic importance seemed to grow. The Nietzschean cult of predators was further developed by Oswald Spengler, who wrote:

> *The animal of prey is the highest form of mobile life*. It implies a
> maximum of freedom for self against others . . . where that self
> can only hold its own by *fighting and winning and destroying*. It
> imparts high dignity to Man, as a type, that he is a beast of *prey*.
> A herbivore is by destiny a prey, and it seeks to escape this
> destiny by flight, but beasts of prey must get their prey. The one
> type of life is of its innermost essence defensive, the other
> offensive, hard, cruel, destructive. The difference appears even
> in the tactics of movement — on the one hand the habit of
> flight, fleetness, cutting corners, evasion, concealment, and of
> the other the *straight-line* motion of attack, the lion's spring, the
> eagle's swoop (22).

According to this anthropological theory, human identity was established when people first began to use weapons, enabling them to kill and dominate. "The tactics of his {man's} living," Spengler wrote, were "those of a splendid beast of prey, brave, crafty, and cruel" (28). The invention of weapons also divided people into heroes who would use the arms, and peasants who would produce them. The "predators" among men were destined to command and "vegetarians" had to obey. Spengler saw history as a succession of cultures, each of which rose through the will to dominate and succumbed to decadence. The last and most "tragic" of these he called the "Faustian" culture of Nordic man. This culture had found the means to control nature in new technologies, yet squandered superiority by sharing discoveries with the world. The sublime egotism of the predator had given way to the morality of the herd.

<21>

Spengler also wrote that predation had been necessary for animals to develop and refine their abilities:

> Cleverness in the human sense, active cleverness, belongs only to beasts of prey. Herbivores are by comparison stupid, and not merely the 'innocent' dove and the elephant, but even the noblest sorts like the bull, the horse, and the deer; only in blind rage or sexual excitement are these capable of fighting; otherwise they will allow themselves to be tamed, and a child can lead them (23).

Such generalizations were dubious. Predators are actually not necessarily more intelligent or even more fierce than the vegetarians of the animal world. Among land animals, the elephant appears at least as intelligent as any carnivore. Boars, which are largely herbivorous, may be the fiercest of fighters. Furthermore, the lives of predators are, contrary to what Spengler imagined, not filled with perpetual combat.

The cult of predators was also very selective. Nobody ever thought of "man the predator" as a crocodile, a frog, a rat, or a hyena. The only creatures that seemed true to the image were large mammals which ironically had sometimes been partially domesticated. This is because, though Nietzsche and Spengler failed to realize it, the extreme aggressiveness which people identify as "savage" is to a very great extent something that has been deliberately cultivated in captive animals. Thus animals destined for the chase were often systematically starved and tormented in order to increase their ferocity. Fox-terriers that were trained to catch rats in France during the late nineteenth century would be placed in an enclosed space with a few captured rats then not allowed to leave until they had destroyed the prey (Digard, 160-166). Nevertheless, rhetoric about "man the predator" and "the blond beast" became common during the Weimar Republic and the Nazi period (Glaser, 123-130; Herf, 65-66, 100).

The Nazis identified themselves with idealized images of predators and implicitly claimed the right to kill. Hitler, for example, told Hermann Rauschning in 1934 that "I desire a violent, domineering, fearless, and ferocious upcoming generation. It must be able to bear pain. It must show no signs of weakness or tenderness. The free and magnificent predator must once again glint from their eyes" (Hermand, *Dreams*, 281). Hitler also stated, referring to the Nazis and Jews: "Who is to blame, the cat or the mouse, if the cat eats up the mouse?" (Fleming, 105). Sometimes this preference for predators was defended on the ground that they were actually gentler and more ethical than other animals. Writing a short time after the end of World War II, Lorenz continued the Nazi tradition of preferring predators to other animals. He maintained that carnivorous

<22>

creatures have an instinctual morality which holds their destructiveness within bounds. Among herbivorous animals such as doves and rabbits, by contrast, conflicts are far more vicious (*King*, 181-199). Perhaps the most fundamental myth of the Nazi period was the idea that predators were closer to nature and possessed greater vitality than other creatures.

Vegetarianism and Other Paradoxes

Hitler was a vegetarian, probably in emulation of the composer Richard Wagner.[2] Several leading figures in the government followed his example, including Hess and Goebbels (Arluke and Sax, "Nazi," 17-18); Himmler, who was influenced by Buddhism, even mandated vegetarian meals for leaders of the SS (Hermand, *Utopien*, 114). It is true that the Nazi leaders never tried to promote vegetarianism beyond the ruling circles. An entry in Goebbels' diary dated April 26, 1942 stated that this omission was dictated by practical necessity. According to Goebbels, Hitler was more deeply convinced than ever that eating meat was wrong, but Hitler could not revolutionize the system of food production while the war was in progress. He planned to promote or even impose vegetarianism among the general population eventually (Kaplan, 5).

Some policies suggest ambivalence about carnivorous activity among the Nazis. The law on Animal Protection of November 24, 1933 banned the use of dogs in the chase (Giese and Kahler, 278). This put an end to traditional fox hunting as it had been practiced among the aristocracy. How could this sort of restraint be reconciled with the Nazi rhetorical celebration of predators? Swept up in the momentum of the Nazi movement, many people simply ignored its contradictions. One possible explanation, however, is that the leading Nazis used abstinence from meat to signify their elite status. Throughout most of history only elites could eat meat on a regular basis, but only elites could readily afford to refuse it. Many Christians, Buddhists, and Hindus have refrained from eating meat to signify not only their regard for, but also their elevation above, animal life (Salisbury, 170). The identification of the eater with his or her food is a very old and widespread feature of human culture, and it is far from absent in secular society of today. That is why people hardly ever eat the creatures such as rats or beetles that they tend to find repugnant, though these might otherwise be a convenient source of protein. In a similar way, many people have feared that eating meat would render them bestial.

---

[2] Hitler was probably not entirely consistent in his vegeterianism, and there has been much debate about the reasons for it. For a discussion of this, see Proctor, *Caneer*, pp. 134-41,

<23>

A further explanation is sublimation. The identification of the Nazis with carnivores was always on the level of a highly stylized fantasy. Protecting this fantasy may have required that the reality of predation be kept at a distance, even when this involved abstaining from meat. They saw themselves collectively as one enormous beast that would kill less out of hunger than for sport.

<24>

CHAPTER 3
ROMANTIC TERROR

And haply sometimes with articulate voice,
Amid the deafening tumult scarcely heard
By him who utters it, exclaim aloud,
"Rage on, ye elements! Let moon and stars
Their aspects lend, and mingle in their turn
With this commotion (ruinous though it be)
From day to night, from night to day prolonged!'
—William Wordsworth, "The Excursion"

IN *CROWDS AND POWER*, Elias Canetti traced the communal identity of many nations to images drawn from the natural world. The Germans, he stated, saw themselves as a "marching forest":

Each individual tree is always taller than a man and goes on growing until it becomes a giant. Its steadfastness has much in common with the same virtue in a warrior. In a single tree the bark resembles a coat of mail; in a whole forest, where there are many trees of the same kind growing together, it suggests rather the uniforms of an army. For the German, without his being aware of it, army and forest transfused each other in every possible way . . . He took the rigidity and straightness of trees for his own law (173).

Canetti argued that the treaty of Versailles, which deprived Germany of its army, was felt by the Germans as far more than simply a humiliating defeat. It was a denial of the primal identity of the people (179-182).

Trees are closely linked with fire, another symbol of crowds. "The forest," Canetti wrote, "is set on fire by men in order to create space for settlements, and there is good reason to believe that it was through the experience of such conflagrations that men learnt how to deal with fire" (77). Fire is like mob action in the suddenness with which it can break out and the ruthlessness with which it can destroy. Domination of the earth began with the mastery of flame, long before people domesticated plants and animals. Yet cozy hearths do not fully satisfy us. Even at its most threatening, fire continues to fascinate people, and they will stare at a conflagration (75-78). Such a preoccupation with apocalyptic destruction runs through the Nazi movement. Speer observed that ". . . fire was Hitler's proper element," adding that "he set the world aflame and brought fire and sword upon the continent" (Speer, 80). The destruction wreaked by

<25>

the Nazis was like the vast fires people have set to clear land for farming and for homes.

Canetti traced the solidarity of other peoples to images that were similarly vivid and intriguing. For the Dutch this was the dyke claiming land for settlement by holding back the sea. For the Jews it was the desert erasing footprints of wanderers as they pass on. But only the image of the marching forest was drawn neither from nature nor human society but blended the two through fantasy. In much the same way, the German character has always been an unstable combination of pagan and Judeo-Christian traditions.

Jew, Christian, and Pagan

In Genesis, God tells Adam and Eve, "Be fruitful, multiply, fill the earth and conquer it. Be masters of the fish of the sea, the birds of heaven and all living animals on earth" (1:28). It is a cliché that the archaic pagan deities, which are immanent rather than transcendent, are closer to the natural world than are their counterparts in the Judeo-Christian tradition. That difference is not quite so clear or abrupt as many people suppose. Yahweh is very closely associated with the elements, especially with weather and terrain. Christ is associated with the cycles of the year in his birth, maturity, sacrifice, and resurrection. The pagan Greeks and Romans did not always show great reverence for the earth and often treated their gods casually. The vast mining operations of the Romans, for example, were a far more aggressive intervention in the natural world than was ever found among the Hebrews. In general, however, pagan beliefs were more intimately bound to specific places than those of Jews or Christians. The need to placate the guardians of streams or forests inhibited the growth of urban or industrial civilization (White, 86). For over a millennium a conflict between pagan nature-worship and Judeo-Christian spirituality has run through German history.

The Romans had been awed by the vast Hyrcanian forest which covered most of Germany. In the first century CE, Pliny the Elder wrote that this forest "exceeds all marvels with its almost limitless age." He continued, ". . . hills are raised up as roots collide or where the ground has fallen away from them. In their struggle with one another, their arches rise as high as branches and curve in the manner of open gateways so that squadrons of cavalry can pass through" (book 16, chap. 8). Tacitus described the Germanic tribes as relatively egalitarian and democratic (110). They worshiped not in temples but in sacred groves (109). Though impulsive and warlike, they practiced simple agriculture. They had no orchards, gardens, or irrigated fields, but they grew grain, kept cattle, and traded in horses (122-123). Reproaching his own countrymen for deca-

<26>

dence, Tacitus described the Germans as what would later be called "noble savages" uncorrupted by urban ways.

The tradition of German identification with the natural world goes back to the battle of Teutoburger Forest in 9 C.E., when Teutonic tribesmen under the leadership of Arminius annihilated an entire Roman army in the depths of the woods. The Emperor Augustus reportedly ran through the halls of his palace vainly shouting for his perished legions. The Romans frequently defeated the Germans, yet they could not secure the territory East of the Rhine. This boundary marked the limit of imperial expansion. Thus the Germans were able to retain many of their traditional practices and beliefs when most of Europe had been conquered and Christianized.

Finally in 772 Charlemagne began to forcibly convert the pagan Saxons and Friesians. This began a genocidal war which was to last 33 years, not even counting many subsequent revolts. The soldiers of Charlemagne desecrated holy places, relocated entire communities, and slaughtered all who refused to accept the new religion (Murphy, 11-26). The laws imposed on the vanquished Saxon peoples made it a capital crime to refuse baptism, to neglect to fast before Easter, to cremate the dead, or to blaspheme Jesus (Gugenberger and Schwiedlenka, 41). In contrast to territories such as Ireland where conversion had been peaceful, the bitter resentments on both sides would linger in German culture for many centuries to come. The pagan deities of the Saxons such as Wotan became demonized (42), while resentment against the new religion continued to fester.

Luther attempted to eliminate pagan elements of Christianity, thereby returning to the simple faith of early Christians or even of the Hebrews. The romantic writers of the early nineteenth century, though often devout Christians, emphasized their pagan heritage. They celebrated primeval forests and were fascinated by archaic magic. The collective identification with the natural world was revived and strengthened when Napoleon occupied Germany in the name of civilization. Just as the Renaissance was fundamentally Italian and the Enlightenment was French, so Romanticism was a German movement. The basic ideas of Romanticism include longing for the absolute, the cult of genius, veneration of nature, nostalgia for the remote past, exaltation of passion, suspicion of science, and salvation through art. All were articulated more thoroughly and remained dominant longer in Germany than in the rest of Europe or North America. Several romantic authors and philosophers of Germany, attempting to resist the cultural domination of France, tried to rally people around their ancestral past.

The Industrial Revolution widened the division between the domains of nature and civilization, thus stimulating both the Enlightenment and Romanticism. The sympathies of the Romantics were with nature, while

<27>

the *philosophes* of the Enlightenment glorified the civilization of human-kind. The Romantics ranged across the entire political spectrum. They included the extremes of religious orthodoxy and nihilism. Virtually all of them, however, in some way questioned the anthropocentric values that otherwise predominated in their era. The romantic longing for nature took forms that were elusive, subtle, and ambiguous, what Friedrich Schlegel called "romantic irony." For Goethe longing for nature was expressed in the search for a science that would be less mechanistic and abstract. For many poets such as Wackenroder and Novalis, it took the form of cryptic utterances that tested the boundaries of language. Others such as Brentano and Eichendorff sought union with nature in the contemplation of landscapes and in the primal vitality of rural life.

By the middle of the nineteenth century, however, the bucolic images of the early Romantics no longer inspired confidence. The ideal of natural harmony was challenged by reports of the harsh conditions faced by explorers in exotic lands. The identification with nature became increas-ingly a taste for extreme situations. In the words of Daniel Worster, "On every hand, in painting, poetry, and music, a superabundance of terror was represented: roaring lions leaping onto the backs of terrified stallions, dreadful torrents plunging over cliffs, thundering volcanoes erupting into lurid skies" (126). The late Romantics sought obliteration of the self in the contemplation of primal landscapes governed by powers vaster than those of human beings. This experience was poised precariously between reverence and revulsion. In literature and the arts descriptions of the horrors of nature grew ever more extreme in order to satisfy an increasingly jaded public. The battlefield became a common metaphor for nature, sanctioned in 1859 by Darwin's *The Origin of Species* (Worster, 115-129).

The Modern Era

For much of its history Germany had remained a loose collection of petty kingdoms, precariously held together by cultural and linguistic affinities; it was finally united only in 1871. The conflicts between tradition and modernity that troubled all of European society in the latter nineteenth and early twentieth centuries were particularly acute in Germany, where industrialization was especially abrupt. The attitudes of the Germans toward the natural world in this period were confused and ambivalent. Farmers abandoned their profession and migrated to the cities, while the urban intelligentsia felt an intense nostalgia for life on the land. Germans celebrated woods that were dense, primeval, and almost unex-plored, but the actual German forests had long been the most elaborately cultivated in the world. Farmers had killed the last wolves of Germany around the middle of the nineteenth century, and the only large animals remaining in the wild were deer which foresters managed for sport.

<28>

German attitudes toward animals reflected the same tension between romantic nostalgia and technocratic control that would run through the entire Nazi movement.

In northern Europe and especially in England, industrialization had drastically altered attitudes toward animals. The new popularity of pet-keeping generated a growing humane movement which included protests against such activities as hunting, animal experimentation, and eating of meat. The Germans, struggling with the dislocations caused by rapid industrialization, often followed their English counterparts in protesting against these practices. Though industrialization had largely created the conditions for the humane movement, in Germany it became a conservative protest against modernity which was linked to a romantic celebration of wildness.

By the middle of the twentieth century virtually the entire globe had been explored by Europeans. Agricultural expansion was approaching its limit as the few remaining wild lands were claimed for settlement. As wilderness approached an end, the momentum of destruction was not extinguished. It turned, particularly with the Nazis, against civilization itself. Late Romantics from Charles Darwin to Richard Wagner had venerated nature as a vast and inexorable power. This was the force that produced violent storms and earthquakes, that drove entire species and peoples to annihilation. Human beings with their technologies were reaching a point where they might begin to claim such power for their own.

By the end of the nineteenth century people throughout Europe were restless and bored after a long period of comparative peace. Many thought of war as a primordial activity in which life could be reduced to its essentials. In *The Storm of Steel* {*Im Stahlgewitter*}, based on his diary as a soldier in World War I, Ernst Jünger wrote of going off to fight, "The war had entered us like wine. We had set out in a rain of flowers to seek the death of heroes. . . . It was a man's work, a duel on fields whose flowers would be stained with blood" (6). Several of his compatriots were later disillusioned. The unrepentant Jünger wrote many decades later in a preface to the English edition of his book that the opposing armies were "two mighty forces of nature locked in conflict" (x). He added:

> It was strange, for example, to hear at night the cry of the
> partridges from the waste fields, or at dawn the careless song of
> the lark as it rose high above the trenches. Did it not seem then
> that life itself was speaking out of the confidence of its savage
> and visionary heart, knowing very well that in its more secret
> and essential depths it had nothing to fear from, even the
> deadliest of wars . . . (xi).

<29>

The coldness and even brutality demanded by war made soldiers one with the natural world.

By contrast, Marie Louise Kaschnitz in her novel, *Der alte Garten* {The Old Garden}, written in secret during World War II and published posthumously, told of a brother and sister in a neglected garden: "The boy had once gone to the circus with his father, and there he had seen lions, bears, and apes that danced and did all sorts of tricks at the command of their tamers. He had this experience in mind and, even if the spiders, beetles, and worms of the Old Garden were not like those proud animals, he thought one could still show those creatures that they were underlings which must obey the will of their master" (16). The boy engaging in wanton destruction at the start of the book was plainly an image of Nazi Germany, possessed by an obsessive desire to dominate.

The Nazis identified civilization with the Judeo-Christian tradition and identified with the pagan past. By claiming a special bond with nature, the Nazis stigmatized their adversaries as unnatural; they showed little tolerance for the environmental activism of their opponents. The Friends of Nature, a socialist-oriented organization devoted to the enjoyment and preservation of the land, had a membership of more than 100,000 and owned more than 200 rural lodges at the time of Hitler's coming to power. Almost immediately the new government dissolved the organization and confiscated all of its property (Dominick, 105).

Enjoyment of the natural world had long been thought of as a delight of peace. War invariably leads to the destruction of landscapes as well as of human beings. In the ancient world and the Middle Ages, war led to the devastation of forests. Wood was needed to build fleets, for weapons, and for siege engines. Furthermore forests were often destroyed so that they could not provide cover for enemy forces. In addition, sacred groves and animals were often destroyed simply as a means of demoralizing the enemy. Ecological sabotage for purely military purposes took several forms from the poisoning of streams to the starting of conflagrations.

In early Victorian times Europeans had viewed nature as violent, lawless, and chaotic, by contrast with the order and discipline of society. Though the Nazis agreed that nature was violent, they reversed this dichotomy. Nature became a realm of absolute order, opposed to the anarchy brought on by civilization. In imposing inflexible authoritarian rule, the Nazis believed they were restoring the natural order to society. Instead of being a source of humility, the Nazis made nature an object of pride. Instead of being personified as feminine, the Nazis made nature "the fatherland." By extending centralized control almost without limits, the Nazis thought they would become nature itself, harsh and implacable yet always orderly.

<30>

The Principle of Leadership

The Nazis retained continuity with the traditions of nature preservation and romantic protest in one essential respect — they were not anthropocentric. The Nazis had little or no conception of equality, human or otherwise. They placed hardly any value on the individual, whether animal or human. "The individual," one scientist explained, "is . . . one arbitrarily selected and interchangeable instance of a genus, race or tribe" (Weber, 259). In the words of another biologist, ". . . race is simply a living force that embraces all being and becoming, maturation and death of human beings . . ." (Garbe, 147). Loyalty to race replaced loyalty to species — that is, to humanity — in the morality of the Nazi movement. They organized their cosmos less around humankind than around the Germanic nation, not as it existed but as they imagined it ought to be. The Germanic nation, in turn, might include certain animals and exclude many citizens. As an article in a major German veterinary journal of 1937 stated, "Through the National Socialist laws on animals, any creature, just like a human being, enjoys appropriate protection on account of its belonging to the national {völkische} community" (Brumme, "Tierarzt," 38). An individual dog could easily have more value than a human being if the dog was "useful" and the man was not.

The highly influential educator Ferdinand Rossner described the Nazi "doctrine of blood and race" as "the third Copernican deed." The first had been the theory of Copernicus itself, which moved the earth from the center of the universe. The second had been the theory of evolution, which dethroned the human species. In a similar way, the doctrine of race was to deprive "human personality" of its special status (367-368). Many people find a lesson of humility in discoveries like those of Copernicus or Darwin, yet in this case they led to arrogance. Instead of simply speaking as fallible human beings, the Nazis would make pronouncements in the name of the natural world.

The Nazi strictures on animal protection were very explicit in their rejection of anthropocentric perspective — animals were not to be protected for the sake of human interests but for themselves (i.e., Giese and Kahler, 13). An intensified hierarchy, however, replaced humanism as an organizing principle. For the Nazis hierarchy was not simply a matter of organizational efficiency; it was a way of fitting into the cosmic order. This conception replaced anthropocentric philosophy with its corollary of human equality. The biologist Ludwig von Bertalanffy wrote "an organic system is basically nothing other than a hierarchically ordered sequence of events in dynamic equilibrium" (Bertalanffy, 19). He considered it self-evident that human society should, like nature, also be ordered in a hierarchic manner. He approvingly mentioned the rule of Mussolini as an example (341). He also praised the forest law enacted by Hermann Göring

<31>

which placed all decisions respecting the government of forests under total central control as a practical application of his ideas (258).

In politics the Nazis understood hierarchal organization as a manifestation of what they called the "Führerprinzip" or "principle of leadership." At the apex was Hitler, the Führer himself, who was identified with the entire people. The nation was often compared to the body and Hitler to the will (e.g., Garbe, 147). Though he did not regularly interfere with the routine of government, his power was unchallenged and virtually absolute. Subordinates with extensive powers were his representatives, and they were involved in perpetual competition (K. Fischer, 295-304). The Nazi hierarchy was never formalized, but was meant to be fluid and dynamic. Hitler did not assign his subordinates specific duties and responsibilities, only vague mandates. In consequence the position of an official would never be secure, and he could only retain it by dominating others.

According to Joachim Fest, this principle was the core of Nazi philosophy. He writes, ". . . with the exception of the idea of struggle and the maxims of the Führer, there was scarcely any article that it {the Nazi movement} would not willingly have abandoned or set aside at least temporarily for the sake of gaining and holding power . . ." (164). In practice, this hierarchic organization was established largely through the policy of "Gleichschaltung" or "synchronization," whereby all organizations from the chess club to the police force were fused in a single bureaucracy with one chain of command. By replacing the murky complexities of parliamentary democracy by a single structure, the Nazis sought to restore a putative primal simplicity in human relationships. This hierarchic structure, embracing not only people but all living things, defined their conception of the natural world. Every individual creature would have a rank and a place, and those that did not fit in could be destroyed.

Just as Stalin and his followers murdered in the name of the downtrodden and oppressed of humanity, the Nazis murdered in the name of nature, invoking animals and landscapes. "Total terror," Hannah Arendt has written, . . . "is supposed to provide the forces of nature or history with an incomparable instrument to accelerate their movement . . . terror executes on the spot the death sentences which Nature is supposed to have pronounced on races or individuals which are unfit to live' . . ." (6).

<32>

This is not to deny that the Nazi government accomplished much in the way of conservation. A vast number of new nature preserves were established, and the municipal park system doubled in size (Dominick, 106). Dictatorial regimes can achieve many goals including those of conservation more effectively in the short run than can democracies, which require elaborate processes of negotiation. Ultimately far more important, however, is the development of customs and traditions that enable communities to live harmoniously with the natural world over long periods of time, a goal that requires active participation of many people.

<33>

PART 2

THE SYMBOLISM OF ANIMALS IN NAZI GERMANY

Fig. 1. "The Large Blue Horses" by Franz Marc (1912). The expressionist paintings of Marc, who had died fighting in World War I, were banned by the Nazis. Like many of the Nazis, Marc had been fascinated by the rhythmic motion of horses, but, unlike the Nazis, he did not wish to subordinate these animals to human agendas. By using seemingly "unnatural" colors (the horses are painted in shades of blue), Marc was attempting to imaginatively reconstruct an equine perception of the world.

CHAPTER 4
GRANDFATHER APE

Is man an ape or an angel?

—Benjamin Disraeli

IN THE OLD Testament God is a father, the sole parent of Adam and Eve. The first human beings rebel, establishing a pattern which runs through the entire Judeo-Christian tradition. The Old Testament is replete with conflicts between fathers and sons: Abraham and Isaac, Isaac and Jacob, Jacob and most of his children, Noah and Ham. Finally this culminates in a conflict between Judaism, the religion of the father, and Christianity, the religion of the son. Even today people generally suppose that Christianity grew out of Judaism, but it is probably more accurate to regard the two as sister religions. The New Testament and the Talmud, the distinguishing books of Christianity and Judaism respectively, were both compiled on a common foundation of the Old Testament or Torah. Both continue to regard that foundation as holy, yet they interpret it differently.

Judaism has long been associated with age, Christianity with relative youth. The proverbial "Jew" was very rarely depicted in the Christian Middle Ages as young; he was usually an old but foolish man, an ineffectual authority figure. He was often identified not only with Judas Iscariot, the traitor, but also with King Herod, the killer of infants. In a more benign aspect, the Jew was also identified with Joseph, the husband of Mary, who was overshadowed by both his wife and child. The Jew was a target for deflected childhood and adolescent rebellion, a caricature of a father. The stereotype of Jews reflects a resentment of God the father, Yahweh of the Old Testament, who visited dreadful tribulations both on his worshipers and their adversaries.

Evolution

Apes have long been maligned in Western culture. Their wrinkled faces suggest extreme age, but their lack of human speech and their narrow foreheads suggest infancy. They are playful, yet they have difficulty in walking upright, features that can suggest senility. Fables stigmatized apes for trying to imitate human beings, while legends sometimes made them into people who had degenerated. Among the Jews there are several stories of people, even entire races, being turned into apes for impiety and idolatry. According to legend, that was the fate of those who built the Tower of Babel (Schochet, 90). Apes had a reputation for lacking dignity and morality (Sax, *Frog*, 86-87). Long before Darwin the essayist Montaigne, chastising

<35>

human pride, had observed in "Apology for Raymond Sebond" that of all animals the apes, "those that most resemble us," were "the ugliest and meanest of the whole herd" (478).

In modern ideologies of progress, sons are superior to their fathers. In popularizations of Darwinian evolution, the father — or grandfather — became not a man but an ape. The theory of evolution could have elicited many responses other than the usual ones of shock, denial, resignation, and heroic acceptance. Since man was "descended from the apes," primates could have been given an honored place in human culture. The theory of evolution could even have triggered nostalgia for prior stages of evolution, but virtually nobody on either side of the debates over evolution took the new ideas about origins as a source of human pride. All tried to put as much distance between themselves and any simian ancestors as possible.

Just as most people regarded Judaism as a preliminary stage of Christianity, they thought of the ape as a preliminary stage of humanity. The image of the ape, much like the anti-Semitic caricature of the Jew, was almost always male, almost always advanced in years if not wisdom. The rhetoric of the period never included references to the ape as a grandmother. The ape was never an infant or a young man. He was the grandfather who had been surpassed and rendered superfluous by his progeny. What troubled people was not simply the evolutionary connection between people and animals. Had evolutionary theory involved human descent from lions instead of apes, people might have had little difficulty in accepting it. Several aristocrats in the Middle Ages had traced the descent of their families to animals such as bears (Sax, *Serpent*, 81-82), which suggested natural vitality and tragic dignity. People had not been psychologically prepared by legend or myth for Darwin's theory of evolution. European legends had often traced family history from a seal, wolf, snake, bird, or other animal, but never from an ape.

Simian imagery was the center of the famous debate between the traditionalist Bishop Wilberforce and the evolutionist Thomas Henry Huxley in 1860, less than a year after Darwin published *The Origin of Species*. Wilberforce had made an allusion to the simian ancestry of his opponent. Huxley replied, "If then, . . . the question is put to me would I rather have a miserable ape for a grandfather or a man highly endowed by nature and possessed of great means of influence and yet who employs those faculties and that influence for the mere purpose of introducing ridicule into a grave scientific discussion — I unhesitatingly affirm my preference for the ape" (Barber, 274-5). Huxley may have carried the day with his eloquence, but his point was largely lost on the public. With neither the patience nor the background to understand the scientific arguments, most people understood only that according to Darwin human beings somehow were descended from apes. Contemporary evolutionary

<38>

theorists point out that the saying is mistaken or highly misleading. Human beings and apes were actually both descended from a common ancestor. But in the Victorian era scientists took a more linear view of evolution; they speculated that an existing ape which had simply stopped evolving might have been the ancestor of humankind.

Crude references to this pedigree became a standard rhetorical tool to ridicule the theory of evolution. Such personal attacks were not only used by the opponents of evolution. Against the explicit advice of Charles Darwin, Ernst Haeckel, the leading advocate of evolution in Germany, turned these taunts around by stating, "…it is an interesting and instructive fact that the discovery of the natural evolution of the human race from genuine apes arouses especially intense indignation among those people who have obviously, so far as their intellectual equipment is concerned, hitherto traveled the least distance, themselves, from the apes" (Wendt, 284).

The distress over evolution was compounded by the recent discovery of the gorilla in Africa, described in sensational accounts by the explorer Paul du Chaillu as a satanic monster (Barber, 276-277). Even such a distinguished Victorian naturalist as Philip Gosse, who was entirely capable of careful observation, would indulge in relatively uninhibited fantasy when trying to describe the gorilla: "The hideous aspect of his visage, his green eyes flashing with rage, is heightened by the thick and prominent brows being drawn spasmodically up and down, with the hair erect, causing a horrible and hideous scowl" (Gosse, 238). For many people, this was the putative ancestor of humankind.

The tie of kinship doubtless also contributed to the impression of perverse eroticism that surrounded the apes, especially gorillas. Even before evolution was proclaimed by Darwin, there were obscure rumors which sometimes found their way into scientific articles about women being abducted by apes (Sax, *Parliament*, 87, 89). People were embarrassed by the sexuality of apes and monkeys in the zoo (Barber, 133; Bölsche, vol. 2, 351), and sometimes the simians were dressed in clothes. "We approach," one popular American author writes around the start of the twentieth century, "the imprisoned baboon with the same feeling of repugnance that would be excited by a debased and brutal maniac" (Sax, *Frog*, 79).

Favored Races

Proclaimed at the height of British Colonialism, the theory of evolution was used to help Europeans and their descendants dehumanize other races. Most early followers of Darwin saw evolution as a hierarchic continuum of progress from "lower" to "higher" forms. For followers of Darwin, the gap between man and his hominid ancestors was filled by apes and by "savages" (Cartmill, 200). Many views championed by Darwin

<39>

himself would be considered blatantly racist today, probably more so than those of most of his contemporaries. In *The Descent of Man*, Darwin theorized that success in the competitive struggle for survival gave advantage to races according to their "grade of civilization" (chap. 6), strongly suggesting that primitive people throughout the world would face eventual extinction. He left open the question of whether or not various racial groups should be classified in a single species. Around the end of the nineteenth century, people often understood the term "Darwinism" as referring not only to an empirical theory but also to the idea that racial improvement comes through competition for survival.

This racism was carried to an extreme by Ernst Haeckel. He had first read *The Origin of Species* as soon as the translation into German came out in 1860, and he was filled with enthusiasm. Darwin had opted not to explicitly raise the issue of human origins in that volume, but, as noted previously, Haeckel immediately proclaimed that human beings were evolved from apes. Lacking the rhetorical skills of Thomas Huxley, he exceeded his British counterpart in zeal. Haeckel constructed an elaborate philosophy from the theory of evolution which he called "Monism," because it was intended to overcome the duality between nature and spirit (Bäumler, 61-63). According to Haeckel, basic principles of organization were the same for all life, whether in a society of microbes or of human beings. The difference was just a matter of complexity (Haeckel, *Evolution*, vol. 1, 161). Since he saw no fundamental discontinuity between human society and the natural world, Haeckel tried to understand human society through comparisons drawn from other forms of life. These analogies laid the foundation for the complete medicalization of all moral and ethical concerns in the Nazi state (Gasman, 34).

One practical effect of the theory of evolution was to discredit nostalgia for an Edenic past. A further consequence was to focus the imaginative energies of people increasingly toward an idealized future. In 1899 Haeckel published *The Riddle of the Universe*, in which he proclaimed that science was close to resolving all of the great mysteries. Haeckel also theorized that the possibility of "atavism" or "reversion" was a constant feature of evolution. In the evolution of almost every higher organism," he wrote, "we observe that the progressive completion of most organs is accompanied by retrograde processes of evolution in single parts" (Haeckel, *Riddle*, vol. 1, 133). The most complex organism for Haeckel was not the human being but the state, viewed as a biotic community (Haeckel, *Evolution*, vol. 1, 161). Just as a person or animal must fight ruthlessly for survival, the state had to battle both other states and corruption {that is, "disease"} from within (Bäumler, 214-215). Haeckel's favorite comparison was between the development of the embryo and that of the state. Just as many cells either die off or live off others in the development of the embryo, so many people

<40>

fail to contribute to the formation of society. While the whole organism is being constructed, individual cells can regress to a more primitive condition, just as individual human beings can lapse into a prior state of social development.

For all the bonding with nature Haeckel found in the theory of evolution, he most certainly did not like to think that he himself might be related to the apes. According to Haeckel, the Germanic race had progressed furthest from the form of ape-men and had thus been able to surpass other branches of humanity in civilization (Gasman, 200). He ridiculed any belief in human equality (Gasman, 12, 39; Haeckel, *Evolution*, vol. 1, 374) and stated that the difference separating refined Europeans from "savages" was greater, far greater, than the difference separating savages from anthropoid apes (Gasman, 134; Haeckel, *Evolution*, vol. 1, 40; Cartmill, 199). Haeckel and his followers interpreted such features as short noses (Haeckel, *Evolution*, vol. 1, 373-374) and wooly hair (Gasman, 39) as indicators of people who had not yet gotten beyond their simian heritage.

But Haeckel was only partially successful in popularizing these ideas outside of scholarly circles. That task remained for his disciple, Wilhelm Bölsche, a romantic novelist and literary critic. In 1901, Bölsche published his *Love Life in Nature: The Story of the Evolution of Love*. Writing with only a superficial knowledge of his subject but with limitless enthusiasm, Bölsche proclaimed "love" to be the guiding principle of evolution. In an extremely florid style, he presented an erotic history of life from microbes to "civilized" human beings. He believed this history culminated in the "new" science of "race hygiene": "It is a long road from the little bird in the Australian bush which put a red berry on its nuptial bower for adornment — to the establishment of a hygienic aristocracy in eugenic mankind" (Bölsche, vol. 2, 337). While Bölsche expressed a fondness for virtually every other form of life, his descriptions of apes — and, to an extent, of "savages" — showed little beside aversion and disgust. Bölsche's book was full of prurient descriptions of apes that sexually molest or attempt to seduce young girls, for example a caged mandrill that responded to a human female by turning around and exposing himself. Bölsche also imagined scenes of animals in the wild like:

> Where the mighty equatorial stream, which for our days has taken the place of the old legendary Nile in romance, traverses the dark continent in a daring curve, there in the primeval jungle did nature create her masterpiece of grotesque atrocity in the monkey type. The defenseless human girl on a solitary path encounters a huge, bull-necked, short-legged goblin plunging toward her; it has a monstrously large head and gnashes its teeth, and it has Herculean strength in its arms, which could

<41>

tackle a panther. Hairiness and nakedness alternate on the body of this woodland imp in a way that intensifies the impression of gnomelike atrocity to the peak of the possible (Bölsche, vol. 2, 350-351).

The images clearly anticipate those of later anti-Semitic propaganda used by Nazis and others, in which hairy Jewish men seduce or assault innocent Aryan girls. Such lurid, sensational passages are doubtless the reason why Bölsche remains perhaps the most successful popularizer of science in all of history (Bäumler, 64-65).

From the beginnings of scientific racism in the seventeenth and eighteenth centuries, comparisons were constantly made between apes and human beings. With the expansion of maritime trade and global exploration during the Renaissance and the Enlightenment, Europeans simultaneously learned of great apes and of the so-called "primitive people." It was some time before they learned to distinguish clearly among these groups, so that early descriptions of "wild men" by Lord Edward Tyson and Lord James Burnet Monboddo conflated the orangutan, the Negro, the Native American, and the chimpanzee. Up through most of the nineteenth century Europeans considered Negroes to be closely akin to apes, often granting Africans only marginally human status on the ground that they had not developed sufficiently. A biologist named Sömmering attempted to prove a kinship between the ape and the Negro by arranging skulls of various primates including human beings according to their relative "primitiveness" and "advancement." As late as 1930, Walter Scheidt, founder of Cultural Biology {Kulturbiologie}, could still describe these findings as "unchallenged" (79). Far from being the link between humanity and nature, the apes seemed more to be the barrier between the two. Bölsche was actually more aware of this paradox than many of his contemporaries. He could not dismiss the revulsion toward apes as cultural since, following Haeckel, he regarded aesthetic judgments as instinctive and therefore in a sense objective. His only explanation was that those apes or savages which failed to develop had either become petrified or had degenerated from a higher state (Bölsche, vol. 2, 332).

Primitivism and Degeneration

Until the middle of the nineteenth century Jews were classified as Caucasian, and they received little attention from racial theorists. Gradually, they came to be thought of as apelike, not on the ground of insufficient development, but because they had allegedly deteriorated. Houston Stewart Chamberlain, a leading theorist of Teutonic supremacy and anti-Semitism, expressed admiration for the ancient Hebrews and even for Sephardic Jews of the modern period. He showed only revulsion for the Ashkenazi Jews,

<42>

whom he maintained had lost their identity through racial mixing starting in ancient Israel. He attributed the rounded heads and hooked noses, supposedly the most Jewish features, to Hittites with whom the original Hebrews had interbred (vol. 1, 274-275, 372-377).

One prominent scientist of the later nineteenth century, Cesare Lombroso, theorized that certain physical characteristics such as large jaws, high cheekbones, and protruding ears were common not only to apes and savages but also criminals (Mosse, *Toward*, 84). "Criminals," he wrote, "are apes in our midst, marked by the anatomical stigma of atavism" (H. Friedlander, 3). In 1932, Spengler, though he generally did not emphasize race, remarked that "one can even observe the Neanderthal type in any public gathering" (37). This sort of sentiment laid the groundwork for a racism that could be particularly virulent and uncompromising. The idea of savage people as undeveloped contained an ambivalence which helped to balance domination with paternalism and even admiration. The other side of the demonization of many indigenous people was the widely-held ideal of the "noble savage." The notion of degeneration could deprive people not only of conventional status but also future promise. They were not even accorded the spontaneity associated with childhood. "It frequently happens," Chamberlain reported, "that children who have no conception of what 'Jew' means . . . begin to cry as soon as a genuine Jew or Jewess comes near them!" (vol. 1, 537).

With the advent of evolutionary theory, simian characteristics became a feature of a wide range of ethnic and racial stereotypes. While originating largely in learned journals, these stereotypes were quickly picked up by cartoonists and pamphleteers. By the late nineteenth century simian features were a standard rhetorical device to mock various races and ethnicities in cartoons throughout Europe and North America. Not only Negroes but also the Irish were regularly depicted as apes. During World War II cartoons and other forms of propaganda constantly depicted the Japanese as monkeys. (Dower, 77-93). Ethnologists of the early twentieth century held that Jews had profuse facial and body hair, a characteristic of apes (e.g., Günter, 26).

Some Nazis viewed Jews as an intermediate creature between ape and human being (Mosse, *Toward*, 143). Popular depictions of Jews and other races considered inferior by the Nazis gave them the features of apes, low foreheads, extended jaws, protruding stomachs, a slouching walk, and profuse body hair. A pamphlet entitled *The Sub-Human {Der Untermensch}* produced by Gottlob Berger's SS Main Administrative Office in 1940 gave the following description of allegedly inferior human beings:

<43>

Fig. 2. "How long will it take before others here in Germany may only be seen behind bars?" Illustration on the front page of *Der Sturmer*, March 10, 1932

> ... that product of nature which, on the surface, is a member of the same species, with hands, feet, and a sort of brain, with eyes and mouth, is nonetheless a creature of a totally other and horrifying kind, a mere approximation of a human, with human facial features — but mentally and spiritually he is lower than a beast. Within this creature reigns a vicious chaos of wild, uninhibited passions, unspeakable destructiveness, the most primitive desires, unconcealed baseness (Fleming, 125).

A cartoon on the front page of the Nazi publication *Der Stürmer* on March 10, 1932 showed a man with simian features, clearly intended to represent a Jew, gazing at an ape in a cage. The caption beneath read, "How long will it take before others here in Germany may only be seen behind bars?"

The Nazis had no official position with respect to human origins. Walter Gross, who headed the Nazi party's Office of Race Policy, advocated complete freedom of scientific research on the question (Deichmann, 270). The Nazis generally accepted Darwin, who seemed to hold out a promise

<44>

of evolutionary progress. A few rejected evolution, however, since it contradicted their notions of the original purity of the Aryan race (Mosse, *Toward*, 103; Kalikow, 194). This ambivalence sometimes led to bizarre blends of Darwinist and creationist ideas. While these notions were totally unscientific, they did show a degree of consistency. They took as their starting point the idea known as "polygenesis," that different races of people were created separately. They then viewed modern human beings as created through a gradual miscegenation of some of these races. Richard Wagner wrote that the "lower races" traced their origin "from the apes," while the Aryans traced theirs "from the gods" (276). The occult writer Lanz von Liebenfels, who influenced Hitler and many other prominent Nazis, believed that the original human beings had degenerated through interbreeding with an ape-like creature depicted in certain Assyrian tablets (Goodricke-Clarke, 94-102). Hitler wrote in *Mein Kampf*, that the mission of the state was "to bring forth images of the Lord and not abominations blending man and ape" (444-445). In a speech of 1927 in Munich, he stated: "Take away the Nordic Germans and nothing remains but the dance of apes" (Waite, 85). The Jewish philosopher Emmanuel Levinas wrote that he and his fellow prisoners in a Nazi work camp were regarded as "a gang of apes" (153).

The theory of evolution has generated all sorts of phrases and theories that have a mythic resonance: "survival of the fittest," "the struggle for existence," "man the hunter." The theory created an iconography of heroic images from the brave fish that crawls forth on land to the caveman discovering the use of fire. The structure of Darwin's theory of evolution is basically that of totemism, the descent of a tribe from a sacred animal. Only two things rendered this prosaic — the mass of scientific evidence and the selection of the "ape" for an ancestor. The Nazis challenged the unity of the human race so the origin of humanity appeared less important. Since the nation was itself an organism, they felt that their true ancestor was less an ape than a primeval biotic community.

<45>

CHAPTER 5
BLOOD OF THE LAMB

One of the elders then spoke, and asked me, "Do you know who these people are, dressed in white robes, and where they have come from?" I answered him, "You can tell me, my lord." Then he said, "These are the people who have been through great persecution, and because they have washed their robes white again in the blood of the Lamb, they now stand in front of God's throne and serve him day and night in his sanctuary; and the One who sits on the throne will spread his tent over them." — Revelation 7:13-15

UNCERTAIN ON ITS feet and constantly calling for its mother, the lamb is a symbol of helplessness, passivity, and innocence. The sight of a lamb arouses protectiveness, and there was a special intimacy between sheep and human beings in the Old Testament. Yahweh looked with favor on the sacrifice of the shepherd Abel, a son of Adam who offered up the first born of his flock. The patriarchs of the Old Testament almost all possessed flocks. Jacob was a shepherd, as was King David. In many passages from the Old Testament, the people of Israel were compared to a flock, while their leaders were called "shepherds" (e.g., 2 Samuel 12:1-4; Jeremiah 3:15, 23:1-8; Ezekiel 34; Isaiah 53:6). Perhaps the most famous such passage is Psalm 23, beginning, "The Lord is my shepherd. I lack nothing. In meadows of grass he lets me lie. To the waters of repose he leads me. . . ."

When the Hebrew people were in bondage, the Pharaoh refused to let them leave even after Yahweh had visited ten plagues upon Egypt. Yahweh proclaimed through Moses that he would strike the first born of all who lived in Egypt from the eldest son of the Pharaoh to the first born of the cattle. "And throughout the land of Egypt there shall be such wailing as was never heard before, nor will be again." At the command of Yahweh, Moses and Aaron directed each family within Israel to slaughter a one-year-old, unblemished sheep or goat and eat the meat with unleavened bread and bitter herbs. Then each family was to take some blood from the slaughtered animal and mark its home, so that it may be spared the punishment of the Egyptians (Exodus 11-12). For Christians the animal is an anticipation of the sacrifice of Christ, who would take the sins of humanity upon himself.

On seeing Jesus for the first time, John the Baptist said, "Look, there is the lamb of God that takes away the sins of the world . . ." (John 1:29-30). When Peter professed his love for Jesus, Christ replied that the favorite disciple should show this love by feeding sheep and lambs (John 21:15-12).

<46>

The Last Supper of Christ, commemorated in the Christian mass, was a Passover meal. The blood then, identified with wine, would initially be the sacrificial animal. The body would initially be the unleavened bread eaten by the Israelites. St. Paul proclaimed, "Christ, our Passover, has been sacrificed; let us celebrate the feast, then, by getting rid of all the old yeast of evil and wickedness, having only the unleavened bread of sincerity and truth" (1 Corinthians 5:7-8). In Matthew we read that at the Last Judgment Christ "will separate men one from another as the shepherd separates sheep from goats" (25:32). In Revelations the "Lamb" became a designation for Christ, who presides over the apocalypse. Those around the throne of God "have washed their robes white again in the blood of the Lamb" (Revelations 7:14-15). To identify such a creature with God was a remarkable paradox in Christianity, one intended to show the mystery of the Deity. Rather than being simply powerful, God transcended the categories of earthly authority.

Christ would often be represented by the sacrificial lamb beside a cross, blood flowing from the wound in its throat into a chalice. Our word "pastor" was originally a Latin term for shepherd. The crosier carried by bishops of the church represents a shepherd's staff, and it is often carved with the figure of a lamb. As in so many other instances, the traditional symbolism of the Jews was turned against them.

In the Middle Ages, Jews were regularly accused of capturing Christian children for the purpose of ritual murder. This was suggested in part by the Biblical story of Abraham and Isaac. Abraham had been commanded by Yahweh to sacrifice his son Isaac on a mountain top. Just as he was about to cut the throat of his son, an angel appeared. The messenger of God pointed to a ram that had caught its horns in a bush, to be sacrificed in place of the boy (Genesis 22:1-14). The idea of ritual murder was also suggested by the Biblical story of the feast of Passover, constantly mentioned in propaganda against Jews. Also frequently invoked in accounts of ritual murder was the killing of the enemies of the Jews, including Haman and his ten sons in Persia, after the triumph of Mordecai which is celebrated at the feast of Purim (Esther 9).

The first widely publicized charge of ritual murder to be directed against the Jews came in 1137 when a 11-year-old boy named William mysteriously disappeared in Norwich, England. His mangled corpse was later found in the neighboring woods. Jews were accused of the murder of several other young boys including Richard of Pontoise {1182}, Hugh of Lincoln {1255}, and Simon of Trent {1472}. In 1235, when Jews were charged with ritually murdering two small children in Germany, the Emperor Frederick II ordered a thorough judicial investigation. The Jews were entirely acquitted, yet neither Emperors nor Popes were always able

<47>

to defend the Jewish communities from eruptions of violence brought on by rumors of ritual murder.

The alleged victims of ritual slaughter by Jews were venerated as "Holy Innocents" and often identified with the children killed by Herod in the gospels. In accounts of ritual murder, the victim was almost always bled to death by a cut to the throat, much as animals are in kosher slaughter. Another example is the story of a young boy murdered by Jews and thrown in a privy, told by the Prioress in Geoffrey Chaucer's *Canterbury Tales* (377). At times anti-Semitic propagandists even depicted Jews standing around the victim and catching streams of blood in outstretched vessels. Like many anti-Semitic beliefs, the notion of ritual murder was not simply an arbitrary invention but a direct inversion of Jewish practice. By tradition so fastidious in avoiding blood, the Jews appeared utterly obsessed with a craving for this mystic fluid. The accounts of murder were a perverse distortion of Jewish customs such as ritual animal slaughter and circumcision. They were also a parody of the Christian mass, which attributed enormous power to the blood of Christ. Proclaimed at a time when Christianity had conquered virtually all of Europe and faith had begun to wane, the cult of the Holy Innocents not only attacked the Jews but also broke with many traditional Christian ideals. The original Christian martyrs had knowingly chosen death rather than deny their faith. The Innocents had made no such choice; they were entirely passive. Christianity had taught that human beings were born in sin. The Innocents, however, seemed to be blessed simply by virtue of youth which left them uncontaminated by experience.

The cult of the Holy Innocents was a celebration of passivity and vulnerability as well as youth. In this respect it was like the Children's Crusade of 1212, when a group of children led by a French peasant boy named Stephen of Cloyes set out for the Holy Land to convert the Infidels, not through force of arms but through the spiritual power of purity. Most died on the voyage or were sold into slavery. As the cult of youth evolved, it retained the mystique of innocence but shed the passivity. Not content to be ritual victims, young men would humiliate and terrorize Jews on feast days such as Easter and Christmas.

The Power of Blood

Perhaps the most tangible point of continuity running through Judaism, Christianity, and Nazism is that all three attribute enormous importance to blood. The Jews showed this by their careful avoidance of blood, most especially in food. Christians, on the other hand, ceremoniously consumed it in the form of consecrated wine. Nazis viewed blood mystically as the carrier of ancestral heritage. The imagery of blood became an obsession in Nazi rhetoric.

<48>

The phrase "blood and soil" {Blut und Boden} has come to seem almost synonymous with Nazi ideology for many people. It began to circulate in the twenties and was further popularized by the Nazi Minister of Agriculture, Richard Walter Darré (Bramwell, 6, 54-63). Never very clearly defined, the phrase was used to designate a bonding between human beings and the ground on which they live. While flocks of sheep were not economically important in Germany, people associated these animals with farmers in the Alpine lands whose allegedly simple lives were often celebrated by writers and painters in the "blood and soil" movement. In the Nazi propaganda film *Der Ewige Jud* {*The Eternal Jew*} directed by Fritz Hippler, clips of Jews tormenting animals were followed by a bucolic scene of lambs relaxing in a field.

Like so many other images and phrases which acquired anti-Semitic associations, "blood and soil" had ironic origins in Jewish heritage. When Cain had killed his brother, the shepherd Abel, Yahweh said to Cain, "Listen to the voice of your brother's blood, crying out to me from the ground . . ." (Genesis 4:10-13). The phrase also recalled ritual slaughter of animals by the Hebrews, where the blood was allowed to run into the ground as an offering to God. In addition, "soil" and "blood" seemed to correspond respectively to the bread and wine of the Christian Eucharist. When the Nazis later appropriated this imagery, their idea of "innocence"was fierceness and brutality; redemption lay not in suffering but in victory, not in the lamb but in the wolf.

"A People of Murders"

Nobody but Julius Streicher, the propagandist who edited the weekly *Der Stürmer*, could repeatedly get in trouble with the Nazi party for taking anti-Semitism to the most perverse extremes. The bizarre fantasies of Streicher sometimes read like the supermarket tabloids of today which mix headlines about space aliens and the second coming of Elvis with stories like "Fur Coat Bites Rich Widow to Death." The publication of Streicher was similarly popular, yet it was anything but harmless entertainment. In May of 1934, Julius Streicher devoted an issue of *Der Stürmer* to the theme of "ritualized murder" by the Jews, ignoring a vast body of testimony from at least the time of Frederick II. He maintained that the Jews were a nation of murderers who lure others to slaughter and take their blood.

Streicher described many cases of ritual murder in lurid detail, adding illustrations of young men and women being held and bled to death as Jews caught the precious liquid in outstretched vessels. One story illustrates with special vividness the connection between the image of the sacrificial lamb and the charges of ritual murder. In 1899, during the Jewish holiday of Purim, a young Polish girl names Agnes Hruza disappeared in

<49>

the wood near Brezin. She was later found dead with her throat slit, and many believed she was a victim of ritual murder. "Agnus" means "lamb" in Latin, and Christ is often referred to as "Agnus Dei" or the "lamb of God." An illustration showed a blond Agnes held by two Jews as a third cut her throat. Just as the blood of the lamb in Christian painting flows into a chalice, a stream of blood from Agnes flowed into a bucket placed beside her (Streicher 95-96). Another illustration showed four bearded Jews drinking blood out of the body of a murdered child through straws. Streicher listed 131 cases of ritual murder, from pre-Christian times to 1932, adding that these were just a few of the hundreds of thousands, most of which went undiscovered (100-103).

Streicher maintained that the Jews were engaged in a plot to perform ritual murder on Adolf Hitler. A medieval custom on Yom Kippur had been to raise a fowl and swing it three times above one's head. The fowl would then be killed in place of the person, who would go on to live (Schochet, 224). *Der Stürmer* gave an inaccurate account of the ceremony, adding that it was ideally performed on a human being rather than on a bird. A plan for the ritual slaughter of Hitler was allegedly documented by a Jewish postcard printed by the "secret Jewish government," in which the face of the Führer had been placed on a sacrificial rooster. Reproduced in *Der Stürmer*, the postcard was surely a clumsy forgery, since the head of Hitler is not in the same style as the rest of the picture and looks as if it had been pasted on. According to Streicher, ritual murder takes place especially at the Jewish celebrations of Passover and Purim. In support of the charges, Streicher quoted many passages which purported to be from the Talmud. "Only the Jew is a human being," proclaimed one. "All who are not Jews are animals. They are livestock in human form. Against them, everything is allowed. The Jew may lie to them, deceive them, and steal from them. He can dishonor and murder them." Further quotations compared all who are not Jews to swine, apes, and dogs. "Every Jew," proclaimed another passage, "that spills the blood of an infidel {non-Jew} makes an offering to God" (94).

Streicher presented a long list of supposed Jewish customs, most of which involved the taking and ritual use of blood from gentiles. According to him the blood of gentiles was mixed in the wine and matzo at Passover. Dried to a powder, it was used to flavor eggs at Jewish weddings. It was drunk by Jewish women to aid in giving birth, and also used as a condiment with fruits and vegetables. It was stored in synagogues and sold at very high prices. Streicher also claimed that the father in a Jewish family would mix a liquid containing the blood of gentiles. At meal times he would dip in his left hand and sprinkle some over everything on the table while saying, "We ask you Father, to send plagues against all enemies of the Jewish religion." At the end of the meal, the father would say, "So may all

<50>

Fig. 3. "Sacrifice of the Jews." Illustration in *Der Stürmer,* May, 1934.

the goyim perish." A note explained that this Jewish practice had a "suspicious similarity to the Christian mass" with bread and wine as the body and blood. The only difference was that the Christian symbols were the Jewish reality (95).

The advertisements at the end of the issue showed just how respectable the ranting of Streicher had become. There were no sensational ads such as those found in tabloids. On the contrary, advertisements were from the most respected companies. They sold everything from tickets to the Berlin Zoo to hotels and insurance. In a tastefully restrained manner which contrasted strangely with the content of the publication, the ads promised men renewed youth through dye for grey hair. They promised women greater attractiveness through girdles and fashionable hats. "Your advertisements in *Der Stürmer* always bring great success," a note in the margin proclaimed (110).

<51>

The leaders of the Nazi movement may have privately shared many of Streicher's lurid fantasies, and they certainly found him useful in inciting the public against Jews. Nevertheless, Julius Streicher, the attack dog of the Nazis, was starting to become too rabid even for his handlers. After many readers had protested, Hitler ordered the issue of *Der Stürmer* on ritual murder withdrawn from the newsstands (Gilbert, 43). The response of Streicher to the criticism was to become even more lurid. He stated that a single instance of sex with a Jewish man was enough to contaminate the progeny of an Aryan woman forever. In seducing German women, Jews were following an injunction of the Talmud to destroy the Aryan race (Victor, 139). A special issue of *Der Stürmer* in 1938 listed 358 cases of these seductions, complete with photographs and detailed accounts. When leading officials in the Nazi party attempted to restrain Streicher, he turned his fury on them, alleging, for example, that Göring had not really fathered his daughters but produced them through artificial insemination. The list of Streicher's enemies grew ever longer until 1940 when a court declared him "unfit for leadership." Stripped of all positions of authority and forbidden from public speaking, he withdrew to his country estate and continued to edit *Der Stürmer* until the end of the war. In 1946 he was condemned to death by the Nuremberg Tribunal (Baird, "Streicher," 237-240).

Today, reading the charges of ritual murder made by Streicher against the Jews, it is remarkable how clearly they reverberate against the Germans of the time. He accused the Jews of being a nation of murderers, yet that is precisely what the Nazis were starting to become. He accused the Jews of regarding other peoples as animals, yet that as well is what the Nazis were doing, not only to Jews but also to Gypsies, Poles, Russians, and others. Appointed Gauleiter of Franconia in 1933, Streicher had ordered 250 Jewish tradesmen in Nuremberg to work as cattle by tearing up grass with their teeth (Gilbert, 40). A perverse identification with the Jews was especially apparent when Streicher's anti-Semitic tirades became obviously pornographic. A notorious lecher himself, Streicher was vicariously enjoying the perversion of his fictive Jews who abused the innocence of Aryan maidens. In his descriptions of ritualized slaughter, Streicher was blatantly projecting Nazi crimes upon the Jews. Rumored to be partly Jewish, Streicher read the Talmud and subscribed to a Jewish weekly. Before his execution, Streicher requested permission of the Nuremberg Tribunal to become an Israeli citizen (Victor, 145). When the request was denied, he went to his death still pledging allegiance to Hitler.

While upholding a nearly absolute ideal of purity, the Nazis were constantly obsessed with images of corruption. Hitler enjoyed the images of Franz von Stuck, his favorite painter, which depicted women erotically engaged with animals. Some of these paintings, with the titles "Sensuality,"

<52>

"Depravity," and "Sin," showed women luxuriating in the embraces of snakes (Waite, 68-69). A painting by Paul Mathias Padua entitled "Leda and the Swan" created a scandal though its blatantly pornographic depiction of bestiality, and Hitler soon purchased it for his own collection (Adam, 153-155). For all the Nazi invective about Jews being bloodsuckers, Hitler enjoyed having leeches draw his blood and called them "sweet, dear little animals" (Waite, 24).

The Nazi image of Jews, like most fantasies, was a combination of unarticulated desire and terror. An illustration on the cover of the special issue of *Der Stürmer* devoted to ritual murder by Jews shows a graveyard over which fly the spirits of young children. In the neck of each is a wound from which springs a stream of blood. Two men intended to represent the Jews are gazing at the sky. One clasps a bloody knife while the other holds a container decorated with a serpent and a Star of David to catch the blood. A caption above the picture reads, "Sacrifice of the Jews" {Judenopfer}. The phrase is ambiguous, in German as in English. Who is performing the sacrifice? Who is the victim?

<53>

CHAPTER 6
THE SACRIFICIAL PIG

"You men! You filthy dirty pigs! You're all the same, all of you. Pigs! Pigs!" —Amy Lowell, *Altogether*

PIGS CAN APPEAR remarkably "human": they are capable of a great range of vocalizations, and even in antiquity people noticed a resemblance between the internal organs of pigs and those of human beings. Their most dramatic resemblance to human beings may be the way that pigs appear to fear death. Boars have long been proverbial for fighting with great fierceness and until they are killed. Pigs taken to slaughter seem to sense the destiny that has been prepared for them and resist it by struggling and attempting to run away.

Nut, the Egyptian goddess of the sky, was depicted as a sow. In Norse mythology, warriors in Valhalla feasted nightly on the flesh of a great boar, Gitamburstli, which was then resurrected the next day. In Jewish tradition, however, the pig became the epitome of all that was unclean and disgusting. One reason is that pigs will eat almost anything, while Jews are traditionally very fastidious in their dietary practices. Another is the large amount of fat, considered unclean by Jewish law, in pork. The prophet Isaiah speaks of idolatrous Israelites as "living in tombs, spending nights in dark corners, eating the meat of pigs" (65:4-5). In the First Book of Maccabees, the Seleucid king degrades the Israelites by forcing them to sacrifice pigs and unclean beasts (1:47). The attitude in the New Testament is similar. Pigs become a refuge of devils when they are exorcized from men (Matthew 8:31; Mark 5:13; Luke 15:15). The degradation of the prodigal son is shown by his working as a herder of pigs (Luke 15: 15-16). Matthew enjoins his readers not to cast "pearls before swine" (7:6).

Since the Jews regarded the pig as the antithesis of everything holy, it was probably inevitable that early Christians in differentiating themselves from the Jews would choose the pig as an emblem. At the same time, they could not so easily overcome their traditional abhorrence of the animal. Christians developed a complex and ambivalent relation to pigs. To distinguish themselves sharply from Jews, they partially sacralized the swine. In peasant communities of Europe, swine would be kept as pets. They would be raised with affection and intimacy. On holidays such as Easter or Christmas they would be ceremonially slaughtered. The entire family would be present to pay last respects (Digard, 226). Finally the pig would be festively consumed. Special ceremonies were used for the disposal and burial of the bones (Farbe-Vassus, 293-322).

<54>

And yet much of the old aversion against swine remained. The attitude toward pigs in Europe reflects many of the paradoxes that surround the Hebrew heritage of Christianity. The Jesus of the gospels is very clearly a Jew. Christians viewed themselves as simultaneously repudiating and yet building upon a foundation in Judaism. Eaten to show defiance of Jewish law, pigs have nevertheless been identified with Jews. Like pigs, Jews were said to be creatures of the flesh, to be filthy and lustful. Many stories of the Middle Ages tell of pigs changed into Jews. Typical is one Swabian legend, in which a Pharisee tested Jesus by asking what was hidden beneath an overturned tub. There he had placed a slaughtered pig, but, unknown to him, his children had hidden there in play. "Your children are under the tub," Jesus replied. The Pharisee laughed, saying it was not his children but his pig. "Very well," answered Jesus, and when the Pharisee looked under the tub he found his children had been turned into pigs (Farbe-Vassus, 93). A chronicle of "wonders" by Johannes Fischart, published in Binzwangen in 1575, reported a Jewish woman giving birth to two piglets (Schreckenberg, 298).

Many ceremonies of the Middle Ages that marked episodes in the life of Christ incorporated ritualized violence against the Jews. Often enough, the enemies of Jesus would be symbolized by swine. In Dannelbourg, France, the enactment of the killing of Judas for his betrayal of Christ was accompanied by the sprinkling of blood from pigs upon the ground (Farbe-Vassus, 174). Until 1312 in Rome the season of Lent was inaugurated by rolling an aged Jew in a barrel spiked with points down the slope of Mount Testaccio. Later, pigs rather than Jews were decorated and seated in fine carriages, then taken to the mountain peak and thrown to their deaths (162). According to late medieval law in Germany, a condemned Jew sometimes had to be led to the place of execution wrapped in the skin of a pig (127). Similarly, pigs executed for eating their young, and for other crimes, would be led to the scaffold in human clothes. A caricature that emerged at the end of the Middle Ages known as the "Jew sow" showed Jews as bearded old men sucking on the teats of a mother pig. The ritualized violence against Jews which accompanied Christian holidays was intimately associated with the festive slaughter of pigs. Unlike the tending of sheep or cattle, the occupation of swineherd has seldom been spiritualized by bucolic associations. Even in their fantasies, aristocrats did not consider that a worthy occupation. It had a special earthiness which was at once its stigma and appeal.

As already noted, this earthiness and romance of the soil was a foundation of Nazi ideology. Overwhelmingly urban themselves, many Nazis were drawn to the image of the traditional farmer. For such men as Hitler and Goebbels, this appeal was at best sentimental, more a cynical means to power than a deeply held belief. For Richard Walter Darré it was

<55>

Fig. 4. Jewish scholars being suckled by a sow, from an anti-Jewish pamphlet published in Germany in 1475.

Fig. 5. Kitchen workers at the Gurs concentration camp with a slaughtered pig. Just as sometimes in the ancient world, Jews are humiliated by being forced to be associated with swine. Courtesy of the American Holocaust Memorial Museum (photo #17725).

<56>

generally sincere. Born to a prosperous German family in Argentina, he came to Germany at the age of ten in 1895. Never losing his Spanish accent, he idealized the history of his reclaimed homeland yet was not entirely able to fit in. He served in the army during the World War I, and then received a degree from an agricultural college in Halle. Unsure of his vocation and troubled by poor health, he was neither fully German nor Argentine, neither farmer nor intellectual.

Always uncomfortable with modern life, Darré sought a place in an idealized vision of the remote past. This was a primeval Germany, as yet untouched by the corrupting hands of Rome and Christendom. It was, so he imagined, a place of rugged peasants, simple, honest, and bonded to the soil. In his essay of 1927 "Das Schwein als Kriterium für nordische Völker und Semiten" (The Pig as a Distinguishing Feature for Northern Peoples and Semites), Darré proclaimed the pig to be the "leading animal" of the Germanic people. Not easily transported over distances, it was not a companion for nomads; it thrived on the acorns of the Northern forests. The pig provided the large quantities of fat necessary to survive the harsh winters of the north. Furthermore, the flesh of the pig spoiled quickly in tropical lands. Finally, the sacrificial pig was the animal favored by gods of the ancient Aryans.

Darré suggested that the Semites might have lost the ability to digest pork by avoiding pigs for so long. The foundation of their desert society was the ass or the camel, beasts of burden which did not become attached to a plot of soil. While swine thrive in the fertile woodlands, the ass and camel do well amid parched sands. Strangely, Darré did not even mention sheep in his discussion of domestic animals in the Near East. Perhaps this omission was simply ignorance of Biblical lore, surprising in somebody with claims to scholarship. However that may be, the mention would have placed in question the sharp contrast he wished to draw between the north and south. Both sheep and swine are animals that are herded, and both can forage more or less on their own. Both are animals preferred on feast days, especially at Easter; in fact the role of swine and sheep are largely parallel in the respective cultures of northern Europe and the Mediterranean.

The analysis by Darré had other faults as well. He interpreted the Biblical story of the first murder as a conflict between agriculturalists and herders. Cain, who offered produce of the soil to God, represented the settled Aryans. Abel, who offered flesh, represented the nomadic Semites. Darré neglected to mention the curse placed on Cain to be a wanderer protected only by a mark on his forehead. The nomadic Bedouins, who are Semitic, had long regarded Cain as their ancestor. Darré assumed that agriculture was necessarily a stable occupation and that farmers could be indefinitely bonded to a bit of land. Constant agriculture over generations,

<57>

however, generally exhausts the fertility of land more rapidly than grazing. The changeless world of the rural village was a figment of his imagination, and the attempt to create it could only lead to imperial expansion as agriculturalists were forced to search for additional territory.

Darré articulated his dream of primal harmony in *Neuadel aus Blut und Boden* {New Nobility of Blood and Soil}, first published in 1930. The peasant culture of Europe had endured for many centuries, yet the pressures and seductions of the modern world were now close to destroying rural ways of life. With support from the state the peasants might not only survive but also form a new nobility. By controlling the food supply, they could dictate to those who lived in cities and in towns. But under capitalism it was the market and not the peasants that set prices, and so it was necessary to free agriculture from the tyranny of the marketplace.

Like corporations, governments need people who are able to articulate poetic visions and yet corrupt enough to let these be exploited; such a person was Darré. A relative novice in politics, Darré attracted the attention of Hitler. When the two met in 1930, the Führer praised the writings of Darré, yet expressed concern that he was soft on Jews. Shortly after Darré joined the Nazi Party and when it came to power, he was given the grandiose title of "Imperial Peasant Leader" {Reichsbauernführer}. Unable to bond his peasants to the land, Darré tied the land to the peasants, forcing them and their descendants to retain it, profitable or not, forever (Schoenbaum, 157). His main accomplishment was the Law on the New Formation of German Peasantry, passed on June 14, 1933. This withdrew small farms from the marketplace and did not allow them to be bought, sold, subdivided, nor mortgaged. Darré hoped this legal bondage would grow over centuries into a bond of love. Eldest sons would work the land, while younger ones would organize to form militias. In 1934, he declared the medieval city of Goslar to be the capital of his new Peasant International, a confederation of farmers that were allegedly destined to rule in harmony with the land.

To serve the government of Hitler, Darré still had to prove his anti-Semitic credentials, and his thoughts turned back to the pig. World War I had begun in a rush of euphoria which turned to bitterness as troops reached an impasse on the Western Front. In response to severe shortages, the government tried to head off riots by rationing food. The state angered farmers by an injunction against using potatoes and grain as food for livestock. Then, in 1915, suspecting that farmers were not abiding by the new laws, the government ordered a wholesale slaughter of at least nine million hogs. This measure was greeted enthusiastically by the general public, especially by the poor. The "swine" became an epithet of contempt used by many sides as German society fragmented along lines of class, income, and profession. "Pigs" were all those that grew fat at public

<58>

expense while others starved or risked their lives in trenches: pampered officials, black-market profiteers, even the farmers themselves (Davis, *passim*). The public anthropomorphically called the events the "pig murder" {Schweinemord}. Apart from gratifying fantasies of revenge, the slaughter of swine brought little relief. The price of potatoes did not fall. Then in 1915 a government survey revealed that far more potatoes were available than previously thought. Fearing they might spoil, Germany even lifted a ban against distilling potatoes for alcohol (Herwig, 285-286).

All of this provided an occasion for Darré to indulge in the sort of anti-Semitic fantasizing that was a trademark of the Nazis. Jews had been long condemned as or "parasites." Since Jews do not eat pork, they seemed aloof from the suffering of the people (Davis, *passim*). The many temporary measures for the conservation of food enacted in World War I included a prohibition on kosher slaughter, instituted in 1916 to "obtain greater quantities of blood for human nutrition" (Brumme, "Blutkult," 404). The ban was not necessarily anti-Semitic in intent, but the idea of letting blood run to the ground must have reinforced stereotypes of Jews as living wastefully at public expense. As the turmoil and hunger in Germany grew, people increasingly placed the blame on Jews.

An essay in the July 1932 issue of *Deutsche Agrarpolitik*, an agricultural monthly published by the Nazis and edited by Darré, criticized the recent turn to feeding pigs industrially produced victuals rather than potatoes and other local products. The reliance on commercial feed, the article argued, undermined German self-sufficiency, interfered with farming tradition, and turned farms into "meat factories" (Schwiechow, 52). Meanwhile, the plight of the German farmers soon grew more desperate and the rhetoric more intense (Schoenbaum, 164-166). In 1937 Darré claimed to expose the "pig murder" as a Jewish plot, an attack on farmers which crippled the war effort and caused the death by starvation of three quarters of a million Germans. The betrayal was supposedly led by the assassinated Jewish minister Walter Rathenau, for whom Darré had previously expressed considerable admiration (Bramwell, 189), assisted by a cabal of Jewish advisors, academics, and officials. Darré published his charges in 1937 in a pamphlet entitled *Der Schweinemord* {The Pig-Murder}. The little book made it almost seem as if the slaughtered pigs were Germans symbolically killed to Judaize the land.

We can explain, though certainly not excuse, the hysterical polemic of Darré as a gesture of frustration. Darré believed the order to slaughter millions of pigs had been an attack on the culture and livelihood of the peasants. Emotional and spiritual longings were clearly present in the neo-pagan agrarianism of Darré, yet he had no skill whatsoever at expressing these feelings. A prolific yet clumsy writer, he would fill his articles with facts, figures, and academic arguments. Unable to explain the

<59>

Fig. 6. "The Civilized Man Being Made into a Domestic Pig." Illustration by Högfeldt to an article by Konrad Lorenz, used to show the difference between degeneration and primitivism.

urgency he felt, Darré disguised his passions with abstract theory and later with anti-Semitic invective. His theory about the pig as the emblem of the Aryans was an intriguing yet absurdly transparent attempt to fuse his own agriculturalist ideology with current political trends. The analysis reflected a combination of wishful thinking and cynical manipulation with no more than a minimum of scholarly argument. It placed all true Germans on the side of the farmers, and it labeled those who ordered the massive slaughter of swine as Jews.

Rather more typical for the Nazis was the view of Konrad Lorenz who regarded the pig as an example of the genetic degeneration that comes through domestication. An article of his published in 1942 contained an illustration, intended to be humorous, entitled "The Civilized Human Being Made into a Domestic Pig." It shows two black Africans, one wearing a chef's hat and the other carrying a chain. The end of the chain is attached to the nose ring of a corpulent white man who is completely naked and stares vacantly at his captors (Lorenz, "Formen," 306). The message is that the effete person who has degenerated genetically through excessive

<60>

civilization now has less value than the primitives. A jingle that became popular in right-wing circles during the twenties called the minister Walter Rathenau a "god-damned Jewish sow" (Gay, 153).

Despite the efforts of Darré, the German farmers continued to be deprived of their autonomy. A regulatory institution called the "communal market" {Markgemeinschaft} was formed to determine where and how much meat every dealer could place in public markets. It also regulated how much farmers might spend for the feeding and lodging of every animal (Vereinigte Fleisch, 19). In the Dresden Stockyard alone, 754,000 pigs, mostly stolen from farmers in occupied territories, were slaughtered on the assembly line from 1940 through 1944 (20). Roger Carras has observed, "No domestic animal is routinely treated with such profound cruelty as the pig, cruelty that is accepted as some kind of perverse norm in even our most sophisticated societies" (119). Pigs are kept in confined quarters where they sometimes do not even have room to turn around, and they are fed only what will yield the greatest quantity of meat and lard in the least amount of time. When the goal was to move people to anger or revenge, leaders like Darré might invite them to identify with pigs. Those who wished to brutalize and slaughter other people, however, would find it psychologically easier if they thought of their victims as swine.

<61>

CHAPTER 7
THE ARYAN WOLF

Homo homini Lupus est.
— Plautus

OR THE VICTORIANS the subjugation of large predators symbolized the triumph of their civilization over savagery. This was illustrated in the circus where a muscular man, perhaps wearing a leopard skin, would crack a whip and compel large cats to obey. Animals were considered admirable according to the degree to which they accepted human domination, and those perceived as rebels such as the tiger or wolf were often demonized (Ritvo, 21-30). This led to a moral crusade for the extermination of wolves and other large predators, especially in the United States during the nineteenth and early twentieth centuries — a goal often pursued with great persistence and cruelty (Worster, 258-290). Bounty hunters in early twentieth century America developed ingeniously cruel ways of killing wolves. After locating a den they might spear the cubs or drag them out with hooks. Alternatively, they might dynamite the den or start a fire at the entrance, causing the wolves to either be burned to death or suffocate. Another technique was to tie the sexual organ of a captured male wolf to prevent him from urinating; after a while hunters would kill the wolf and use the urine to attract his family. Hunters would lie in wait to shoot the wolves at they came (Hampton, 121-124). The most efficient means of killing wolves was to leave out a buffalo carcass laced with strychnine or some other poison (108-114). A self-righteous rhetoric reminiscent of the worst persecutions of witches or heretics often accompanied such exploits.

The Fear of Decadence

The other side of pride in the accomplishments of science and technology in the late Victorian period was the fear of an accompanying slackness or "decadence." Though seldom clearly defined, the word suggested weakness of will, sentimentality, lack of purpose, and self-indulgence. Many Victorians supposed that the cure for decadence was military life, which reputedly fostered courage, fierceness, and discipline. This idea was dramatized at the end of the nineteenth century in the enormously popular *Jungle Books* of Rudyard Kipling, often regarded as the poet of the British imperialism. The most popular stories were of a boy named Mowgli who was adopted and raised by wolves. The wolves met in a sort of parliamentary assembly, rather like the constitutional monarchy of Great Britain. There were checks and balances, yet it was quite clear

<62>

that the author's sympathy is with the monarch, an aging wolf named "Akela." His authority rested on superior abilities. The adversaries who challenged him in the assembly really only spoke for the rabble. Lacking the strength of Akela, they instead used stealth and cunning. All constantly invoked the "law of the jungle," which determined in meticulous detail how and under what conditions the leader of the pack might be deposed.

As Margaret Blount put it, "The Jungle is essentially a place of rules and order, and the *Jungle Books* are *about* rules and order, and about an outsider who learns to conform and to pass on to a different {and, one feels, lesser} kind of society. It becomes even more obvious that the Mowgli stories are partially disguised school or soldier stories when one thinks of the way the scout movement took them over" (230). Fear of decadence made Europeans look to the rule of instinct for firmness and reliability. From this perspective authority was a natural condition that the sentimentality of a democratic age had undermined. The jungle of Kipling was no place for bleeding hearts, and the penalty for violation of the laws was usually death.

Mowgli was almost a Nazi superman. Animals regarded him with fear and admiration. He fitted into and even dominated the society of the jungle. His status was won not only by obeying the rules but also by killing — a rite of passage which he had to constantly repeat. The forces of decadence and anarchy threatened even in the wild. The greatest danger came from the red dogs or "dholes." They invaded the jungle in huge numbers, flouting precepts and traditions. Mowgli led the dholes into a trap where he and his friends the wolves brutally slaughtered every member of the enormous pack. It is hard to know whether to credit chance or poetic intuition, but the scene was an uncanny anticipation of Nazi Germany. Kipling showed us genocide worked by one group of canids, ostensibly law-abiding and heroic, against others who were unable to conform.

The Jungle Books quickly became huge international bestsellers and were translated into all major European languages. Konrad Lorenz acknowledged *The Jungle Books* as an early influence (Lorenz, *King*, xviii), and many other thinkers also looked to wolves as a model for a warrior society. By having Mowgli outgrow the society of wolves, Kipling implicitly cautioned the reader against taking his portrayal of the jungle too seriously. The tale is in the tradition of many Victorian adventures for boys, with no sex and plenty of violence. The British with their enormous empire were able to take their fantasies of violence to exotic corners of the world while remaining relatively civilized at home. In Germany this was not feasible; the nostalgia for savagery was not so readily satisfied. Almost all features of the modern world including democracy were frequently considered decadent, and the cult of the wild beast became especially

<63>

vehement. One way to read *The Jungle Books* is as an allegory of human evolution and history in which the young boy representing humanity begins as an animal, but the wolves rather than apes are forerunners of human beings. The tales end when the animals rejected Mowgli; he asserted his superiority by threatening the wolves with fire and left to make his way in civilization.

According to Eliade, "Numerous Indo-European and Turko-Mongol tribes had eponyms of beasts of prey {primarily the wolf} and regarded themselves as descended from a theriomorphic mythical ancestor. The military initiations of the Indo-Europeans involved a ritual transformation into a wolf: the paradigmatic warrior appropriated the behavior of a carnivore" (*Stone Age*, 36). The Volsungs, a legendary warrior clan of Scandinavian and German mythology, were very closely identified with the wolf. Sigmund the Volsung was raised by wolves, and he sometimes put on a pelt to attack people as a werewolf. Romulus and Remus, the legendary founders of Rome, were suckled by a she-wolf. In earlier versions of the tale, the wolf was probably their biological mother. *The Jungle Books* were a protest against the slackness and decadence of a civilization that had turned its back on heroic tradition, thus severing a link with both the past and with the natural world. The wolf had often been celebrated as a romantic outlaw in other works of the same period, for example in the popular story, "Lobo," by the American naturalist Ernest Thompson Seton, at the end of the nineteenth century. Perhaps even more than the lion or bear, the wolf has remained a symbol of martial culture.

Hour of the Wolf

When an extended period of comparative peace in Europe drew to a close, people throughout the western world once again began to see the fierceness of predators in a positive way. This led to an increased interest in canids, particularly because of their ability as fighters. For the cult of the wolf seemed to offer the Nazis a promise of the discipline sometimes associated with "civilization" without its accompanying decadence, of nature without anarchy. As an animal that had been extinct within Germany for almost a century, yet lived on in figures of speech, folk tales, and iconography, the wolf suggested a sort of primeval vitality that had been lost. And the fact that no wolves survived in Germany made it easy to appropriate the animal for symbolic purposes, since experience could seldom contradict the prevailing rhetoric. Unlike governments in the United States and other countries, the Nazis did not have to deal with farmers who feared that predators would attack their livestock. In 1934 Germany became the first nation in modern times to place the wolf under

<64>

Fig. 7. Eighteenth-century German engraving depicting the punishment of Jews
in this world and the next. In both instances they are degraded by animals which
Jews have traditionally considered unclean. First, they are hanged, and the one on
the right is string up together with a large dog. In Hell, they are forced to ride on
pigs. One of them continues to read a book, presumably the Talmud, which reminds
him of his shame.

<65>

protection (Giese and Kahler, 227), a gesture that was not much more than symbolic within the original national boundaries. The Nazis were already looking toward Poland and other countries where wolves could still be found.

Hitler and his followers could find further support in traditional symbolism, since dogs and wolves are unclean according to Mosaic Law. Wolves are the enemy of flocks and shepherds, and the people of Israel were, as we have seen, frequently identified as sheep (e.g., Psalm 23). In the Old Testament, wolves are repeatedly associated with destruction and with the enemies of Israel (e.g., Jeremiah 5:6, Ezekiel 22:27, Zephaniah 3:3). Dogs by contrast are generally associated with carrion and viewed with disgust (Menache, 28-29). In Proverbs we read, "As a dog returns to its vomit, so a fool reverts to his folly" (26:11). In Rabbinical literature, keeping dogs is often condemned as "abhorrent behavior of the uncircumcised" (Menache, 30-31). Sometimes, association with dogs or wolves was used as a means of demeaning and tormenting Jews. In late medieval Germany, Jews convicted of crimes were sometimes suspended from a gallows by the feet instead of the neck, with two vicious dogs or wolves, also suspended by their feet, on each side (Kisch, 186-187).

There had been a wave of werewolf trials in late medieval France, so the wolves and Germans seemed to share a common enemy. The Jews in Germany had been liberated from the Ghetto and from several restrictive laws by the Napoleonic occupation. As a consequence, Jews tended to sympathize with France against the Germans, while Germans tended to identify Jewish with Gallic culture (Lotter, 17). The Germans often stigmatized both the French and the Jews as antagonists of nature. Hermann Hesse published a highly lyrical story entitled "The Wolf," in which the animal, a symbol of natural beauty, is martyred by the unappreciative Gallic farmers. Hermann Löns wrote a similarly poetic sketch of a wolf whose den in the forest has been destroyed and was trying to escape from cars and human beings (*Isengrins*, 3-11). The Teutonic peasants defending their lands with great brutality during the Thirty Years' War were celebrated as "werewolves" in an immensely popular novel by Löns, published in 1910 (Mosse, *Crisis*, 25-26).

The Nazis were constantly invoking dogs and wolves as models for the qualities they wanted to cultivate: loyalty, hierarchy, fierceness, courage, obedience, and sometimes even cruelty. Hitler's code name was "the wolf." He also sometimes went by the nicknames "little wolf" and "uncle wolf," while his various headquarters were referred to as "Werewolf" {Wehrwolf}, "Wolf's Gulch" {Wolfschlucht}, and "Wolf's Lair" {Wolfschanze}. He referred to the SS as "a pack of wolves" (Ehrenreich, 212). A plan to infiltrate groups hostile to the Nazi government was known as "operation werewolf." The members of the Hitler Youth used by the

<66>

desperate government as soldiers at the end of World War II were also known as "werewolves." Hitler called himself "a wolf . . . destined to burst in upon the seducers of the people" (Steinhart, 101), and he told a servant, "I am the wolf and this is my den" (Waite, 16). Hitler also explained that crowds of people cheered him rapturously because they realized that "a wolf is born." (Ehrenreich, 212).

After the assassination of Heydrich, Richard Wolf {sic}, a high-ranking SS officer wrote a poem entitled "The Führer's Wolves," which began:

> The lead wolf was killed —
> The pack huddled together
> And forms — still fired up from battle —
> With their bodies alone
> A ring of loyalty around the chief
> Who chose the pack to protect him.
> The strongest wolf springs up again!
> He bravely surveys the field with flaming eyes —
> And full of rage strikes his fangs into the heart of the enemy,
> While the pack forms up around the knoll (Baird, *To Die*, 216).

In a similar manner Joseph Goebbels described the Nazi delegates to the Reichstag in 1928, saying ". . . we come as enemies! Like a wolf tearing into the flock of sheep, that is how we come!" (Koonz, 53).

The Wolves of Schenkel

Rudolf Schenkel began his innovative study of wolves in 1934, shortly after the Nazi rise to power. He published it in 1949, not very long after the final defeat of the Nazis. Working in Basel, Switzerland, he may have been influenced by the proximity of Nazi Germany, the proverbial "wolf at the door." In studying wolves, he was demythologizing them; nevertheless, the Nazi mystique comes through in his accounts of lupine behavior. Schenkel described in intricate detail cruel games played by dominant wolves, adding that the victim always belonged to another "race of wolves" than the perpetrators. He added that certain wolves were victimized repeatedly and gradually lost the status of a "social partner." They were "deprived of any social privileges and, amid the continual attacks, were sometimes given fatal wounds." Clearly, the dominant "race" of wolves corresponds to the Nazis while the others are their victims like Jews and Gypsies. Schenkel explained in a note he did not employ word "race" {"Rasse"}, obsessively used by the Nazis, with any claim to scientific exactness (89). But Schenkel could have used a number of other words which would have been less politically charged; he could also have

<67>

attempted a more exact definition. The note sounds as if it might have been added as an afterthought, perhaps because the implicit comparison between wolves and Nazis was starting to make the author uncomfortable.

Schenkel described wolves as governed by a "domination hierarchy," adding that the hierarchy for females differs from that for males. This corresponded exactly to the hierarchal structure that the Nazis endeavored to create in their society. The hierarchy of women in Nazi Germany was somewhat distinct from that of men. As early as 1926, Elsbeth Zander received permission to consider herself the leader of all female Nazis (Koonz, 72). As Claudia Koonz put it, ". . . several woman Nazis independently organized into what one woman leader called 'a sort of parallel movement,' separate from the Nazi party yet supportive of it" (71).

Schenkel emphasized repeatedly that hierarchy is a model that only described the behavior of wolves approximately. He did not make any attempt to offer a precise definition of rank within lupine society. The element of rank is situation-specific and continuously in flux (Schenkel, "Wölfen," 87). Furthermore, he insisted that lupine society can never be reduced to any simple formula and that the gestures of wolves were a language capable of communicating virtually endless nuances (112). Later authors often described wolves as hierarchal but neglected to add these qualifications.

For a long time, the idea of lupine society as strictly hierarchal was taken for granted in much popular and professional literature. Among the earlier observers to express reservations about the idea is Barry Lopez, who has written, "But the term "alpha" {top animal} — evolved to describe captive animals — is still misleading. Alpha animals do not always lead the hunt, break trail in the snow, or eat before the others do. An alpha animal may be alpha only at certain times and for a specific reason, and, it should be noted, is alpha at the deference of the other wolves in the pack" (Lopez, 33). In 1979, Randal Lockwood, complaining that the concept of "dominance" in wolf packs had been used overly freely, did an extensive study of various behaviors that had been associated with rank, such as success in competition for food, sexual privileges, grooming, and many others. The result was that little correlation among these behaviors was discovered, and Lockwood concluded that the concept of a dominance hierarchy was of little use in predicting behavior within a wolf pack. As an alternative model to describe the social structure of wolves, he suggested "role differentiation" (Lockwood, 235-236). Other studies indicated that the concept of "dominance" had limited but genuine applicability (Hoof and Wensing, *passim*), but a consensus has emerged that social behavior within a wolf pack cannot be accurately described with any simple model including hierarchy (Moran, 214; Steinhart, 120-123).

<68>

Leopold and His Successors

The cult of the wolf continued to influence Western culture long after the end of the Nazi regime. Aldo Leopold, the founder of the American environmental movement, went to Germany in 1935 in order to learn about German methods of forestry, then considered the most sophisticated in the world. He generally stayed aloof from politics, and it is uncertain what if anything he may have heard about the German concentration camps. While Leopold was impressed with the German ability to plan in terms of cycles lasting hundreds of years, he was troubled by the artificiality of the German woods. Every aspect of the environment in Germany had been placed so far as possible under human control. The intention of preserving a maximum yield of timber while at the same time a maximum density of deer for hunting meant that young trees had to be protected with fences or wire. Leopold felt that Germany was pervaded by nostalgia for wildness. The United States by contrast still had many wild landscapes but was in danger of losing them (Flader, 142; Worster, 285). The foresters of Germany were already making attempts to restore their original landscapes (e.g., Schoenichen, 110-112), which resembled those Leopold would propose in the United States. Leopold expressed strong admiration for the nature protection {*Naturschutz*} movement in Germany, which was already reintroducing raptors and some predators (Meine, 355).

On his return from Germany, Leopold co-founded the Wilderness Society and began to work for the return of wolves and other predators, inspired in part by the German example. The greatest contribution of Leopold to the ecology movement was an ethic of the "land," a word that resonates mystically though his writing. "Conservation," he wrote in 1948, "is getting nowhere because it is incompatible with our Abrahamic concept of the land. We abuse land because we regard it as a commodity belonging to us. When we see land as a community to which we belong, we may begin to use it with love and respect" (*Sand*, viii). This rhetoric echoes that of many German nationalists, with the attack on Judaism and capitalism, as well as the longing for community. "Abrahamic" is used here as a euphemism for "Jewish," and the word is certainly inappropriate.

Leopold shows no trace of the brutality or the chauvinism that characterized the Nazi movement. Furthermore, the suggestion of anti-Semitism is partially muted by the fact that Leopold does not attempt to criticize the ancient Israelites from an attitude of presumed superiority. Leopold interpreted American history partly in terms of an Old Testament paradigm, as had many early colonists over a century before. Like the Jews in the Holy Land, the European immigrants to America had come to a "land of milk and honey." They had then, like the Israelites, nearly

<69>

exterminated the original inhabitants, and were in the process of destroying the fertility of the countryside (Leopold "Conservation," 636).[1]

Since the Nazi period the cult of the predator, especially the wolf, has not faded. Novelty shops everywhere in America are full of t-shirts and sterling jewelry with romantic depictions of wolves. This new craze for wolves, now several decades old, started with Farley Mowat's best-selling book *Never Cry Wolf*, first published in 1963, a fictionalized account of the author's sojourn in Alaska. The mystique that Mowat conveyed about wolves was very similar to that in Nazi Germany. His focus was primarily the alpha couple in a pack. Mowat stressed the fidelity of wolves which he contrasted with the lack of loyalty in dogs, their close relatives corrupted by human society (92-93). Especially notable was his account of the eugenic importance of wolves, an idea which he claimed to have heard from Native Americans. Wolves, according to Mowat, tested the caribou and then selected those which were weak or ill as prey, thus ensuring the vigor of the herd. "The caribou feeds the wolf," he reported an Eskimo friend as saying, "but it is the wolf who keeps the caribou strong. We know that if it were not for the wolf there would be no caribou at all, for they would die as weakness spread among them" (199-200).

---

[1] Contemporary historians and climatologists doubt this view. The people of Moses may not have entered Palestine as conquerors, and they do not necessarily bear more or less responsibility for its decline in fertility than the many other societies that lived in the Holy Land before and after ancient Israel. Long before the Israelites, it had been subject to terrible droughts and to flooding, as is recorded by the Sumerians and other peoples of the Near East. Only gradually though millennia of excessive irrigation had its fertility been reduced. For a discussion of the ecology of the region, see Attenborough (*passim*).

<70>

CHAPTER 8
THE JEWISH DOG

I am his Highness' dog at Kew;
Pray tell me, sir, whose dog are you.
— Alexander Pope

HANS FANTEL WAS just entering his teens when Hitler invaded Austria in 1938. Initially, the young man joined most of his companions in celebrating. A few weeks later the Gestapo came to arrest his neighbor, a lawyer named Mr. Eisler, whose dog attacked the intruders and was shot. Fantel was not particularly concerned about the neighbor, but he had played with the dog. The housekeeper who looked after him reassured young Hans that "It doesn't matter. . . . It's a Jewish dog." As he pondered this, the teenager found it made little sense. Did dogs actually have creeds? For the first time, he began to doubt Hitler (Fantel, *passim*). What could the housekeeper have meant? It was probably not simply that the dog was owned by a Jew, since the Nazis generally had no hesitation about using confiscated Jewish property. That was certainly not how Fantel understood the phrase. Furthermore, the notion of a Jewish dog was not new. The epithet "dog" was traditionally applied to Jews as an expression of contempt. In Shakespeare's *The Merchant of Venice*, Shylock, the Jewish moneylender, complains to Antonio, his Christian customer:

What should I say to you? Should I not say
"Hath a dog money? Is it possible
A cur can lend three thousand ducats?" Or
Shall I bend low, and in a bondsman's key,
With bated breath and whisp'ring humbleness,
Say this, "Fair sir, you spet on me on Wednesday last;
You spurned me such a day; another time
You called me "dog" . . . (Act 1, Scene 3, Lines 120-127)

Heinrich Heine, a German-Jewish poet, had written a narrative poem entitled "Princess Sabbath," about a Jew named "Israel" who must assume the form of a dog on every day but Friday (Heine, 263-267).

The housekeeper, of course, was using the term "dog" literally, while "Jewish" was relatively metaphorical, but the two were often associated. To give one very mundane example from everyday life, a sign on the door of a hotel in a Bavarian village in the 1940s read, "Dogs and Jews not welcome" (Engelmann, 80). Fantel gave us a hint as to the meaning of the

<71>

housekeeper's phrase when he said that the dog was a mongrel. The rest is not terribly hard to imagine. It would have been a dog that conformed to many popular stereotypes of Jews. It may have been relatively small with rather irregular features. The dog may also have been more intelligent than strong, the opposite of the "heroic" canine and lupine images that were popular at the time. From the romantic era through much of the twentieth century, Europeans were obsessed with this duality of civilization and savagery, and dogs could represent either of these forces.

Struggle for Existence

The widespread keeping of pets was a middle-class custom that was established in the late eighteenth and nineteenth centuries (Ritvo, 85-86). Nazi revulsion against this was part of a widespread revolt against bourgeois culture in the early twentieth century, a revolt which also embraced Bolshevism and artistic avant-gardes. Keeping animals simply as companions involved the cultivation of softer emotions. Historically, bourgeois pet keeping reflected a greater emphasis on individual autonomy, so an attack on it was nearly inevitable in the Nazi movement.

The Nazis favored wild animals over domestic ones at least in rhetoric, largely because wild creatures seemed untouched by human personality. The Darwinian phrase "struggle for existence" was commonly translated into German with the more severe expression "Daseinskampf," giving the impression of life as a perpetual battlefield (Bäumer, 64). This phrase was echoed in *Mein Kampf* or "my struggle," the title of Hitler's autobiography. Victory in the battle of life might be expected to go to the greatest warriors. Ernst Haeckel had written that: "A 'moral ordering' and 'a purposive plan' of the world can only be visible if the prevalence of the immoral rule of the strongest . . . is entirely ignored" (Haeckel, vol. 1, 112). Nevertheless, it was hard not to notice that large predators were everywhere dying out. Furthermore, the most powerful people very seldom looked or acted like mighty warriors. The world of everyday observation had virtually nothing to do with the martial images evoked by popular Darwinism. For many people the supposed "right of the strong" took on a moral aspect: the warriors, the wild predators, had been meant to rule, but they had been cheated of their patrimony. The primeval Aryan warrior spirit might still be present in the German people, much as the heroic lupine character survived in at least some dogs.

<72>

The Mystique of Breeds

A breed is an artificially created species. Up through the Middle Ages breeds of domestic animals were vague and approximate to the extent that they existed at all. Systematic mating of animals only really began in the latter eighteenth century when the Englishman Robert Bakewell developed the technique known as "inbreeding," that is crossing animals that were already related genetically (Digard, 48-49). This enabled breeders to produce animals that were specialized and uniform, thus conforming to the pattern of industrial production. Cattle and pigs were bred to produce the greatest quantity of meat with the minimal investment of food. Breeds of horses, dogs, and other animals were also created according to aesthetic criteria or to perform practical tasks. By the second half of the nineteenth century, stud books were kept for cattle, dogs, and horses, in which standards were fixed and detailed blood lines were recorded. Highly competitive shows were held in which animals were judged as representatives of their type. The breeding of animals first produced the concepts of "race" and of "pure blood" (Digard, 56), later adopted by the Nazis. In the latter nineteenth century dog shows preserved and even popularized feudal concepts of a natural hierarchy by birth. They featured a eugenic pursuit of moral and aesthetic perfection that mirrored the enormous emphasis on pure family lines, on "pedigree," in aristocratic houses (Thurston, 98; Ritvo, 82-121).

Breeds were also romanticized; applying a mystique adopted from vinoculture, the animal fanciers viewed thoroughbreds as a product of centuries in which these creatures gradually adapted to the climate and soil of a region (Digard, 50). Fraudulent histories traced the pedigrees of animals back for centuries, much like the questionable genealogies of aristocratic families (Ritvo, 82-121; Derr, 59). The more imaginative canine historians even attempted to trace modern breeds back to Neolithic times (Derr, 56). Around the beginning of the twentieth century, Max von Stephanitz bred dogs to recreate what he believed was "the primeval Germanic dog" {germanischer Urhund}, an animal we know today as the "German Shepherd." This dog was intended to embody the virtues of the German people, and its inception clearly anticipated the Nazi attempts to breed human beings back to a primeval Aryan stock (Wippermann, 195).

A follower of Haeckel, Stephanitz frequently drew parallels between breeds of dogs and the people who lived alongside them, categorized on the basis of race, class, politics, and ethnicity. He wrote that feral dogs "are the products of free-love on the most modern and broad-minded scale, and are all convinced Bolsheviks in creed and conduct" (Stephantiz, 44). Stephanitz claimed that, "creatures of pure blood, where by proper breeding all unevenness has been eliminated . . . far surpass all mongrels." He also did not hesitate to apply that lesson to human beings, concluding

<73>

that, "Physical beauty, which in female descendants of connections with unequal members of the Human Race is often startlingly conspicuous, is generally combined with mental degeneracy. This is a well-known fact. The Law forbidding intermarriage between members of highly cultured peoples with women of a lower race is therefore thoroughly sound and appropriate" (50).

Stephanitz promoted a theory of the dual origin of the dog, whereby certain breeds such as pinchers were traced to domestication of the jackal. Other dogs had varying amounts of jackal blood, but the German shepherd was entirely a descendant of the wolf (18, 22-23). These dogs were the companions of Germans from primeval times. The German love of dogs was simply "part of his nature" (195). "It is hard not to understand," Stephanitz wrote, "how the warlike proud German held in high esteem his courageous hunting comrade who helped him in his struggle with the rampaging wild-ox, the destructive boar, or the greedy beast of prey" (172). Alfred Rosenberg, their chief ideologist, later found it "tragic" that people took so much care with the pedigree of horses and asses while being so careless about the breeding of human beings (77), a sentiment that would be echoed by many other Nazis. Even in contemporary society, thorough-breds win the prizes while mongrels are often abandoned or euthanized. In much the same way, the Nazis resolved to "euthanize" those who were not racially pure.

The Bourgeois Hound

In the latter nineteenth and early twentieth centuries civilization and restraint were regularly contrasted with instinct. Freud valued the ability of reason to hold instinct in check, though he doubted that the victory over savage impulses could ever be complete. The life of civilized man was a constant struggle between sexuality on the one hand and repression on the other. In the last years of his career, this duality was replaced by that of eros and death. Thomas Mann dramatized the tension between instinct and civilization in his story "A Man and his Dog," first published in 1919. It is an account of a pet dog named Bashan that acknowledges the rules of his human master yet cannot resist the call to chase the creatures of the woods. The man tolerates the hunting instincts of the dog, observing that Bashan can never catch anything larger than a mouse. Hares are able to dodge Bashan without great difficulty. On the few occasions when birds are not able to escape by flight, they can outmaneuver Bashan.

When Thomas Mann wrote the story, he was beginning his political transformation from a German nationalist contemptuous of democracy to a supporter of the Weimar Republic. This is symbolized by a change of pets. The first dog of the master in his story is named Percy, a hound of high pedigree who is aristocratic and disciplined yet sickly and erratic.

<74>

Noble yet doomed, he represents the feudal order. Bashan, his successor, is normal and healthy apart from a few spells of moodiness. The new dog represents the social order of the bourgeoisie. The health of Bashan is based on precarious compromises; he can indulge his instincts including the lust for blood only in strict moderation. When these instincts are overly indulged an incipient savagery comes out.

A metaphor that runs with varying degrees of explicitness through almost all Western culture from the eighteenth century to the present is civilization as the taming and restraining of an animal. This creature is the "beast within," a part of the human psyche that lingers as an archaic heritage, rather like a caged beast of prey at the zoo. The restraint applies especially to sexuality and lust for blood, impulses that would otherwise be destructive and overpowering. In Freudian terminology this restraint was "repression." The founder of psychoanalysis accepted this with a melancholy regret as necessary, but many of his more impetuous followers saw human fulfillment as "liberation" of the beast.

Dogs of War

Dogs were not only models of the ideal of "pure blood" but also provided an object for eugenic experimentation. In 1934 H. Vogel told the German Society for Scientific Breeding that, "When I speak of the importance of race in breeding, I do it with the specific intention of drawing connections between the successfully tested methods of animal breeding and the substantially unexplored tasks of systematic biological improvement of the human race" (Wolfschmidt 18). A publication of a society of rabbit fanciers declared in 1942 that, " . . . Since the National Socialist assumption of power, German rabbit breeding has made unheard of progress, . . . has received a new aim. The people concerned with it were imbued with new organizational and eugenic impulses" (Remak, 56). The German Society for Animal Psychology, which was to direct most research and public policy relating to animals, originally grew out of experimentation in the breeding of dogs. When tests on various hounds convinced scientists that it was not sufficient to breed for physical characteristics, they turned their attention to mental ones. The result was a new domain of study based on a strict biological determinism (Effertz, 1). Werner Fischel, head of the Research Institute for Animal Psychology in Münster during the Nazi period, was very explicit about the reasons for studying dogs when he wrote, "While we have many catalogs of instincts of the insects and the birds, we hardly know anything useful about those of dogs. The increasing importance of the dog in war compels us to research them. We need the martial abilities of dogs, but far too little is known about their instincts for fighting. These are now more important than any purely theoretical constructs about the nature of instinct" (68).

<75>

Fig. 8. SS guard posing proudly with his dog. Courtesy of the United States Holocaust Memorial Museum (Photo #08870).

Soldiers at the front constantly used dogs for tracking, carrying messages, guarding prisoners, and occasionally even for combat. Qualities such as physical courage and aggression made such dogs models for human soldiers. The SS was responsible for the care, training, and breeding of these dogs, activities that required an extensive organizational structure and even special institutions for the production of food (Wipperman, 31). When dogs were captured on the Eastern front, however, the Russians used them against their former masters. They would starve the dogs, attach explosives to them, and let them free. The dogs would immediately head for the German lines where they were used to being fed, at which time the bombs would explode (Delort, 462).

The martial partnership of man and dog is dramatized in the novella *Auf den Marmorklippen* {*On the Marble Cliffs*}, published during World War II, by Ernst Jünger, then a German officer of the occupying army in France. It is a veiled account of the "night of the long knives" in 1934 when Hitler purged his rival Ernst Röhm, and dissident Nazis were rounded up and shot. The tale described a rebellion in a mythic land against the dominion of the devious "Old Forester," probably a representation of Hermann Göring. On both sides, men and dogs fought together, and the author used various dogs to represent many qualities including faithfulness and cruelty, human civilization and animalistic abandon.

Another side of the Nazi preoccupation with dogs was their use in guarding the inmates of concentration camps and other prisoners. The

<76>

teeth of these dogs inspired enormous fear, probably beyond that evoked even by the human guards with their weapons (Wippermann, 198-199). The SS had a central Institute for Canine Training and Research in Orienburg (197-198). Auschwitz contained a special regiment recruited from the SS Death's Head Brigades, which was devoted to caring for dogs. Members would sometimes set dogs on prisoners simply for entertainment (199-200). Heinrich Himmler called for dogs trained to herd prisoners like livestock (Wippermann 200); The grotesque idea perversely reflected the traditional symbolism of both Jews and Christians as sheep. The Nazis even declared a special "Day of the Dog," in which large wagons depicting the service of dogs paraded down the streets to marching music (196).

The archives of the United States Holocaust Memorial Museum contain a description, written by former inmate Willy Furlan-Horst, of the kennel for dogs used by the SS to guard prisoners at the concentration camp in Dachau. The dogs had been trained to jump on a prisoner who made any sudden or irregular move. There were about sixty kennels, each with its own doghouse and a large exercise area. Furlan-Horst contrasted this with the cramped quarters of the inmates where three or four men sometimes had to sleep together in a single bed. The dogs, he remarked, "were SS family after all" (USHMM, document RG-4.019*01, 1, 3). Such concern, however, did not apply to all canines. Dogs in the Third Reich, like people, were divided into two basic groups — those dogs that served the Third Reich, and enemies. Once, in occupied Rotterdam, when a dog barked at a German patrol, an officer immediately shot the dog and arrested the owner (Engelmann, 317).

The Führer's Dogs

With systematic consistency, Hitler had himself photographed with hounds in order to "humanize" his public image (Wippermann, 202). Biographers are generally agreed that Hitler's dogs actually did come closer than any human being to sharing intimacy and friendship with him. Even today it is hard to separate out legend, truth, and propaganda about these dogs. One primer for children in Nazi Germany narrated how two little girls go to visit the Führer. They were very impressed when he gets his puppy, Wolf, to jump for a piece of sausage. One of the girls said, "My goodness, Herr Hitler, you really do have an excellent way of training dogs" (Kamenetsky, 183). The first of Hitler's dogs to achieve fame was Fuchsl, who leaped into Hitler's trench during World War I and stayed with him about a year and a half. Eventually Fuchsl disappeared, presumably stolen, and Hitler was devastated. After his mistress Eva Braun attempted suicide, Hitler gave her two fox-terriers, Stasi and Negus, to ease her loneliness. The most famous of Hitler's dogs was Blondie, a female German Shepherd.

<77>

When the Russians captured Berlin, Blondie was given a cyanide capsule and shared death with Hitler and Eva Braun in their bunker.

Hitler remains mysterious in spite of massive scholarship, but the best indicators of his attitudes are probably remarks made in unguarded moments. What comes out most strongly in accounts of Hitler's relation to his dogs is a streak of pathological jealousy. Hitler said toward the end of his life that he trusted only his dog Blondie and perhaps his girlfriend Eva (Waite, 413). Incapable of close relations with human beings, he would spend long periods of time with his dogs. In the bunker toward the end of his life, he would go daily to the kennel and caress a puppy named "Wolf" whom nobody else was allowed to touch (414).

The surgeon Ferdinand Sauerbruch reports that in 1942 he was summoned to the headquarters of the Führer, a place that impressed him as a "madhouse." Led by an assistant into Hitler's office, he found the elegant room completely deserted. As he looked around in perplexity a huge dog entered, began barking furiously, bared its teeth, jumped on him, knocked him over, and placed its teeth at his neck. Sauerbruch had worked with dogs all his life and knew exactly how to pacify them; he lay completely motionless for a while, then he began to speak gently and stroke the dog. Hitler entered in a furious mood after a frustrating meeting with his generals and was overcome by jealousy. "What have you done with my dog?" he screamed at the terrified Sauerbruch. "You have deprived me of the only creature who was truly faithful to me, taken my companion away . . . ," Hitler continued; he then announced that he would have the dog shot and the visitor arrested, but after some flattering words from Sauerbruch, Hitler relented, sparing both dog and man (545-549).

The novelist Günter Grass has often focused on the more mundane features of daily life in an attempt to strip Nazism not only of legitimacy but also of its satanic glamour. In his novel *Dog Years* {*Hundejahre*}, Grass tells the story of a few generations of dogs together with their human masters. The dog Harras is used as a stud to produce Prinz, who is presented to Adolf Hitler. Those who raised Harras suddenly find themselves surrounded by celebrity and controversy. After being presented to the Führer, the dog and his ancestors become a center of pride, intrigue, and metaphysical speculation. When Harras runs away from Hitler, authorities report a massive search in rhetoric that blends jingoism with the philosophical terminology of Heidegger. Prinz is later adopted by Walter Matern, a former member of the SA. The disillusioned Matern has previously poisoned Harras, the father of Prinz, as an indirect way of taking revenge on the Nazis. As the novel ends, Matern wanders with the ageing Prinz after the war in search of understanding and forgiveness.

The ancestor of Prinz had been a Lithuanian shepherd dog that mated with a wolf. Such intimacy with the enemy of sheep was a betrayal of her

<78>

calling and left her descendants unsuited to life in a village, but this lupine descent was precisely what attracted the Nazis. Prinz showed his inheritance in not only in his black color but also in his fits of rage. On dying, Hitler bequeathed the dog Prinz to the German people, signifying that the barbaric element in the German character will not perish with his regime. Prinz had precisely the same ambivalence as the dogs in the tales by Mann and Jünger, all of which are torn between their predatory instincts and civilization.

Wolf and Jackal

The Nazi regime, intended to last a thousand years, fell after barely over a decade, though the cult of the wolf implicit in much of Nazi literature survived the regime. In *King Solomon's Ring*, initially published in 1950, Konrad Lorenz gave the cult of the wolf perhaps its most articulate formulation. Lorenz revived Max von Stephanitz' theory that the modern dog was domesticated separately from the jackal and the Northern wolf (Mech, 37-38). Lorenz calls these respectively "aureus dogs" and "lupus dogs." While Max von Stephanitz had believed the origin of both was in Europe, Lorenz maintained that the aureus dogs were descended from the Mesopotamian jackal. This change made the two types correspond to the Semitic and Aryan peoples.

The descriptions by Lorenz were filled with a sort of rhetoric that recalls the Nazi period. "The wolf packs," he declared, "roam far and wide through the forests of the North as a sworn and very exclusive band which stick {sic} together through thick and thin and whose members will defend each other to the very death" (Lorenz, *King*, 119). Anybody familiar with the Nazi period will recognize here on every point a canine equivalent of the idealized descriptions of primeval, Aryan tribes whose putative qualities the Nazis and other nationalists endeavored to emulate. The jackals and their descendants were, according to Lorenz, not oriented toward the pack but solitary; while capable of absolute obedience, they lacked the deeper traits of loyalty and affection. This corresponded to the anti-Semitic propaganda in Nazi Germany which had described Jews as superficially clever but lacking emotional refinement and creativity. In accord with his earlier theory about the difference between the races — human and animal — of north and south, Lorenz attributed the "infantile" character of aureus dogs to "age-old domestication" (120-121).

Another scientist in Nazi Germany argued that there was a northern and a southern psychology which crossed the lines of species. To demonstrate this, he did a detailed study of chickens in various countries in the north and south of Europe. He observed such matters as the speed with which they picked up grain and the colors they responded to, and compared their mental profiles with the people who lived alongside them.

<79>

The conclusion was that the "races" of chickens paralleled those of human beings (Jaensch, *passim*). The Nazis considered Jews people of the desert and spiritually barren, while Germans, as people of the forest, were profound, mysterious, and orientated toward the light (Mosse, *Crisis*, 4-5; Herf, 140, 151). Lorenz suggested that the contrast between the populations, both human and animal, of north and south was the same as that between wildness and domestication. This prompted Jaensch, author of that article on chickens, to remark that the idea of Lorenz: "must absolutely be investigated and can further research into both animals and questions of race in human beings. The Northern Movement {i.e., National Socialism and related trends} is indeed without doubt also a protest against the damage done by domestication among people of culture" (252).

The climax of *King Solomon's Ring* came at the very end when Lorenz repeated the description of a battle between wolves from an article of his written during the Nazi period ("Formen," 372-373). According to Lorenz, when two dogs or wolves fight, the defeated one would eventually offer its neck to the other:

> A dog or wolf that offers its neck to its adversary in this way will
> never be seriously bitten. The other growls and grumbles, snaps
> with his teeth in the empty air and even carries out, without
> delivering so much as a bite, the movement of shaking
> something to death in the empty air. However, this strange
> inhibition from biting persists only as long as the defeated dog
> or wolf maintains his attitude of humility (*King*, 188).

Despite his frequent use of illustrations, Lorenz did not provide a picture of this event, perhaps out of an unacknowledged uncertainty about it. Furthermore, the two warring canids, in contrast to most of the animals in his book, were never individualized, much less named. Lorenz went on to generalize that among all "higher" animals, the vanquished would always signify submission by offering the most vulnerable part of his body to the victor, thus releasing an inhibiting mechanism (Lorenz, *King*, 194). He later repeated the observation about fighting dogs or wolves in his book, *On Aggression*, adding that he had observed this not once but many times (Lorenz, *Aggression*, 13).

Lorenz shared this extreme biological determinism with other Nazis. His theory of imprinting {*Prägung*} held that behavior was inherited not only in general tendencies but also in precise and elaborate patterns of behavior (Deichmann, 180-182). In his studies of wolves, Rudolph Schenkel had maintained that although such patterns were found in the behavior of birds and reptiles, the responses of mammals were too variable and subtle to be described in such a way (*Wölfen*, 2, 21). Though he did not

<80>

explicitly mention Schenkel, the observation about wolves by Lorenz was probably intended as a response, a demonstration that intricate social interactions were indeed inherited by dogs and wolves. The accuracy of Lorenz' observations of fighting wolves was later disputed by Schenkel in an article entitled "Submission: its Features and Functions in Wolf and Dog," and published in 1967. Schenkel stated that Lorenz had completely misinterpreted the behavior of the respective canids, perhaps confusing victor and vanquished. "It is always the inferior wolf," Schenkel wrote, "who has his jaws near the neck of his opponent" (320). The posture that Lorenz had interpreted as submission was, according to Schenkel, actually one of readiness to attack. Still more significantly, Schenkel challenged the concept of submission articulated by Lorenz. Submission, Schenkel maintained, did not occur in a truly serious fight, which would end in death, mutilation, or flight of one party. Rather, submission was found only in minor or ritualized fighting where the conflict was mediated by affection. Lorenz did not reply, and subsequent research has confirmed the view of Schenkel (Mech, 92-93). Additional support for Schenkel comes from Lorenz's own original description of the confrontation, since Lorenz says that the supposedly victorious wolf or dog that has not bared its neck is actually the one to leave the scene (Lorenz, *King*, 373). Common sense suggests that this is not a sign of victory but of retreat.

If the criticism directed at Lorenz is correct, he made an error of great magnitude in a matter on which he himself chose to place major emphasis. How could such a mistake have been made by a future Nobel laureate? The answer can only be that the enormous power of animal symbolism can direct and sometimes overwhelm observation. Lorenz described the canids according to the model of Nazi bureaucracy, in which relationships were structured by unambiguous gestures of authority and submission. Both groups were conceived as strictly hierarchal within their society and ruthless toward those outside.

<81>

CHAPTER 9
OUR COMRADE IN ARMS, THE HORSE

Theirs not to reason why,
Theirs but to do and die:
Into the valley of Death
Rode the six hundred.
— Tennyson, "The Charge of the Light Brigade"

A S THE RENAISSANCE was drawing to a close, the Spanish novelist Cervantes gave us perhaps our most vivid image of a doomed yet noble struggle against modernity — Don Quixote on horseback in full armor charging at windmills. The updated version of this is the charge of Polish cavalry against Nazi tanks. One division after another of cavalry and mounted artillery advanced against motorized troops, only to be destroyed by aircraft and armored vehicles. Since the middle ages, cavalry charges had been heavily romanticized. They were daring and spirited, and they could bring either great victory or disaster. They were so much a part of legend that many commanders were reluctant to give them up as World War II approached, even though more sober advisors realized that they were nearly useless in a modern war. The Polish army with its proud military tradition had 40 mounted regiments (Ellis, 182). In late afternoon on September 1, 1939 a Polish officer raised his saber and horsemen came charging out of the woods into German machine gun fire. After another such charge two days later, the Polish front collapsed (Ellis, 182-183; Piekiewicz, 8-9). Though the courage and gallantry of the Poles occasionally intimidated the German invaders (Ellis, 183), these massacres signaled a very diminished role for the horse in combat, and an end to what little remained of the chivalric tradition in war.

With the advent of modern weapons, horses gradually came to play a less significant function in war, but there have been a number of partial revivals. The First World War, particularly on the Western Front, was largely one of attrition, as adversaries bunkered down in trenches and tried to outlast one another. The Second World War was conducted at a more rapid pace; speed and mobility were decisive. In World War I the Germans used one horse for every seven men; in World War II they used one horse for every four (L. Buchner, 137). More than a million horses were taken by the Germans from the Soviet Union, while vast numbers were also taken from Poland and other captured territories. Still others were purchased from neutral counties (L. Buchner, 137-138). Rather than being used in cavalry, horses generally assumed the rather unromantic roles in transport. Much of the Second World War was fought in areas that were rendered

<82>

Fig. 9. "German Soil," by Werner Peiner. Photo: Becker Collection/Werner Library

inaccessible to motorized vehicles by the rough, uneven ground and the lack of paved roads or railroad tracks. Horses could cross rivers far more easily than motorized vehicles, which made them especially important in Holland and other areas of soggy terrain (Etz and Sohn, 231-232).

The Horse as a Companion

As we have seen, the fundamental division the Nazis made among animals was between predators and herbivores. Predation provided the model for dominance, conquest, and the idea of a master race. The horse, perhaps alone among animals, seemed to bridge this division. Though not predators themselves, they are intimately associated with battle. In a sense they might be similar to slaves, yet they do not seem to show what Nietzsche had called "slave morality." They seem to take their servitude with a sort of equine grace, and the erect carriage of a horse suggests pride. This earned horses respect and even admiration from the Nazis. Martial, yet not very wild or ferocious, horses could sometimes symbolize the disciplined, professional soldier (Gorny, 91-96). As one author of the Nazi period put it, "A mute comrade and loyal helper, who fulfills every duty until the final breath — that is our comrade in arms, the horse" (Norman, 11). The final phrase {Kriegeskomerad Pferd} comes up constantly in the rhetoric of the two world wars.

Officers liked to have themselves photographed sitting proudly on horseback. In his memoirs of life in the German cavalry during World War II, Max Kuhnert reported many experiences of friendship and camaraderie with horses, as he was constantly shifted from one battleground to the

<83>

next. All of these relationships, however, were ephemeral and superficial. Only his horse Siegfried seemed to command real loyalty. Max learned to understand and respond to Siegfried's gestures, glances, and grunts. When Max was unable to get oats for his horse, he searched until he found an old sofa and took out the straw used as stuffing. He carefully treated a wound of Siegfried and covered the horse with a blanket at night (130-131). The horse was a figure of tenderness in an otherwise indifferent world. Rudolf Höss, the commander of Auschwitz, reported that when the pressures of work became intense he would withdraw to the stable at night to find "peace among my beloved horses" (Glaser 239).

The Horse as Totem

Rural life and war were the constant themes of Nazi art and propaganda, and the horse figured prominently in both. Horses were romantically celebrated in the monumental sculptures the new regime erected in public squares. Sculptors such as Arno Breker and Josef Thorak exemplified the official style, which featured muscular young men in highly theatrical poses, engaged in either battle or sport. They conveyed vigorous motion but virtually no pathos; in fact, the facial expressions are either vacuous or simply brutal. Often, these gigantic figures were accompanied by horses, rearing and charging with their manes blowing in the wind. In these celebrations of masculine power, the horses suggested female submission, even though they were allied with their masters in pursuit of further conquest. Hitler, not much of a rider himself, often carried a riding whip in his hand, no doubt because he liked this symbolism. Typical of the monumental equine images were the enormous sculptures produced by Thorak for the Mars Field in Nuremberg (Adam, 195, 204).

These larger-than-life statues reflected one side of Nazi ideology. Heinrich Himmler liked to adorn his banal fantasies with the pageantry of archaic mythologies. The Ahnerbe {Ancestral Heritage}, the research branch of the SS, tried to promote the idea of the horse and related animals as the totems of ancient Aryans. The "stag of the sun" had supposedly been the symbol of the Nordic culture. The idea, however, never won much acceptance (Gugenberger and Schwiedlenka, 168), probably because it was so obviously at odds with the reality of a war in which horses were simply exploited.

While monumental sculptures unequivocally served the Nazi agenda, the "blood and soil" ideology could be subtly subversive of it. The ideal of bonding with the soil conflicted with the Nazi goal of conquest. The ideal of regionalism conflicted with the Nazi centralization of power. Finally, the emphasis on traditional techniques of agriculture conflicted with the Nazi desire to increase production through modern equipment. "Blood and soil" painters of the Third Reich used horses to symbolize

<84>

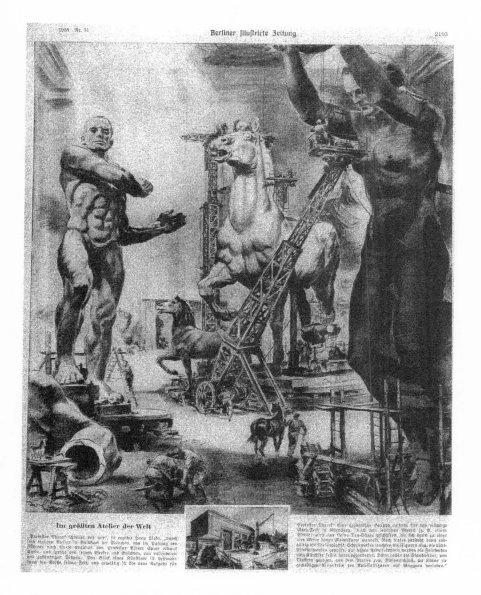

Fig. 10. This article from the Berlin *Illustriete Zeitung* in 1938 calls the studio of Josef Thorak "The Largest Atelier in the World." The colossal sculptures depict both horses and human beings in very theatrical poses and with exaggerated muscular development.

<85>

selfless service and work. They depicted farm life in highly anachronistic terms: no tractors or other modern devices, and peasants performing ceremonies in traditional costumes. A favorite subject painted by Julius Paul Junghanns, Willy Jäckel, and others, was a solitary farmer with a plough or cart drawn by horses, moving with steadiness and intensity (Adam, 131, 135, 137). A Nazi art magazine described the people and animals of Junghanns as "monuments of a speechless, heroic attitude and strength" (132).

In a few genre landscapes from the Nazi period there was even a latent protest against the prevailing ideology. An example is "German Soil" by Werner Peiner (Adam, 130-131). It showed a lone farmer holding a harrow drawn by two horses, one white and one black. In the distance, dark clouds were gathering over a village. The isolation of the individual stood in contrast to the Nazi emphasis on race and ethnicity, and the clouds suggested approaching war. In a regime that profoundly mistrusted organized religion, Peiner made a church steeple the vanishing point on the horizon where the furrows in the field converged. The peasant was bonded with his animals but alienated from the rest of his society. The small figure was overwhelmed by the expansive landscape which made even his hold on the soil appear tenuous.

The Fate of Horses

The Nazis celebrated the horse in rhetoric yet brutally exploited the horse in practice. Horses shared the deprivations and danger of the men at the front. It was not easy to obtain, train, feed, and care for the horses. Two and three quarters of a million horses and other beasts of burden were employed by the Germans in World War II (L. Buchner, 141), and very few survived the war (Etz and Sohn, 233). About 865 died each day, 52,000 during the siege of Stalingrad alone (Piekalkiewicz, i). Vast numbers were lost to disease, exhaustion, cold, starvation, and weapons. According to Piekalkiewicz, 75% were killed by the Allies, while 17% died from exhaustion and heart failure (244). In the Caucasus and other mountainous areas, mules were generally preferred as being more sure-footed. These too had massive difficulties to contend with. Since it was impossible to get sufficient quantities of oats and hay, they had to subsist almost entirely on grass. Their saddles and shoes were often deficient. They often traveled in single file over narrow mountain pathways in foul weather, and many fell off the cliffs. They were severely overworked and exposed to the cold. Those that survived the elements were mostly lost to enemy fire (A. Buchner, 213-214).

Though not sympathetic to the Nazi leadership, the military historian Bidermann constantly spoke reverently of their army. He was infatuated with the military virtues of courage and loyalty as well as with the

<86>

pageantry of uniforms and medals. Nevertheless, he dropped the sancti-monious tone to mischievously write that horses which had been reported as killed by enemy fire were actually often shot for food by the Germans themselves. He added that the kitchen help was expert in the preparation of horsemeat. "It is stringy, hard and sweet-tasting, but it was still avidly devoured" (139-140). The officers, however, were well aware that horses were being eaten. A report of an army headquarters dated January 5, 1945 in Crimea on the Eastern Front told of a corps distributing six different recipes for horsemeat (NA, Microcopy T-314, Reel 80).

The animals in the war effort required massive care. The need was so great that a special academy for veterinary officers was opened in Han-nover. Of the approximately 10,000 German veterinarians in the Third Reich at least 6,000 were called for military service (L. Buchner, 140). This mobilization meant that other animals were deprived of veterinary care, but few pets in any case were able to survive the hunger, bombing, and other miseries. Because of the harsh conditions, relations between people and animals in the Third Reich generally became more utilitarian and less intimate.

In Crimea on May 4, 1944, the retreating Germans slaughtered about 30,000 horses to keep them from falling into enemy hands (Meyer 90). The poor animals were led in rows to a precipice, then shot and hurled off the cliff (Piekalkiewicz, I). Very likely, Max Kuhnert's beloved Siegfried was among them. Despite widespread hunger these horses were not butchered and eaten. The routine resembled the mass executions of Jews or partisans, who would also be shot in such a way as to make them fall into mass graves. The slaughter, in addition to violating the animal-protection laws, was unnecessary from the point of view of rational self-interest. It was clear that the war was lost, and the killing of the horses was part of a scorched-earth policy. The retreating Nazis left a trail of arson and devastation behind, which culminated in orders for the destruction of France and Germany. Perhaps a perverse kind of possessiveness also inhibited the Nazis from letting the horses return to the enemy alive.

Inge Müller, a poet of East Germany, chronicled an incident that happened very shortly after the war in her poem "Fallada 45." A horse was trotting through the streets of Berlin after the driver of his wagon had been killed. People shouted and came running up from their cellars bearing knives, clubs, and any improvised weapon that came to hand. Without even bothering to kill the horse, the frenzied mob tore its body apart for meat (33).

<87>

PART III
TREATMENT, THEORY, RESEARCH

CHAPTER 10
THE MYSTICAL TECHNOCRACY

*.. . .over the entrance to the gates of the temple of science are written
the words:* Ye must have faith.   — Max Planck

VEN TODAY, IT is disconcerting to watch Leni Riefenstahl's propaganda film, *Triumph of the Will*. The gesticulations of Hitler before
an audience appear so bizarrely exaggerated that our impulse is to
laugh. Yet there remains something stirring about these operatic pageants
with their meticulously choreographed banners and costumes. The film
leaves a contemporary audience uncomfortably torn between amusement,
fear, intoxication, and revulsion. The movie was technically innovative,
but conceptually it was an unbroken string of banalities. The Führer
chatted amiably with men and women in traditional Alpine costumes; he
smiled at adorable children; he commemorated the German soldiers who
lost their lives in the first World War. Framed by scenes of crowds singing
in unison and marching in step, the platitudes took on a menacing aspect.
The abiding impression was of enormous power. The hierarchic system
obliterated all individuality, and everybody appeared to act with a single
will.

The Nazi leaders were proudly irrational and fairly open about their
fascination with destruction. Nazi science, by contrast, was often highly
rational and utopian. The difference between their politics and their
science was largely a matter of style; both activities contributed to their
eugenic programs. The policies of the Nazis were sometimes explained in
the eerily sophisticated language of what they called "racial hygiene." They
regarded everything from forced sterilization to mass murder as a means
to produce a genetically healthy population. Such ideas were articulated
in highly technical terms in biological and medical publications. Nazism
was not without an internal logic. Only when viewed from the outside was
its horror fully apparent.

Science is never precisely free, but always practiced within the context
of a culture which sets both goals and prohibitions. For science to develop
in its present form, researchers needed to overcome many inhibitions. To
study metallurgy and geology they needed to put aside inhibitions about
extracting ores from the earth (Merchant, 29-41). For the development of
modern medicine and biology, they needed to overcome inhibitions about
cutting open dead bodies. They also needed to permit experiments on
animals and within limits on human beings.

<91>

Science during the Nazi period did away with many remaining prohibitions. Scientists in key positions had at their disposal human subjects such as Jews and Gypsies, over whom they possessed the power of life and death (Caplan, *passim*). By experimenting without inhibitions on human beings, the Nazi scientists considered themselves more scientific than researchers in England and the United States. As Robert Proctor has stated, "The Nazis depoliticized problems of vital human interest by reducing these to scientific or medical problems, conceived in the narrow, reductionist sense of these terms. . . . Confronting crime with the knife of the surgeon, justifying genocide on the grounds of quarantine, racial hygienists allowed a reductionist biologism to obscure the political character of social questions" *(Racial Hygiene, 293)*. Like their counterparts in the Allied countries, Nazi researchers favored argument over rhetoric. Their bigotry may seem obvious in retrospect, but that is also frequently the case with American and British scientific writings of the early twentieth century. In 1927 such a distinguished spokesperson for science as the philosopher Bertrand Russell could remark that Negroes were "on the average inferior to white men," casually adding that the ability of Negroes to work in the tropics made their extermination "highly undesirable" (Proctor, *Racial Hygiene*, 179).

Much of the science and medicine developed in Germany during the Nazi era was abruptly dropped without being refuted or formally discarded. Since Nazi science proceeded in part from blatantly racist assumptions, most researchers later sought to conceal rather than publicize the articles they had written during the era of Hitler. One problem for later researchers has been that even an attempt at refutation of Nazi science acknowledges its seriousness, yet until a refutation takes place, the Nazi works are subject to possible revival. These difficulties are most dramatically illustrated by the controversies that erupt from time to time about the use of data from experiments done by Nazi doctors on unwilling human subjects, data that some medical professionals believe has the power to save lives (e.g., Farnsworth, *passim*).

The dilemmas posed by the theoretical work of Nazi scientists are similar, though they are usually considered less serious. Konrad Lorenz, for example, was a member of both the Nazi Party and its office of Race Policy, and he wrote many essays in support of Nazi eugenic policies. To what extent is it possible to use ideas developed in the service of the Nazi movement without sanctioning its ideology? To what extent, in science or in art, is it possible to separate the man from the work? Scholars had to ask this question in 1996 when a doctor by the name of Howard A. Israel took a close look at a widely used reference book known as *The Pernkopf Anatomy*. He noticed that the signatures of artists on many illustrations incorporated swastikas and insignia of the SS. It turned out that Eduard

<92>

Pernkopf, who directed the writing of the book, had been an early member of the Nazi party. After the incorporation of Austria into the German Reich, he became dean of medical facilities at the University of Austria. Some anatomical drawings in his book may be based on cadavers from concentration camps. Medical experts still regard *The Pernkopf Anatomy* as a masterpiece both because of the scientific accuracy and the aesthetic quality of the illustrations (Wade, *passim*; Proctor, *Cancer*, 273-276). Can one use it without honoring the author? If not, can one forgive the author his politics, so long as that they did not affect his medical work? And what if it should turn out that cadavers of concentration camp victims were indeed used as models? The fact that we need to ask this sort of question at all shows how deeply anchored science is in its social and historical context.

Perhaps the greatest reason researchers have been reluctant to investigate Nazi science is that it challenges our traditional idea of scientists as necessarily on the side of progress. Despite the high value they accord to objectivity, scientists are as prone as political and religious leaders to romanticize their intellectual predecessors. Like other institutions, science has its heroes and martyrs, from Bruno to Einstein. Many people still resist the idea that a fine intellect could be morally indifferent or even perverse. To avoid implicating science in the crimes of the Nazis, they prefer to describe the work of Nazi researchers as "pseudoscience." The distinction, however, is not very clear. How, exactly, do we distinguish genuine science from the counterfeit? One may not do that by refuting theories since all science, however legitimate, is subject to eventual refutation. Furthermore, science is subtly pervaded by judgments of value and from time to time involves bold theorizing. As Stefan Kühl put it in his study of Nazi genetics, this distinction "between science and pseudoscience fails to recognize that science is socially constructed within a particular historical context" (140).

The scientific theories developed under National Socialism are like land mines scattered by the Nazis. To seek them out and attempt to defuse them may be dangerous since it risks setting off an accidental explosion. Simply to leave them buried, however, will only prolong and perhaps even increase the hazards. People who wish to legitimate anti-Semitism and racism could deliberately rediscover and resurrect Nazi science. Even more significantly, Nazi theories may be absorbed through oral and secondary sources. The forces in our culture that once produced the discipline of Nazi racial hygiene could, if we are not aware of them, again produce the same developments. The distinguished biologist Francis Crick, for example, proposed in the early sixties that all people be subject to reversible sterilization through a chemical that would be placed in food. Authorities would then license those who were considered genetically desirable to take

<93>

the antidote and have children. Crick apparently did not realize that the Nazis had been making such experiments in reversible sterilization, one of which would have involved an additive to flour (Kaye, 48-49).

Holism

The great revolt against the mechanistic world view was the Romantic movement of the eighteenth and nineteenth centuries. This movement found its earliest and most articulate support in Germany. Herder, Goethe, and countless others saw the mechanistic view of the world as a denial of life. German scientists of the Nazi period maintained that their science was that of Northern peoples. They insisted that their science was holistic and not based on a duality of matter and spirit, in contrast to the mechanism of Judaic thinking. The following description, by a Nazi biologist named Spanger, was typical:

> The idea of a science of organic form, which has been
> legitimized by Plato, Aristotle, Goethe, and Hegel, battles
> eternally with a science that makes formal laws the ultimate
> knowable element of being. It is impossible to mistake not only
> a one-dimensional logic but also an aesthetic and, finally, a
> religious element in that science based on form. As this science
> awakes to new life, we hear calls for "synthesis," "totality," and
> "the creative power of thought" (Weber, "Organismus," 58).

Over and over, the Nazis celebrated the creativity of Aryan science with its putative power to move beyond dispassionate analysis and grasp the whole. Another biologist explained, "For thousands of years Northern man has taken the unity of body and soul, together with their meaningful integration in nature, as the foundation of his world view, in contrast to the dualism of body and soul in the Orient" (Krogh, 415). The aspiration of the Nazi biologists was "totalitarian" in a very literal sense since they sought to overcome the fragmentation of knowledge and experience by integrating everything into a single structure.

The term "ecology" was first coined in the 1860s by Ernst Haeckel to designate this holistic, Romantic field. At first he used the theory of evolution to oppose all teleological and anthropocentric world views. He searched for organic laws that would be distinct from those governing inanimate matter. Particularly in his late works, pantheism replaced the transcendent God of religious tradition, while a strict evolutionary hierarchy replaced traditional notions of human equality. Beings were ranked according to their perceived complexity, and the state was considered as much an organism as the individual. Some people must be subordinate to others, while all were subordinate to the state. On this

<94>

foundation Haeckel put biology in the service of an ideology that was blatantly racist, chauvinist, and anti-Semitic.

The most pernicious use by Haeckel and his followers of the analogy between the individual creature and the environment was the medicalization of virtually all ethical and social questions. If all creatures including people are part of a larger organism, what happens if that organism gets sick? When we speak of an individual being ill, we usually refer to the presence of unwanted microorganism, or "parasites." For Haeckel, illness of the body politic generally referred to the presence of human "parasites," often identified by race or religion. The medical professional fighting disease became an image of absolute ruthlessness. Just as the doctor destroys an infection, even at the cost of removing an infected limb, so diseases of the collective organism were to be destroyed. Haeckel often spoke of groups of people as cancerous growths or malignant viruses. As the Nazi physician Fritz Klein later explained: "Of course I am a doctor and want to preserve life, and out of respect for human life, I would remove a gangrenous appendix from a diseased body. The Jew is the gangrenous appendix in the body of mankind" (K. Fischer, 514-515).

It is important to realize, however, that an organic hierarchy is not the only alternative to mechanist thought. Carolyn Merchant has pointed out that pre-modern culture employed two variants of the organic approach to nature and society. The first modeled the cosmos on the medieval manor house, with intricate relations of mutual dependence in a hierarchic structure. The second was modeled on the medieval village, where differences were leveled in the interest of community. Ecologists in the late nineteenth and early twentieth centuries applied the hierarchic variant in attempting to understand not only human societies but communities of bees, ants, bacteria, and other organisms. It was only in the late twentieth century, after the experience of fascist tyranny, that the egalitarian model based on village life became favored among environmentalists (70-78).

The Status of Biology

The foremost place among the sciences passed from physics and mathematics to biology, a discipline that is less mechanical and more intuitive. In the words of Walter Greit, who headed the Reichsbund für Biologie, "The leadership of our National-Socialist state and our conception of a people {Volk} is penetrated and inspired by foundations in biology. Legal provisions are derived from the laws of life. Their worth proceeds from the degree to which they are thought through in biological terms and on biological foundations" (233). The Nazis often quoted the words of Bavarian cabinet minister Hans Schemm that "National Socialism is applied biology" (Weinreich, 34).

<95>

As everything from popular culture to history became increasingly biological, the discipline of biology itself started to change. Martin Bormann, perhaps second only to Hitler in authority, wrote in an anti-Christian position paper in 1941:

> When we National Socialists speak of a belief in God, we do not mean what naive Christians and their clerical exploiters have in mind. . . . The power of nature's law is what we call the omnipotent force or God. The claim that this universal force could care for the fate of each individual, of each bacillus here on earth, that it might be influenced by so-called prayers or by other astounding things, rests on a large amount of naiveté or on profit-minded impertinence. We National Socialists, on the other hand, demand of ourselves that we live as naturally as possible, that is to say in accord with the laws of life. The more precisely we understand and observe the laws of nature and of life and the more we keep to them, the more we correspond to the will of this omnipotent force (Remak, 103-104).

But what are the laws of nature? How can we observe them? The Nazis tried to find a sanction for their policies in metaphors drawn from the natural world. Such observations, however, can be placed in the service of almost any agenda. Just as advocates of Natural Theology such as William Paley at the start of the nineteenth century found cause for pious devotion in the study of nature, the Nazis found in it a justification for a militaristic police state. One popular writer on biology during the Nazi period proclaimed, "The animal kingdom is the model for the organic state of National Socialism, the 'biotic community' or, still better, the 'living space' {*Lebensraum*} and our 'vital society.' This shows us the proper bond for nation to its territory and the relationships with other peoples and their governments!" (Bäumer, 262).

In what certainly reads like a defense of genocide, one widely published biologist of the Nazi period theorized that under natural conditions the race best adapted to the environment would be victorious over others. The increase of criminal activity and hereditary illness, however, demonstrated that the natural controls of selection {*Auslese*} and extinction {*Ausmerzung*} were no longer in operation.[1] Legal measures, therefore, had to replace these biological mechanisms (Weber, "Umweltbegriff," 257-259). As another biologist put it, natural selection must be replaced by "artificial selection" (Reche, 80). Others argued that since the "fittest" individuals were most likely to perish in modern war biological selection had to be

---

[1] This is actually not the case. For a discussion of some of the ways in which natural selection continues to operate in modern society, see Gärtner (*passim*).

<96>

imposed by artificial means (e.g., Dittrich, 55). In other words, the "weak" should be killed because they would not automatically die out.

All societies attempt to legitimize their institutions through analogies with the natural world. The democratic institutions of England and France, for example, are justified by appeals to "natural rights." These analogies are ultimately very intuitive and belong far more to philosophy or religion than to science. The analogies do not proceed directly from experience or observation of the natural world but they are mediated by highly abstract analysis. The Nazis, however, used such analogies to put the rhetoric of science in the service of their social programs, thus creating a mystical technocracy.

The calls for holism served many purposes. They expressed nostalgia for a simpler age before the Industrial Revolution with its specialized division of labor. More importantly, they reflected an unconscious desire for a corrective to the mental compartmentalization necessary to carry out acts of extreme brutality. Totalitarian governments such as those of Hitler and Stalin fostered an extreme inconsistency in behavior. Even the most brutal guards at concentration camps would not be brutal all the time. Thus Rudolf Höss, the commander of Auschwitz, might be a mass murderer at work yet fairly gentle in some aspects of his personal life. What makes this possible is a sharp separation between the personal and the public realm. The consolidation of power, in other words, is accompanied by psychic fragmentation (Todorov, 141-157). Perhaps, however, the important question is where the fault lines of human perception are drawn. The Nazis reduced the significance of the divide between human beings and animals, but they stressed the divide between sickness and health. The division between the individual and the society faded into insignificance while the gap between one race and another became enormous.

Popular Culture

The scientific and philosophical ideas of German biologists penetrated the entire society by means of the educational system. A decree of November 1934 from the Ministry of Science, Training, and Public Education demanded that students at all levels be instructed in the meaning of the animal protection laws. At the beginning of 1937, the Minister of Public Education in Thuringia inaugurated an educational program which featured entire weekends devoted only to animal protection (Giese and Kahler, 274). In February of 1938, new requirements for the certification of veterinarians made animal protection a recognized academic field (276). In many respects such educational initiatives did not differ greatly from programs in much of the Western world, but they were subtly penetrated by Nazi ideology.

<97>

Analogies to the ecology of woods and fields were used in Nazi Germany to explain social lessons. A teacher in elementary school might explain to the class that "the cuckoo and woodpecker are necessary to the life of the woods as police, because they take on the struggle against parasites." She would explain that "in the nation of animals the activity of the individual serves, above all, the community." Turning to plants, she might say that roses "have weapons to protect their own lives and those of their descendants." Then with respect to fruit, she would impart the lesson that "Every living thing wishes to preserve its own kind. The preservation of species serves the whole" (Otten, 75). Probably the most persistent lessons were the subordination of the individual to society and the necessity of diligence against enemies. Walter Schoenichen, probably the most popular German writer on biology in both the Weimar Republic and Nazi Germany, often described landscapes in extremely anthropomorphic terms. A landscape, in his view, was an organism that could be "sick," "wounded," "tamed," or "domesticated." Such expressions, of course, are not unique to the Nazis. Here in America, we often speak of "the taming of the West." But authors of the Nazi period used such expressions with a consistency and a seriousness which made them far more than simply figures of speech.

Analogies between the government of human society and the raising of livestock were also very common. Edwin Bauer, director of the Kaiser Wilhelm Institute for Breeding and Research wrote, "Every farmer knows that should he slaughter the best specimens of his domestic animals without letting them procreate and should instead continue breeding inferior individuals, his breeds would degenerate hopelessly. This mistake, which no farmer would commit with his animals and cultivated plants, we permit to go on in our midst . . ." (Weinreich, 30-31). Minister of Agriculture R. Walter Darré by contrast compared society to a garden:

> If . . . the garden is to remain the breeding ground for the
> plants, if, in other words, it is to lift itself above the harsh rule
> of natural forces, then the forming wheel of a gardener is
> necessary, of a gardener who, by providing suitable conditions
> for growing, or by keeping harmful influences away, or by both
> together, carefully tends what needs tending, and ruthlessly
> eliminates the weeds which would deprive the better plans of
> nutrition, the air, light, sun . . .

In other words, getting rid of undesirable people was like weeding a garden. Darré went on to say that the breeding program for human beings should stand at the very center of a culture (Bauman, 113-114). The Nazis did not simply anthropomorphize the biotic community; they also militarized it.

<98>

Nature became a sort of grand battlefield similar to those of the World War II. Walter Schoenichten could say, "The spruce trees, hardened by battle with the elements, are the first line of defense for the forest in the high mountains" and "the confusion of branches reaching in all directions marks the forest of spruce as a battle zone" (H. Fischer, 134).

For the Nazis, kinship was more a matter of geography than of anatomy. They claimed a closer relation to the trees and animals of their homeland than to foreign people. The nationalistic gardener Willy Lange attempted to break down the barrier between garden and landscape, allowing them to blend subtly. He insisted, however, on banning nonnative plants from his garden, a policy that he qualified only by his belief in a theory of "plant physiognomy." According to this theory German gardeners might use plants that resembled native flora in appearance, even if these were imports, provided the plants helped dramatize the primeval German landscapes (Wolschke-Buhlman, 187). Other gardeners such as the more doctrinaire Alwin Seifert insisted on extirpating all foreign plants, comparing this to the battle against human invaders (Wolschke-Buhlman and Gröning, 145-147).

The Nazis realized, probably more clearly than the great colonial powers, that dominance over a region involved not only military might but also an extension of the ecosystem (Weber, 255-258). They planned to "Germanize" large areas of Poland and Russia, supplanting native people and landscapes (Schama, 70-72). The Nazis debated and discussed this project, known as the "Eastern task" {*Ostaufgabe*} in systematic detail. Their proposals included using those Slavs whom they could not assimilate into the German population as slave labor. The Nazis devoted considerable research to finding plants that resembled those of familiar German landscapes yet could thrive in the climate of the newly conquered territories in the East. They carried out several botanical expeditions to the Balkans in order to find appropriate flora that would be resistant to disease. Auschwitz contained a botanical station for the breeding and testing of newly discovered flora (Deichmann, 122-131).

The subordination of the individual organism to the biotic community was a theory that served for an era of total war, of conflict that was waged through technologies of mass destruction. The idea complemented a militaristic nationalism, since it fused the entire population together with the landscape into a single body. Furthermore, it directed the aggression not only against enemy soldiers but also against civilians and entire environments. Germany was meant to be an enormous predator, killing devouring, digesting, and eliminating its victims.

<99>

CHAPTER 11
ANIMALS, NATURE AND THE LAW

> I was desperate. The swine who stole my dog
> doesn't realize what he did to me!
> — Adolf Hitler

T HE GERMAN HAS two characters . . ." wrote William Shirer in *Berlin Diary*. "As an individual he will give his rationed bread to feed the squirrels in the Tiergarten on a Sunday morning. He can be a kind and considerate person. But as a unit in the Germanic mass, he can persecute Jews, torture and murder his fellow men in a concentration camp, massacre women and children by bombing . . ." (entry of December 1, 1940). Perhaps the most dramatic illustration of this divided character is the animal protection laws sponsored by the Nazi government. Both formal sociological studies and extensive anecdotal evidence confirm the intuitive judgment that cruelty to animals correlates with antisocial behavior. To take a single example, Albert DeSalvio, the notorious "Boston Strangler," trapped cats and dogs in crates then shot them with arrows as a young man (Serpell, 85; Lockwood and Hodge, *passim*). The Nazi experience strongly suggests that the reverse does not always apply. Those who are humane toward animals are not necessarily kind to human beings.

The Laws of 1933

The Nazi laws on treatment of animals were notable for their detail, as well as for their medical and legal sophistication. The laws were partially based on humane and nationalistic ideals, but their spirit was primarily technocratic. On April 21, 1933 the Nazis passed a law on the slaughtering of animals (Giese and Kahler, 164-175, 300-305). This was a barely concealed attack on the Jews. The text of the law did not specifically mention either Jews or kosher slaughter. That would have made the law vulnerable to challenge since the German constitution of 1919 specifically guaranteed freedom of religion (Jentsch, 49). The new law, however, mandated that animals be anesthetized or stunned before being killed. This could be done through electric shock or through a blow to the head with a special hammer or ax (168). The provision effectively banned kosher slaughter, at least as traditionally practiced.

In a radio address in August 1933, Hermann Göring announced restrictions on animal experimentation:

<100>

The German people particularly have always shown their great
love of animals and the question of animal protection was
always near their hearts. For thousands of years the German
people have always looked upon their household and farmyard
animals as their companions, in the case of horses as their
fighting companions, and as God's creatures. To the German,
animals are not merely creatures in the organic sense, but
creatures who lead their own lives and who are endowed with
perceptive facilities, who feel pain and experience joy and prove
to be faithful and attached. . . . Under the influence of foreign
conceptions of justice and a strange comprehension of law,
through the unhappy fact that the exercise of justice was in the
hands of people alien to the nation — because of all these
conditions, until now, the animal was considered a dead thing
under the law (Göring, 70-71).

He went on to announce that a new animal protection law was being
formulated which would bring "unity" to domestic life (75).

In the interim period before the laws were promulgated, Göring issued
a decree provisionally banning vivisection under penalty of being sent to
a concentration camp, though he made exceptions for a few prestigious
research institutes. On November 24, 1933, the Nazis passed a detailed law
on animal protection (Giese and Kahler, 19-123, 277-83). The introduction
to the law stated clearly that animals were not to be protected for the sake
of human beings but "for their own sakes" (18). In the amended version
of 1938 the first section stated that the German regulations, in contrast to
"various foreign laws," "protect all animals and make no distinction
between pets and others, between higher and lower animals, or between
creatures that are useful and those that are harmful to human beings" (19).

The first provision of the German animal protection law of 1933 set a
maximum penalty of unprecedented severity — two and a half years in jail
plus a fine — for anybody who would "needlessly torment or mishandle
in a rough way" an animal. The legislation categorically prohibited some
practices such as taking the legs off living frogs. It regulated other practices
such as castration, restricting conditions under which it could be performed and mandating supervision by a veterinarian. Furthermore, it
placed limits on the work that could be demanded of animals on farms, in
mines, and in other environments. Additional provisions restricted animal
experimentation, which could be practiced only under very specific
conditions and with explicit permission of the Ministry of the Interior.

The uniform regulations made it possible to consolidate all organizations devoted to the care or protection of animals just as Göring had
predicted. On December 5, 1933, less than two weeks after the passage of

<101>

the animal-protection law, the Berlin Animal Protection Agency was given authority over policies relating to animal protection in all German-speaking lands. Renamed the Government Animal Protection Alliance {Reichstierschutzbund}, its headquarters were moved to Frankfurt on the Main. The 600 to 700 organizations for animal protection in Germany were absorbed into this Alliance as local branches. The Minister of the Interior was given the authority to dissolve any other organizations for animal protection, though the consolidation encountered little resistance. Membership, according to the charter of the Alliance adopted in 1938, was restricted to those of "German or related blood" (Giese and Kahler, 130-151).

While the Animal Protection Law of 1933 was probably the strictest in the world, it was still less strict than Nazi rhetoric had led many people to expect. The issue of animal experimentation is the best example. Hitler had originally intended to ban that entirely, but Dr. Morrel, his personal physician, persuaded him to compromise in the interest of German research (Händel, 135). An official commentary on the law, published in the newspaper *Preussischer Staatsanzeiger* on December 1, 1933, about a month after it was passed, justified the continuation of some experiments on animals with the statement: "It is a law of every community that, when necessary, single individuals are sacrificed in the interests of the entire body" (Giese and Kahler, 294).

Rather than providing clarity, amendments only added to the vagueness of the first provision. According to the expanded version of the laws passed in 1938, treatment of an animal was to be considered "rough" {roh} when it "corresponds to an unfeeling state of mind" (Giese and Kahler, 20, 24, 277). This may sound at first like a meaningless bit of legalese, but the definition probably helped to undermine enforcement of the law in any traditional way. The major focus switched from the effect of treatment on an animal to what the act supposedly revealed about the perpetrator. Nazi ideology held most crimes to be the result of hereditary defects and considered races such as Jews to be lacking in feeling, so this elaboration of the law of the animal protection law could be used as a pretext to class somebody as racially polluted.

Medical researchers would soon have men and women that the state considered genetically inferior available as unwilling subjects for experiments (Deichmann, 238), but even then animal experimentation was by no means eliminated. For one thing, the cost of using human subjects could be considerable. In addition, the need to avoid publicity limited the scale on which unwilling subjects were used. Perhaps most significantly, experiments on human beings often required animals as a control in order to explain the results. Thus Dr. Hans Nachtheim performed a series of experiments in the late thirties and early forties which involved inducing

<102>

epilepsy in human beings, both children and adults, without their consent by injections of the drug cardiazol. Fearing that the ill-health of his human subjects might impair the validity of his results, he performed the same experiments on rabbits (Deichmann, 234). Dr. Gerhard Schrader, attempting to develop a new pesticide to kill plant lice, inadvertently created an especially potent nerve gas. Officials immediately ordered tests on animals of various sorts, none of which survived. The army ordered more extensive tests on monkeys and baboons, which vomited, excreted uncontrollably, lost control of their bodily movements, and went into convulsions as they died. After further tests on animals the army tried the gas on prisoners of war, with much the same result (Parker, 43-44). By stressing the continuity between human and animal life, Nazi ideology may even have helped to encourage experiments on animals.

The Animal Protection Law of 1933 inaugurated a long series of further laws, reportedly composed under the supervision of Hitler himself (Ferry, "animaux," 55), to regulate the treatment of animals. These continued to be issued and refined almost until the very end of the regime. The laws specified in great detail practices that were forbidden such as releasing tamed animals into the wild, using animals in public amusements, use of blinders on horses, cockfights, bullfights, clipping the ears of dogs, and so on. The intense emphasis on avoiding pain in the laws on animal protection seems at odds with the sort of spirit the Nazis generally tried to encourage. In some respects, the Nazis represented a reaction against the humane movement since they emphasized hardness and strength. They generally viewed Christian virtues such as pity with contempt. Nevertheless, the Nazi animal protection laws took the humane ethic in some respects to its ultimate extreme. The many approving commentaries on the laws written during the Nazi period show virtually no awareness of this contradiction.

Euthanasia

The law of November 1933 placed no restriction at all on euthanasia for animals and even mandated it under certain circumstances. Point four of section two states that it is forbidden to "retain or procure a fragile, ill, overworked or old animal for which further life is a torment for any purpose other than . . . to procure a rapid, painless death" (Giese and Kahler, 32). The expanded version of 1938 states that, when there is uncertainty as to whether "further life is a torment," an expert must be consulted (58). Although I know of no instances when owners were actually forced to euthanize their pets, this would certainly have been possible because the law did not distinguish between emotional and utilitarian relations with animals.

<103>

The laws could not be used to challenge the practice of euthanasia, only the methods employed. One owner was called before the court when he attempted to drown a litter of unwanted kittens. They were taken out of the water after one and a half hours, and the bodies were thrown in the garbage; later they began to move. A number of people in the area complained, and the act was judged "foreign to the spirit of the people." A veterinarian decided after careful consideration that the humane alternative was either to painlessly decapitate the kittens or else to smash their skulls in with a single, powerful blow (26-27). In another case, however, the drowning of a litter of puppies was permitted, provided they were placed in a permeable sack which would be left in the water for the entire night as soon after birth as possible (27-28). This technocratic encouragement of euthanasia mirrors the Nazi policy toward human beings.

On January 14, 1936, the government passed "Law on the Slaughter and Holding of Fish and Cold-Blooded Animals." Fish, like mammals, had to be anesthetized prior to killing. This could be done by a hard blow above the eyes or with electric currents. Exceptions were made with a few fish such as flounder and for frogs, which could be simply decapitated. Eels could be killed by making a slit and taking out the heart. Removing the entrails of living crustaceans was forbidden, as was placing them in a pot of water and bringing it to a boil. Lobsters and other crustaceans, however, might be killed by placing them in water that had already been brought to boil, making the death swift and sure (Giese and Kahler, 178-189).

Transportation

From the perspective of half a century, all of these laws with their tangle of contradictory motivations make a strange impression. They were inspired by authentic compassion, bureaucratic tidiness, lust for power, and xenophobic fear. Such contrasts are probably nowhere quite as disconcerting as in the laws regulating transportation of animals. These included an elaborate law on animal protection in trains, passed on September 8, 1938 (Giese and Kahler, 190-220), and a separate law on transportation in motor vehicles, passed on November 13, 1937 (261-272). Simply in terms of their humane value, none of the other laws are so unequivocally positive as these. In even more detail than usual, the laws provided for the amount of space granted during transport for a variety of animals, including horses, calves, swine, and chickens. These laws mandated that the animals be given sufficient food and water during journeys and that the stalls be well-tended. There are injunctions against loading sick or fragile animals which might be damaged in transport. All of this was an admirable corrective in a farming industry which was growing

<104>

increasingly mechanized as the desire for productivity forced out all other priorities.

Yet in context these laws seem particularly disturbing. The laws on transportation of animals reflected a mental association between the stockyard and the concentration camp. The irony that runs through the entire series of laws — solicitousness toward animals combined with brutal treatment of human beings — is especially obvious here. German officers occasionally held their men accountable for cruelty to animals. Meanwhile, they were taking Jews and others to concentration camps in trains and trucks under conditions of extreme crowding and privation that would certainly not have passed inspection under the laws governing transportation of animals (Goldhagen, 269-270, 328).

The trains and trucks that carried prisoners to concentration camps were disguised as transporters of the meat industry. The Ministry of Transportation, which was primarily responsible for the enforcement of the law on moving animals, must have been deliberately neglectful here. Certainly the government would not have had police continuously stopping the cattle cars for inspection to see if animals inside were given the treatment mandated by law.

The law suggested that opponents of the state counted less than chickens on the way to the slaughter house. Mass executions of Jews and others were an open secret, not officially acknowledged but widely rumored (Laqueur, *passim*). What did people felt when they watched cattle cars and vans drive by? Was there a sense of pride at the humane practices of the German nation? Was there horror at the suspicion that the vehicles might carry doomed human beings?

Nature Preservation

Walter Schoenichen saw the laws on nature protection in the Third Reich as an extension of the animal protection laws, which not only forbade mistreatment of other creatures but also obligated owners to care properly for domesticated animals. He argued that the landscape itself was an organism which had been domesticated, and so the same restrictions must apply to it (128). Woods were the quintessential German landscape, and he regarded foresters as sylvan "doctors." He recommended various "therapies" for overcoming the illness brought on by civilization and for bringing the woods closer to their primordial condition. He also recommended "taking the question of race into account in all reforesting" (111).

Like the protection of animals, the goal of protecting nature had become a means of domination. The first major piece of legislation regarding the environment was the hunting law of July 3, 1934. Just as Hitler had presided over the animal protection laws, the laws for the protection of nature were the province of Hermann Göring. A lover of

<105>

medieval pageantry, he had himself declared "Imperial Hunting Master" {*Reichsjägermeister*}, a resonant title which sounded grandly archaic but actually had no precedent. Like the other laws, the one for the protection of nature was intricately detailed, and the provisions were almost exclusively directed to the avoidance of pain. Laws prohibited the setting of traps. Buckshot was not allowed, and a number of other kinds of ammunition were also considered inhumane. Hunting was only allowed in season and restricted by the right of property. Endangered species were placed off limits completely. A hunting license carried certain duties such as the obligation to feed game in winter.

But the provisions missing from this law as well were as significant as those included. As long as game was hunted in accord with regulations, there were no limits at all. The sort of orgiastic escapades of killing, celebrated in old pictures from Rubens to photographs of Teddy Roosevelt, could continue as before. Dietrich von Haugwitz and his family had no trouble procuring ammunition and organizing a large hunting party on their estate in early 1945. He later found it amazing that they should have been able to keep weapons and even purchase ammunition despite the desperate fighting that was still in progress. The hunter, personified in Göring, seemed to emerge as a sort of godlike figure, presiding over life and death in the woods. "The German hunter," read an official statement on enforcement of the laws, "rules over and protects the creatures of his homeland; they are no longer, as was once the case, without a master, but are rather common property of the German people in whose name he acts" (Giese and Kahler, 221-222). Göring became like those medieval princes who could force peasants to abandon cultivated land and tear down their houses in order to extend the royal hunting preserves. The laws even looked beyond the current German borders to hunting grounds in future conquests. Included among the animals that could be hunted was the bison, found not in Germany but in the woods of Lithuania (227).

With the law for the protection of nature, enacted on June 26, 1935, Göring obtained the additional title of "Imperial Forest Master" {*Reichsforstmeister*}, and was "empowered to protect of all of nature including plants, animals that cannot be hunted, and birds" (Giese and Kahler, 236). He was also empowered to appropriate land for the preservation of nature, with no obligation to compensate the dispossessed (246). Furthermore, Göring was given absolute power over all organizations devoted to protection of the natural world, to change, combine, or dissolve them as he might wish (258). As German troops swept eastwards, Göring claimed the forests as a Teutonic heritage, demolished villages, and began to create enormous game preserves. In similarly grandiose fashion, Hitler spoke of reforesting the entire Ukraine (Hermand, *Dreams*, 281).

<106>

In the comfort of their castles and hunting lodges, the Nazi leaders drew up plans to landscape the forests as a sort of fantasy park. The most ambitious of Göring's follies was a plan to repopulate the woods of Lithuania and Poland with the aurochs, extinct since the early seventeenth century. Just as the Nazis sought to recreate the original Aryan people through selective breeding, they claimed to have re-created the aurochs through crossing various bovines including the American buffalo. By repopulating the woods with these creations, Göring imagined that he would bring back the primeval forests where the Germans had lived in the time of Arminius, but not one of the animals proved able to survive in the wild (Daskiewiczf and Aikhenbaum, *passim*; Schama, 68). Meanwhile, the German soldiers hunted for Jews and performed mass executions in the woods.

Enforcement

Especially in the early years of the Nazi regime, the government sometimes tried to uphold fastidious standards for animal protection. The famous zoologist Karl von Frisch was reprimanded by the Ministry of the Interior when he cut up anesthetized earthworms in an experiment. One of the worms moved slightly in spite of being numbed, and this was reported to the Ministry by a student (Frisch, 114). Like many other laws, however, those on treatment of animals often obscured a reality that was close to chaos.

The enforcement of the laws was erratic, which is hardly surprising in view of the turmoil in Germany. The leaders of Nazi Germany were willing to violate them if it suited their purposes. When his poodle was attacked by another dog, Martin Bormann reportedly ordered the offending hound seized, soaked in gasoline, and set on fire (Comfort, 247). Jost Hermand, sent as a boy to a camp run by the SS in occupied Poland, reports being ordered to do many things that were in blatant violation of the animal protection laws. Though barely entered into adolescence, he had to slaughter chickens and rabbits. He was forced to twist the heads of pigeons and even to swallow live toads at the command of a senior boy (*A Hitler Youth*, 49-50). Ironically, while the laws on slaughtering were allegedly intended in part to avoid coarsening the public, these brutal exercises were done for precisely the opposite reason — to harden and toughen German youth.

Consistent enforcement of any law requires regular patterns of daily life which virtually always break down in time of war and social upheaval. Germany was becoming a country in which murder might easily go unpunished while filching cigarettes could result in death. Furthermore, the very complexity of the Law for Animal Protection of 1933 was an obstacle to consistent enforcement. Influenced by a Prussian preoccupation

<107>

with bureaucratic detail, the law was full of qualifiers and special cases. Additionally, the interpretation and enforcement were divided among several ministries and other agencies of the government in a way that would make confusion inevitable. The law was murky about both underlying principles and administrative structures (Hoelscher, 75-76). Nevertheless, the Animal Protection Law of 1933 still proved viable enough to be retained with a few modifications in the Western sector of Germany until July 24, 1972 when the Federal Republic of Germany replaced the law with a less stringent code. Although kosher slaughter was explicitly permitted in 1945, the law of 1933 on methods of slaughter remained in effect until 1997 (Jentzsch, 51).

Pets

Just as the law on methods of slaughter was directed against Jews, the Law on Animal Protection of 1933 was directed against the French. The basic concept behind the German laws on animal protection was largely the "biotic community" {*organische Lebensgemeinschaft*} uniting animals and people, while French law granted privileges to a "civilized being." French animal protection was based on the *Loi Grammont* of 1850. This provided protection from public abuse to domesticated animals which were felt to have entered human society, but it gave no protection at all to wild animals (Digard, 88). The German laws were imposed in Alsace and other incorporated areas of France during Nazi occupation, though not on the Vichy government of Marshal Pétain (Giese and Kahler, 16). Because of this, animal protection is still sometimes resented in France as a sort of cultural imperialism (e.g., Ferry, "*Animaux*," 56; Ferry, *Order*, 91-107). Many in France perceived the laws less as elevating the status of animals in general than as lowering the status of pets.

One might expect that for people under extreme conditions animals and their welfare would sink into insignificance. Experience shows that is not necessarily so. People in difficult times often find reassurance in their relationships with pets, which offer relatively unconditional affection. Bonding with animals can be psychologically very important to people who live in isolation (Serpell, 87-99). Ernst Jünger occasionally speaks with awe of animals the soldiers encountered on the front in World War I. An aura of mystery especially surrounded a tom cat with one forepaw shot off which would sometimes visit him in the trenches. He thought that this cat was the only creature on familiar terms with both sides (*Storm*, ix, 38). In 1943 as World War II waged on and much of Germany lay in ruins, membership in the Society for Bird Protection in Germany surged to a peak of 55,000 (Dominick, 83). In 1944 while most of Germany went hungry, a book on the animal protection laws of the Third Reich was published by popular demand in a third edition (Giese and Kahler, 7).

<108>

The Nazi animal protection laws contained little aspiration toward universality. Both legal documents and public announcements repeatedly emphasized their specifically German character, and violations were sometimes referred to as "foreign to the spirit of the people" {*volksfremd*}. The Nazi government tried to deny the comfort offered by animals and nature to many people. Gypsies, living on the fringes of European society for centuries, had learned to exploit sources of food that were shunned by the majority; at times they hunted hedgehogs. These were protected (Giese and Kahler, 242), and Hermann Göring had given them special status as "useful animals." To make the hunt for hedgehogs more difficult, Gypsies were forbidden to own dogs. This regulation, which had precedents before the Nazi period (Wippermann, 195-196), was among the earliest that restricted the contact of despised groups of people with animals.

Laws were designed, whether consciously or not, to confirm the identification of Jews with the decadence of urban civilization. A decree of February 15, 1942, prohibited Jews, whom the Nazis considered naturally cruel to animals, from having pets (Wippermann, 196). The decree was a preliminary step toward deportation of the Jews to concentration camps, where conditions would not be compatible with the animal protection laws. Since there was a lack of shelters, the pets confiscated from Jews were almost always euthanized. Jews were also forbidden to hunt, a favorite activity of rural people. The literature of the period, especially that of victims, documents how precious contact with animals often became for those living under Nazi domination. The Jewish philosopher, Emmanuel Levinas, forced to work under severe conditions as a French prisoner of war, reports that friendship with a stray dog reaffirmed the humanity of the prisoners. The prisoners named the dog "Bobby." "He would appear at morning assembly," Levinas writes, "and was waiting for us as we returned, jumping up and down and barking with delight. For him, there was no doubt we were men" (153). The family of Anne Frank kept several cats when they were hiding from the Nazis in Amsterdam, and Anne often wrote about the cats in a playful, affectionate way.

Misha Defonseca has reported how, as a young Jewish girl in Poland when she was hiding in the woods to escape the Nazis, she was startled by a stranger:

> What's that? Who's there? — behind me, watching me! Slowly I lifted my head and looked over my shoulder. There, just a few feet in back of me, stood a splendid creature studying me curiously. It was a long, thin dog — gray, shaggy and twice my size. I was struck immediately by its beautiful face: high cheekbones, large erect ears, and beautiful eyes (90).

<109>

Misha shared some of the provisions in her knapsack with the stranger, who turned out to be a mother wolf. The young girl is adopted by the wolf pack, and the wolves share their prey with her. Even if this account was distorted by fading memory or artistic licence {and it is difficult to believe},[1] it still illustrated the emotional importance that animals can have for people living under extreme conditions.

In "The Dog," a story from Idna Fink's collection *A Scrap in Time (25-31)*, nature itself in the figure of a hound offered resistance to the Nazis. Jewish children in a ghetto in Poland had a dog that they name "Ching." One day some SS officers took the dog and stroked him gently to get Ching to reveal the location of the children. The hound refused and drove the SS men away. A year later the men again interrogated the dog. "In an instant," the narrator reported, "they expanded the scope of the Nuremberg laws to apply . . . to Jewish-owned dogs" (29). The SS men hung Ching from a post and executed him in place of the children.

In Juri Weil's *Life with a Star*, a Jew named Josef Roubicek developed an increasing closeness to animals as he was gradually deprived of his rights. He referred to the work camps as "menageries" and the death camps as "circuses." His companion as he waited to be summoned to a camp is a stray cat named "Tomas," with whom he occasionally shared scraps of precious food. Though laws forbade Josef from adopting a pet, Tomas eventually moved in with him, thus placing both parties at greater risk. Finally Tomas was shot by the Nazis, but the courage of his animal companion inspired Josef to resist them. Victor Klemperer, a Jew who was saved from the concentration camps by being married to an Aryan woman, had his cat, dog, and canary all killed after a judicial process. The tragedy moved him to observe "that is one of the horrors which the Judgment of Nuremberg did not report on and for which, were it in my power, I would set up an enormous noose, even if it cost me eternal bliss" (*LTI*, 119).

Love of Animals?

Of course we expect legal documents to be dry, but the Nazi laws on animal protection are curiously joyless. There is almost no mention of what might give pleasure to animals and people, only the avoidance of pain. There is very little about giving animals recreation, and there are only the most abstract references to affection or love. A preface to an official publication of the laws on animal protection stated that ". . . the German people has from time immemorial had a great love for animals and was always aware of its great ethical obligation to them" (Giese and Kahler, 11). This putative love of the German people for animals, frequently alluded to in Nazi rhetoric, is worth further examination. The Nazis did

---

[1] Since the original publication of this book, the Holocaust memoir by Misha Defonesca has been revealed as a fake.

<110>

not recognize or respect the nearly unconditional love that often characterizes not only close friendship and marriage but also relations between people and their pets. Their government tried to direct the attention of its citizens away from personal relationships to more abstract ideals such as the race or the state. The laws on animal protection show this odd reluctance to individualize animals, which can indeed make the reader wonder how far the vaunted of love other creatures extended beyond providing a painless death. Even the case histories in the commentary on the Nazi laws almost never include the name of a single animal or the mention of a single trait that is not generic.

Nazis were certainly capable of kindness toward animals. As a young man in Vienna, Hitler used to save bread to feed squirrels and ravens in the park (Waite, 41). Many other leading figures in the Nazi government kept pets. For many Nazis, a fondness for animals was psychologically tied to an incapacity for intimacy and friendship with human beings. Hitler showed little or no emotion at the death of friends but wept when his canary died. He appeared to enjoy films of people killed and beaten, but he could not endure depictions of animals being harmed (Victor, 62). Himmler, head of the SS, also had, in the words of his doctor, a "positively hysterical" reaction to hunting. "How can you find pleasure . . . ," asked the man who directed the concentration camps, "in shooting from behind cover at poor creatures browsing on the edge of a wood, innocent, defenseless, and unsuspecting? It's really pure murder" (Fest, 111).

It is impossible to generalize from the practices of the Nazi elite to the population in general. As in so many areas, the highest officials were exempt from what they imposed on others. Hitler, Himmler, Göring, Goebbels, Bormann, and the rest hardly conformed to the ideal of an Aryan superman; they were not blond, tall, or athletic. To some degree, pet-keeping, like exemption from these physical expectations, was a privilege of rank. The ownership of pets was often scorned as bourgeois sentimentality when practiced by ordinary citizens. Near the end of the war, Hermand reported that as he left Potsdam: "I remember how indignant some of our fellow passengers were when they noticed that I was carrying my dachshund, Tinga, in my hand luggage — how terribly inappropriate and sentimental amid the universal human suffering and hunger." One passenger remarked that the dog would make "a good lunch" (*Hitler Youth*, 89).

The Drive to Power

Animal nature or "instinct" is closely associated with sexuality in both popular and academic culture. Michel Foucault has argued in his *History of Sexuality* that what Freud and many others saw as a conflict between "repression" and "liberation" of sexuality was two facets of a single process.

<111>

According to Foucault, "Power" {*le pouvoir*} in intellectual matters consists primarily in setting the terms of discussion. Far from being an era of sexual repression, the Victorian period was an era in which elites such as doctors, biologists, politicians, social workers, and clergy vastly extended their domination over the body and sexuality. They did this by surrounding sex with a mystique involving specialized vocabularies, medical technologies, elaborate etiquettes, and institutional controls. This domination involved discouraging unregulated discussion of sex, but the amount and variety of verbal attention to sexuality increased enormously.

The conclusions of Foucault have now gained very wide acceptance, but his extreme emphasis on relations of power in his interpretation of history impresses me as, like all monocausal interpretations, not entirely correct. Everybody experiences some longing for power, yet very few people become obsessed with this desire. On the other hand, those few unfortunately often do rule the world. Foucault's analysis certainly does much to explain the paradoxes in Nazi attitudes toward sexuality. The Nazis sounded very conservative when they complained of the alleged promiscuity of Bolsheviks and Jews. At the same time, they often advocated polygamy and single motherhood. All of these apparently contradictory positions, however, were designed to bring sexuality and reproduction in Germany under their control.

Something similar is involved in human relations with animals in the modern period, most especially in Nazi Germany. Even if the preoccupation with power was not, contrary to Foucault, the driving force of history, it was certainly an obsession of the Nazis. Few groups have ever been so maniacally preoccupied with power as were Hitler and his major deputies. Just as the apparent "repression" and "liberation" of sexuality worked symbiotically toward an agenda of domination and control in the modern period, so did the Nazi concern with animals and the environment. Just as the control over sexuality in the modern period involved the participation of social and medical scientists, the control over animals and the environment in Nazi Germany involved participation of ecologists, veterinarians, zoologists, and other specialists. As Yi-Fu Tuan has shown in *Dominance and Affection*, kindness can be as much an expression of domination as cruelty.

This obsession with power, in turn, resulted in policies that carried technocratic control to extremes. Detlev Peukert described the agenda of the Nazis as follows: "The application of meticulous scientific research closely backed up by state power would make possible a eugenic process of selection and elimination whereby poverty, misery, illness, and crime would finally be abolished. 'All' that was necessary was to realize the dream of total scientific knowledge: to wrap human beings — including their ancestors, no less — in an information network which would yield exact

<112>

forecasts of every individual's future social behavior" (234). One might add that this complete regulation of human life was especially apparent in the ways the Nazis attempted to control seminal moments — birth and death. Both reproduction and death were placed under the control of the state. This extreme regulation had already been largely achieved with livestock. The Nazis subjected the lives of animals, often using humane pretexts, to even greater centralized control. This agenda sometimes involved kindness as well as cruelty, but both were forms of domination. Simultaneously, the strategic blurring of the boundary between animals and people helped the Nazis extend these extreme controls to the lives of human beings.

<113>

CHAPTER 12
ANIMAL PSYCHOLOGY

.. . . we must note that during the Nazi period scientific research on human evolution was in no way suppressed or directed into specific ideological paths. Scientists themselves chose to place their work in the service of racial ideology and racial policy.

—Ute Deichmann, *Biologists under Hitler*

ONE BOOK ON my shelf which exemplifies many paradoxes of the Nazi period is *Das Tier in der Landschaft* {*The Animal in the Landscape*} by Walter Rammner. I noticed it completely by chance at a sidewalk sale in New York and was immediately struck by the graphics. Then I saw that it was published in 1936 in Germany. Sensitively written, it celebrates German rivers and mountains but is entirely without chauvinistic rhetoric. The author cautions against trying to reduce nature to "survival of the fittest" or any other simple formula. How, one wonders, could such a book be written and published in a country that has just instituted the anti-Semitic Nuremberg laws and that was about to embark on a project of racial extermination? Is there any trace at all of the massive brutalization of the public which accompanied the Nazi rise to power?

Actually, there is, but it lies not in the content of the book so much as in the language. The subtitle of the book is *Die deutsche Tierwelt in ihren Lebensräumen* {The World of German Animals in their Living Spaces}. The word *Lebensraum*, meaning "living space," was a term often used in the Weimar Republic and the Nazi period to justify German imperialist ambitions. I have no idea what the author may actually have thought about politics. Even if he was indifferent or even opposed to imperialism, the rhetoric of the era still helped to form his vocabulary, which must surely have influenced his thought. Few naturalists were as thoughtful as Rammner, and none escaped the influence of Nazi ideology.

The study of animals is one major area in which scientists under patronage of the Nazis made universally acclaimed scientific contributions. The German Society for Animal Psychology was founded in Berlin on January 10, 1936. It established an academic network and a journal, *Zeitschrift für Tierpsychologie*, in which matters of animal behavior might be reviewed and discussed (Kalikow, 136). The first issue, published in 1937, contained articles by Karl von Frisch, Nikolaus Tinbergen, and Konrad Lorenz, who would all later share a Nobel Prize in 1973. Many other authors represented in the issue would go on to have distinguished careers both during and after the Nazi period. Like most Nazi publications intended partially for export, even nonscientific ones, this journal was not

<114>

filled with jingoism or overt anti-Semitism. The articles in it were for the most part reasonably technical. Nevertheless, the politics of the journal came through unmistakably. The first issue closed with a report of the meeting of the German Society of Animal Psychology in February 1937, which was attended by numerous public officials as well as scientists. "The chair concluded the series of lectures at the first annual meeting of the German Society of Animal Psychology," the report stated, "with the praise of our Führer, the warmhearted patron of German science" (Effertz, 191). Linking the discipline of zoology with the Nazi agenda soon enhanced the status of the profession. In spite of the war effort, the amount of government funding for zoological research in Germany nearly tripled in 1940-45 over what had been spent in the previous half decade (Deichmann, 116).

While most of the debate in *Zeitschrift für Tierpsychologie* was conducted in terms that were not overtly political, the scientists often spoke in general ways of extending their findings about animals to people. Otto Koehler, a leading scientist and a member of the SA (Deichmann, 200), put it later during the Nazi period, "The mission of animal psychology is to point out the common psychological features of human beings and animals and, in this way, to write an evolutionary history of human awareness" (Koehler, 85). For the most part, contributors to the journal were apolitical scientists. They wished to advance their research and appeared not very concerned about the source of their funding. A few would be touched by the brutality of the Nazi regime. Both Frisch and Tinbergen, as well shall see, were to experience serious harassment. But Lorenz, one of the editors of the journal, put his research in the service of government ideology. He soon emerged from relative obscurity to become a leader in an emerging field. In 1938, immediately after the Nazis took over Austria, Lorenz joined the Nazi party. Shortly afterwards he was given funding by the Minister of Education, Bernard Rust, to start his own research institute at the Institute for Comparative Psychology at Albertus University in Königsberg (Kalikowa, 206-207; Lorenz, "Formen," 395).

Oscar Heinroth's studies of the behavior of birds had laid the groundwork for the emerging field of ethology in the decades before the Nazis came to power. He had shown how the courting behavior of many birds was inborn and unique to certain species. Konrad Lorenz and others attempted to generalize this biological phenomenon to the behavior found in different races of human beings. He expressed fear that the mixture of races would lead to the confusion or destruction of genetically programmed patterns of behavior that were the basis of harmonious life in society. Heinroth sometimes took issue with these generalizations in his private correspondence with Lorenz, but he offered no objection when Lorenz, publicly claiming Heinroth as a predecessor, placed his writings in the service of a racist agenda. In a tribute to Heinroth in 1941, Lorenz stated:

<115>

We can safely predict that soon the laws of inborn behavior will
be shown to determine the deepest layers of human personality
and the investigation of these in animals will be taken for
granted just as it already is in genetics. We also predict that
these investigations will be of great importance for both
theoretical and practical policies of a racial-political nature.
And, if today these policies are already being instituted in many
locations both within and beyond the boundaries of greater
Germany, that is the accomplishment of Oscar Heinroth.

Lorenz concluded by claiming the mantle of Heinroth for himself. He
observed that the Institute for Comparative Psychology which he headed
had been founded precisely on the 70th birthday of Heinroth ("Oskar
Heinroth," 46-47).

The contribution of Lorenz to the initial issue of *Zeitschrift für
Tierpsychologie* was an article entitled "Biologische Fragestellung in der
Tierpsychologie" {Asking Biological Questions in Animal Psychology},
in which he proposed a theory that all organisms have a goal to increase
and spread their own kind. He maintained that the behaviors of organisms
were purposeful in the sense of "species preservation" {Arterhaltung}.
Lorenz strongly denied that this involved any mystical teleology, and he
considered this principle established with near certainty through observation (24-25). However, in terms of such a goal, it is hard to explain why
people smoke or why mountain lions eat their young. The formula
described the aspirations of one group of animals — the Nazi party. The
theory of an instinct for species preservation was a way of justifying an
ideology of national and ethnic supremacy through analogies with the
natural world. With varying degrees of explicitness this theory conflated
"is" with "ought." Lorenz would later argue that lack of patriotic enthusiasm was the mark of an "instinctual cripple" ("Formen," 388). As we will
see shortly, Lorenz would also make his descriptive formula into an ethical
precept by proclaiming a morality based on promoting the German people.

While many people regarded Nietzsche as a prophet, it took later
thinkers to give his ideas about domestication the authority of science.
Identifying the civilization of people with the domestication of animals
had been suggested repeatedly by Nietzsche. It had been articulated as a
scientific theory by Eugen Fischer, one of the fathers of Nazi racial hygiene.
Fischer argued that the distinguishing characteristics of human races were
the same as mutations in domesticated animals (E. Fischer, 488-490;
Lorenz, "Formen," 293-294, 400). This observation provided a foundation
for many subsequent generalizations embracing animals and human beings.

<116>

Fig. 11. Page from an anti-Semitic German children's book published in 1936 titled *Trau keinem Fuchs aug gruner Heid, und keinem Jud bei seinem Eid* {*Trust No Fox in a Green Meadow and No Jew at His Oath*}. A Jewish family wishing to enjoy their vacation gazes at a sign saying "Jews Are Unwanted Here." Note that the "Jewish" dog is mangy and "degenerate," much like the Jews themselves. Courtesy of the American Holocaust Museum (Photo #40039).

Lorenz accepted the theory of Spengler that peoples went through cycles of productivity and decline, yet he contended that the reason for deterioration was not spiritual, as the historian believed, but genetic ("Formen," 293, 400). Convinced that the human race faced possible extinction through genetic deterioration, he developed an elaborate theory which attempted to justify eugenic measures through analogies with domesticated animals. The first comprehensive statement of this by Lorenz is a long article entitled *"Durch Domestikation verursachte Störungen arteignen Verhaltens"* {"Disturbance of Characteristic Behaviors through Domestication"} published in 1940. He argued that the two processes of civilization and domestication produce precisely the same biological patterns. In his view, the period prior to civilization had been difficult but noble:

In prehistoric times when small clans in wide territories that
were thinly populated by their own kind had, with great effort,

<117>

to combat hunger, cold, predators, and barbarians, all those qualities that we regard as beautiful, good, heroic, and honorable possessed a high value in terms of natural selection. A tribe whose members were not always ready to stand up for one another, whose parenting was inadequate, or who showed a disturbance in other inborn social behaviors was consigned to extinction, as is the case today with all wild animals" (Lorenz, "Domestikation," 67).

But the comfort and security of civilization soon led to genetic decline. When animals are domesticated, Lorenz argued, natural selection no longer works. While irregularities are generally eliminated through natural selection in the wild, they are prized for their novelty or their cuteness by human owners. The result is a proliferation of forms, in contrast to the consistency of features found in wild animals. Since external characteristics are linked with emotional reactions, Lorenz argued, such irregularity in appearance entails a comparable disturbance in instinctive behavior. He added that he had invariably found this to be the case in practice. Precisely the same pattern, Lorenz believed, could be observed among men and women in cities as among domesticated animals, where one also observed a vast range of physical forms and behaviors.

In the view of Lorenz this was "entropy," the decay of a complex and highly differentiated form into increasingly random variations. It signaled genetic decline very similar to that found among domesticated animals, and it should be regarded as an illness (Lorenz, "Domestikation," 69; Deichmann, 189). In the short run, entropy meant social breakdown and disease. People would lose the instincts that inhibited violent behavior and indiscriminate breeding, and they would not care properly for their young. Entropy would mean human extinction if not checked in time. Lorenz conceded that in his capacity as a scientist he was not authorized to make value judgments. He noted, however, that human beings have an instinctive revulsion against this entropy of higher and more complex forms. The instinct, however, might also be lost eventually as human beings were bred to prefer decadence and degeneration.

He also discussed several characteristics which he believed were found among both human beings in civilization and animals in domestication. The physical characteristics found in both included, for example, "pug-dog heads" {*Mopsköpfe*}, shortened extremities, and limp bellies. The mental characteristics included dulled reactions, lack of feeling, and heightened sexuality (Lorenz, "Domestikation," 53-55). Lorenz supported his view with 35 illustrations, the great majority of which contrasted racial health and degeneration in various pairs of animals and of human beings. Though Lorenz did not make the connection explicit, the description of the

<118>

"civilized" man corresponded very closely to contemporary caricatures of Jews in the famous cartoons from the publications of Julius Streicher.

The Nazis did not simply consider Jews an "inferior" race; the Jews were allegedly not an authentic people at all (Aycoberry, 5). The Jews could not be a distinct race since they were allegedly so mixed that they had lost any primordial identity (Kittel, *passim*; Weinreich, 40-45, 111). Like Gypsies, they did not have a single territory, and so they were not integrated into any sort of landscape. Their instincts had reportedly degenerated, and, lacking any sense of shame, they would indulge in indiscriminate promiscuity (Stengel, 165). They represented the entropy, the degeneration which the Nazis believed was a result of urbanization and miscegenation.

Every degenerate animal was, as the housekeeper for Hans Fantel had put it, a sort of "Jewish dog." The following description by Lorenz is typical:

> . . . with phenotypic inferiority the refined modes of social
> behavior are disturbed far earlier and far more seriously than
> the outward appearance. One can predict with absolute certainty
> of a crooked-legged, pot-bellied, pale-beaked grey goose, such as
> is all too easily produced through careless breeding, that its
> social behavior will be other than normal. With the pure-
> blooded wild goose the view of the old Greeks that a handsome
> man can never be bad and an ugly man can never be good is
> fully valid. This, however, is unfortunately no longer the case
> even with the most racially homogeneous European peoples. I
> imagine that even by the time of the Classical Greeks it was no
> longer fully the case. But inborn patterns that are deeply
> imbedded in genetic inheritance are far, far older than all
> traditional cultures, so it required great, indeed geological,
> spans of time to adjust to things like the separation of the
> original unity of those signals which indicate goodness and
> beauty (Lorenz, "Domestikation," 58-59).

The letters of Lorenz to his mentor Oscar Heinroth are full of anti-Semitic asides, and on one occasion in 1939 Lorenz refers to the "ugly Jewish nose" of the shoveler duck (Klopfer, "Lorenz," 204-205).

Lorenz believed it was imperative to institute aggressive measures before decline became fully irreversible. His solution was also drawn from domestication. He believed that just as degeneration could be prevented in animals by making them conform to a standardized breed (Lorenz, "Domestikation," 60), it could also be prevented in people by eugenics.

<119>

In another article from the same year, Lorenz developed this idea further; he voiced eugenic ambitions far beyond anything that even Adolf Hitler or Heinrich Himmler had envisaged. Not simply content with creating a master race, he spoke of creating a new species. He claimed that the guidance of instinct would lead us on to ever higher biological forms, provided we had the will to stop indiscriminate or careless breeding. Identifying the theory of evolution with National Socialism, he urged that the necessity for this be reinforced in young people through education. Lorenz even proposed a new morality in which the Golden Rule would be replaced by his maxim: "You shall love the future of your ethnic group {*Volk*} above all else" (Lorenz, "Nochmals," 32), a moralistic version of his early theory that all creatures have a drive to species preservation.

Lorenz and the "Appropriate" Instincts

Parts of both the articles on eugenics by Lorenz, together with additional materials, were incorporated into a book-length work entitled "*Die angeborener Formen möglicher Erfahrung*" {"The Innate Forms of Possible Experience"}, an essay so ambitious it might be called a "scientific theory of everything," which was published in an expanded issue of the *Zeitschift für Tierpsychologie* 1943. This may be the most coherent justification of Nazi ideology ever produced. A vast range of social and biological phenomena were reduced to instinctive reactions. A similar range of social and ethical recommendations revolved around the demand that only those with the appropriate instincts be allowed to reproduce. He closed with remarks that the struggle against entropy in human beings was part of the battle of harmonious form against chaos and decay throughout the universe. The creation of new forms through controlled evolution, according to Lorenz, was like the work of an artist creating beauty (390-395, 407).

To publish such an exceptionally long — 393 pages — and wide-ranging essay in a scientific journal was virtually unprecedented. Furthermore, it appeared at the height of the war when resources were scarce. The editors, and probably the government authorities, obviously felt it had far more than routine importance. It attempted to integrate the field of animal psychology into the context of Nazi ideology. This gave the discipline greater status and gave National Socialism greater intellectual respectability.

The extent of Lorenz's Nazi involvement was not known until revealed in the 1990s by Ute Deichmann in *Biologists under Hitler*. She disclosed that Lorenz had not only joined the Nazi party but was also a member of its Office for Race Policy. Still more significantly, in 1942 he participated in a study of 877 offspring of mixed German-Polish marriages to determine their potential for assimilation into German culture. Those considered

<120>

asocial or of inferior genetic value were sent to concentration camps while others were sent away to be "Germanized" (193-197, 323). These activities finally came to an end in June of 1944 when Lorenz was captured by the Soviet army (Deichmann, 185).

Other Scientists

Most of the scientists who made major contributions to the emerging field of ethology did not fare very well under the Nazi government. Together with his wife, Katherina, Oscar Heinroth devoted himself to preserving the Aquarium of the Berlin Zoo despite Allied bombings and interference from SS men. Both were in perpetual danger and were thankful when they could eat the zoo animals killed in the blitz. Wounded in air attacks, Heinroth declined to leave the city and died shortly before the fall of Berlin (Heinroth, 133-134).

Karl von Frisch, the great empiricist among animal psychologists in the early twentieth century, deciphered dances of bees during World War II. Though he was completely uninterested in politics, fellow researchers found his approach to science overly mechanistic and not Germanic in spirit. In addition, some of his colleagues criticized him for offering employment to Jewish scientists. The law required Frisch, as the head of a research institute at the zoology department of the University of Munich, to document the Aryan ancestry of all four grandparents. He was unable to do this for his maternal grandmother, and this raised the prospect that he might be partly Jewish. Such "scandals" were very common in Nazi Germany. Nobody could ever be sure that he or she might not be subjected to such allegations, whether the "Jewish blood" be real, fabricated, or imagined. Since the Nazis did not have any definition of a "Jew," the entire concept of "Jewish blood" was in any case close to being meaningless.

Allegations of Jewish blood might be either prosecuted or ignored on the basis of political convenience. The Nazis were reluctant to remove Frisch from his position because his research had great practical importance. A disease was killing bees and thus threatening production in German orchards. After intense debates the Ministry of the Interior finally declared von Frisch a "*Mischling* second class" (i.e., one-fourth Jewish) but postponed his removal from office until the end of the war. The introverted von Frisch simply poured his energies into research with greater intensity and found solace from human stupidity in the more orderly society of bees.

Nikolaus Tinbergen was the most deeply ambivalent of the scientists. After the Nazis came to power, contact was severely reduced between the scientists of Germany and those outside the Reich. The Dutch were considered racially close to the Germans, so Tinbergen as a citizen of the Netherlands had the privilege of working with either group. He chose for the most part to work with the Germans, perhaps because he found their

<121>

work more dynamic and innovative. He became a very close collaborator of Lorenz before he experienced the brutality of the Nazis. During the period of Nazi rule Tinbergen and Lorenz published one joint paper. They did further work together which remained unpublished (Lorenz, "For-men," 252). Furthermore, they constantly praised and cited one another in their publications. Perhaps the longest and most ambitious publication by Tinbergen in this period was a long, theoretical article entitled "*Die Überspringbewegung*" {"The Bypass Motion"}, published in the journal of the German Society for Animal Psychology in 1940-41. He began it with a tribute: "I am further indebted with great gratitude to my friend Dr. Konrad Lorenz, who has read the manuscript and offered very valuable criticism" (3). Tinbergen continued to contribute to the journal for nearly two years after the Germans captured the Netherlands in May of 1940.

The University of Leiden, where Tinbergen was employed, was a major center for resistance against German occupation. In November of 1940, the Germans announced the dismissal of all Jewish officials including professors, and a student strike immediately broke out. Within a few weeks, the Nazis permanently canceled classes and disbanded all student organizations, though the university remained officially open and professors continued their research. In May of 1942, the government fired a prominent faculty member. Almost the entire remaining faculty including Tinbergen resigned in protest, and the university was forced to close completely. Two months later the increasingly desperate occupying forces started rounding up the recalcitrant professors and placing them in hostage camps (Warmbrunn, 146-149).

Though he had not been a leader in the protests, Tinbergen was incarcerated. The experience was traumatic for him, but perhaps it was not unproductive. He passed the time in the camp with relatively unstructured observation of herring gulls. He also managed to write a children's book about a young gull entitled *Klieuw*. In 1942, as the war in Holland drew to a close, Tinbergen was released (Deichmann, 200-203). His book for children was published shortly after the war, and the study of the herring gull later became the foundation of Tinbergen's most important scientific work.

In many ways the history of the German Society for Animal Psychology was typical of work in many scientific fields during the mid-twentieth century. This was a time in which science moved from being an activity of relatively isolated individuals, connected by informal networks and motivated largely by personal interest, to being a far more corporate activity. Increasingly, the cost of research and the growing specialization forced scientists to work as teams governed by bureaucratic structures and supported by government or corporate funds. This sometimes meant greater status, yet it also meant reduced autonomy. Scientists had less

<122>

power to set their own agendas, and the result in Germany was that their work was, in varying degrees of directness, placed in the service of Nazi aspirations.

Today, people often divide those who lived in the Nazi period neatly into collaborators and resisters, but the example of the zoologists shows how inadequate those categories generally are. Apart from Lorenz, very few if any could be unequivocally called "collaborators." Many of them occasionally tried to make a stand for scientific autonomy. At the same time almost none of them offered anything approaching consistent resistance to the Nazis. Perhaps the most notable feature in this history is the degree to which professional solidarity seemed to cut across lines of politics. For the most part, those who were critical of the Nazis and those who supported them continued to work together harmoniously both during and after the Third Reich.

The Rehabilitation of Lorenz

Lorenz was not released by the Soviets until 1948, by which time the initial shock over the concentration camps had already begun to subside. He had a surprisingly easy time winning rehabilitation within the scientific community. The Allies were conducting an intense yet brief period of "denazification," in which they tried to remove the entire legacy of Nazi Germany. This could not succeed very well since there was never any consensus about exactly what Nazism was. The Communists generally saw Nazism as a final stage of capitalism, while Western officials thought it was similar to Communism. The poor coordination in the British, Soviet, French, and American zones of occupied Germany also helped make the denazification campaign haphazard if sometimes severe. According to the "Report on the Educational Conditions in Postwar Germany" produced by Alfred E. Mann for the Rockefeller Foundation in 1947, the Russians removed from office only those academics for whom they had no use. The French dismissed about 75% of the personnel at educational institutions, while the British dismissed about 20% (RA, series 1.1, Box 5, folder 24, 23). The campaign was most severe in the American zone. People who had been members of the Nazi party were not permitted to hold any office above that of laborer, and about half of the educational personnel at all levels were removed (24-25).

Most of the academic facilities in Germany lay in ruins. There was widespread hunger, and the few animals that had survived the war were generally sacrificed for food. Hardly any animals were left for the purposes of research. According to the report by Alfred Mann, the Russians were particularly insistent that all rations be distributed to human beings. A few laboratory animals considered particularly valuable were maintained in secret with food that was designated for people (63-64). At the University

<123>

of Göttingen, enough animals were retained for classroom demonstrations but not for experiments. Experiments on relatively inexpensive animals such as mice, toads, and frogs were still conducted at a very few institutions such as the University of Heidelberg (39).

As the Cold War grew more intense, denazification quickly gave way to more immediately practical concerns. Scientists generally wanted to put the trauma of the recent past behind them and get on with their work, and they saw the denazification program as an obstacle. Their sole remaining resource was expertise, and they wished to make full use of that. Both those scientists who had been critical of the Nazis and those who had supported them united around professional concerns. Otto Hahn, President of the Kaiser Wilhelm Society, angrily denounced the American government for destroying German universities (27).

Even Karl von Frisch, who had suffered under the Nazis, worried that the scrutiny of academics in Germany during denazification was impeding research. Toward the end of the war, his facilities in Munich had been destroyed in an air raid, and he had accepted a position in Graz, Austria. In 1948, he made arrangements to return to his old facility in Munich, which by then had been completely rebuilt. He discussed the move at length in correspondence which is preserved in the Rockefeller Archive. Not once did Frisch betray even a trace of the bitterness, anger, or triumph that could have been expected after his experiences. Instead, he was concerned almost exclusively with the quality of the research facilities that he could find in various locations. In 1948, he complained that the Nazi movement had led to a break between Austrian and German science (RA, record 1.2, series 7050, Box 6, folder 57). He also recommended Lorenz as his successor at Graz, though without success.

Asked to report on the suitability of employing his old friend and colleague Konrad Lorenz, Tinbergen initially gave a very conflicted response. Despite his close work with Lorenz in the Nazi period, Tinbergen reported nothing more specific than "I know absolutely nothing about our German colleagues. Lorenz was in the Army, Department of Herrenpsychology [sic][1] since 1941."

Even more disingenuously, Tinbergen falsely reported that "From 1942 on, I have not published anything. . . ." (Deichmann 203). In fact, he had been the primary author of a long article appearing in 1943 in the *Zeitschift für Tierpsychologie*. The date of submission had been March 1, 1942 (182). Simply publishing scientific articles in a Nazi journal was hardly a crime, and Tinbergen had gained credibility by association with the Dutch resistance, but Tinbergen may have lied to protect Lorenz as well as himself. Precisely that same issue of *Zeitschrift für Tierpsychologie*

---

[1] This is Tinbergen's neologism combining English and German. He means "military psychology."

<124>

contained the long article by Lorenz entitled *"Angeborener Formen möglicher Erfahrung,"* which, as already detailed, was filled with Nazi rhetoric and ideas. With the support of Tinbergen and others, Lorenz obtained a position at the Max Planck Institute in Wilhelmshaven in 1951 (Deichmann 199).

The popular publications of Lorenz, especially *King Solomon's Ring,* extended his rehabilitation beyond the scientific community to the general public. Translated into English, the book became a bestseller in the early fifties. The contents were primarily ideas and observations that he had first published in journals during the Third Reich. This enabled researchers to cite Lorenz without encountering the most sordid aspects of his past. Ever a shrewd politician, he applied his psychological theories to the marketing of his books. During the Nazi era he had, as we have seen, presented the characteristics of "entropy" as genetic degeneration which exercised an almost diabolical appeal as "cuteness." *King Solomon's Ring* is a veritable orgy of cuteness. In cartoons he drew to illustrate *King Solomon's Ring,* Lorenz portrayed both people and animals, himself included, with the characteristics he previously considered genetically degenerate. He gave himself a sharply receding forehead and sometimes an incipient pot belly. This could reflect both pragmatic calculation and sincere regret by Lorenz, but Lorenz never openly discussed or faced up to his Nazi past.

It is hard to see how Lorenz could have been awarded the Nobel prize if the committee had actually read his articles in biological journals published during the late thirties and early forties rather than simply his popularizations. This is not to deny that these articles contained valuable ideas and information. But, in addition to supporting Nazi policies, they used methods of argument which were often very dubious. Lorenz regularly falsified quotations (Deichmann, 190-193). He was also not above calling people who disagreed with him on certain key issues "instinctual cripples" who were genetically unfit to reproduce (Lorenz, *"Nochmals,"* 31; Lorenz, *"Formen,"* 338), an allegation that could be serious indeed in a regime which practiced involuntary sterilization and worse.

The program put forward by Lorenz during the Nazi era was nothing less than to extend technocratic regulation to a point where the breeding and future evolution of the human species would be directed by experts. As the state appropriated the full power of the natural world, the effects of "domestication" would be overcome. The notion sounds paradoxical, yet perhaps we ought not to be surprised by it. As scholars increasingly realize, the concept of "wildness" including that of predators has always been largely a creation of human culture. The attempt to create wildness through elaborate eugenic controls was merely taking this to its ultimate conclusion. It is like the artificial wildness of contemporary zoos and safari parks,

<125>

where the demand for authenticity becomes the basis for increasingly complex manipulation. While Lorenz praised the consistency of features in wild animals, the implicit model for this quality may have been manufactured objects. He wished to produce people almost like products on the assembly line, complete with quality control.

<126>

PART IV
SACRIFICE AND DEATH

CHAPTER 13
SLAUGHTER

"Listen to the sound of your brother's blood, crying out to me from the ground. . . ." — Genesis (4:10)

AFTER THE FLOOD, Noah built an altar for Yahweh and offered sacrifices. The odor reached Yahweh, who said: "Never again will I curse the earth because of man, because his heart contrives evil from his infancy. Never again will I strike down every living thing as I have done" (Genesis 8:20-21). Yahweh blessed Noah and his sons then told them:

> Be fruitful, multiply and fill the earth. Be the terror and the dread of all the wild beasts and all the birds of heaven, of everything that crawls on the ground and all the fish of the sea; they are handed over to you. Every living and crawling thing shall provide food for you, no less than the foliage of plants. I give you everything, with this exception: you must not eat flesh with life, that is to say blood, in it . . . (Genesis 9:1-5).

After investing human beings with new power and responsibility, Yahweh sent a rainbow as a sign of his covenant. Jewish tradition dates the eating of flesh by both animals and human beings from this time.

Abstinence from blood became a distinguishing feature of Hebrew culture. In most totemic systems of belief, the life of the slain animals merges with that of the hunter. The sharing of blood is an essential part of the "mystic solidarity of predator and prey," which Eliade identified as the basis of Paleolithic religion (*Stone Age*, 5). Both parties are joined in the endless circulation of cosmic energy. In many traditions of folk medicine, drinking the blood or eating the heart of certain animals brings strength and protection against weapons (Meyer, 79). In *The Odyssey*, Odysseus entered Hades to find his dead companions were pale and could not speak. He gave them blood from a sacrificed sheep to drink, at which time they temporarily regained their former vividness. The Norse hero Sigurd became invulnerable in battle by bathing in the blood of a dragon. Even in our secular society of today, the eating of red meat still suggests fierceness. The Hebrews had broken with archaic animal cults. By not partaking of blood, the Hebrews distanced themselves from both predator and prey. Nachmanides, a medieval Jewish teacher, later explained the prohibition against eating of carnivorous fowl by stating, "Every bird of

<129>

prey is invariably unclean for fear that its bloodthirstiness would be communicated to the partaker of its meat through its blood" (Welfeld, 55).

The sight of a bleeding wound evokes horror and fascination. The blood of animals from a fish to a human being appears much the same. The flow of blood suggests the return of life to its primal, undifferentiated state. Adrenalin in blood from freshly killed animals can serve as a drug, inducing a state of artificial excitement. Up through much of the twentieth century, people regarded blood as the life force and the carrier of heredity (Montagu, 280-290). Because human beings bear many obvious resemblances to animals, any taking of blood without exception can easily suggest the killing of human beings. The contemporary Yiddish author Isaac Bashevis Singer has told how, growing up in an Orthodox Jewish family in Poland, he "heard and read that the souls of the dead were reincarnated in cattle and fowl and that when the slaughterer killed them with a kosher knife and said the blessing with fervor, this served to purify these souls." Already a skeptic, he wondered "What about those cows and hens that fell into the hands of gentile butchers?" (19-20).

The composer Richard Wagner, who anticipated Nazism in both his vehement anti-Semitism and his love of grandiose spectacle, often attributed magical power to blood. According to his essay "Heroism and Christianity" {Heldentum und Christentum}, humanity was originally a single race. It divided into various races when people gave up their original vegetarian diet for meat, thus absorbing the blood of animals and becoming bestial. This led to a contamination of their blood, which was further spread by sexual intercourse. Finally, only the "noble" Germanic race was left. The Germans as well were "tragically" corrupted when they sacked Rome and mated with the conquered people. Even the most polluted races might be redeemed through a vegetarian diet, provided they also partook of the Eucharist, which was the original blood of unspoiled man (275-280). Hitler was obsessed with pollution of blood or "Blutschande." He had the notorious Nuremberg racial laws of 1935 named "Laws for the Protection of German Blood and Honor" (Waite, 22-25). The most sacred relic of the Nazi movement was the "Blood Flag," carried by the Nazis in the abortive coup in Munich. One German newspaper, reporting on a ceremony in which people swore oaths of allegiance to Hitler, referred to Nazism as "the religion of blood" (30).

Ritual Slaughter

The Biblical prohibition against eating flesh with blood in it is the origin of kosher slaughter, which is practiced by both Jews and Muslims. This is a way of killing animals for food by a single cut to the throat so that the creature will die quickly from loss of blood. According to tradition this cut does not precisely take the life of the animal; instead that life is

<130>

returned to God in the form of blood running into the ground. The Jewish ritual, known as "shechita," is more restrictive than that of Muslims. Jewish tradition requires that the killing be performed with a knife that is exceptionally broad and extremely sharp; it may not have even the smallest notch. Tradition, according to most though not all Rabbinical authorities, also mandates that animals should not be stunned before killing.

Ritual places a highly emotional activity under control; even the most arbitrary rules impose discipline. Jewish and Islamic traditions demand that the person who performs slaughter uphold especially high moral standards so as not to be degraded by his work. Observing the performance of shechitah in many abattoirs in the United States, Temple Grandin found that the shochets, those who perform ritual killing, would never tease or abuse an animal, even though some of the slaughterhouses used painful means of restraint which might otherwise have encouraged such behavior ("Behavior," 210-212).

Ritual slaughter is a tradition that goes back to remote antiquity. Among the Babylonians, Greeks and other ancient peoples, just as among the Hebrews, the killing of animals was a ceremonial act. It was performed in public by a priest and accompanied by prayers and pleas for forgiveness from the animal, similar to those used in traditional hunting societies (Burkert, *Homo*, 1-12). We might doubt the point of such rituals today. Animals certainly do not understand the literal meaning of our prayers, whether they are in Hebrew, Arabic, Greek, Navaho, or English. On the other hand, animals can sense the moods of human beings, as people who keep dogs will attest. Furthermore, ritual addresses a need for familiarity and routine, shared by both man and beast (Grandin, *Thinking*, 145-146). Archaic rituals may have created an atmosphere in which death seemed meaningful even to the animal.

The interval between the cut and loss of consciousness must have initially been a time for prayer or lamentation. The Muslim ritual slaughter, known as "halal," must still be accompanied by prayers to Allah. At one time the prayers were probably directed instead to the slaughtered animal. In ancient Greek ritual sacrifice of a bull, which is similar in many respects to kosher slaughter, women would begin to wail as soon as the cut was made (Burkert, *Homo*, 5). Kosher slaughter was a partial secularization of these practices, though the public rituals which accompanied animal sacrifice among the Hebrews were eventually stopped. Saint Paul proclaimed that ritual sacrifice was no longer needed since Christ had made the ultimate sacrifice (Hebrews 10:4-10). Furthermore, many Christians held with Saint Augustine that only human beings have souls, a doctrine that deprived animal sacrifice of any meaning. If the spirits of animals either vanished at death or simply did not exist, they could not be offered

<131>

as a gift to a deity. The sacraments of Christianity all center either, like marriage, around the relations between human beings or, like communion, around the relation of a person to God. There is almost nothing in Christian ritual that regulates or sanctifies relationships between human beings and other creatures. Christians have often considered kosher slaughtering and related practices to be idolatrous.

Modern people on encountering ritualized slaughter often feel transported into a barbaric past. Ritual killing of animals evokes associations of archaic human sacrifice. A good example of this reaction occurred in Newark, NJ in 1988. When bags containing the remains of sacrificial animals used in a Santería ceremony were found in an alley, there was massive public outrage. The religion of was Santería widely presented in respected American publications as Satanic (Stevens, 13-14). In fact it is a blend of Catholic and West African practices which upholds a morality at least as strict as that of mainstream Christian churches.

The Debate on Kosher Slaughter

Like many ancient practices, kosher slaughter is hard to adjust to a modern secular society. Modern abattoirs will kill not one but thousands, sometimes hundreds of thousands, of animals in a single day. The need to keep production competitive allows little time for humane practices, let alone religious meditation. Kosher slaughter can become a bit like the contemporary electronic church where a minister will bless a list of names on a computer printout. There are, furthermore, complications that arise when kosher slaughtering is combined with modern hygienic requirements. Since it is not sanitary to have animals fall in their own blood, animals have sometimes been hoisted and turned upside down before killing.[1]

Veterinary authorities now generally agree kosher slaughtering is painless, though it requires a great deal of skill and care (Brumme, "Tierarzt," 34). Loss of consciousness after the cut is not instantaneous but generally comes only after a lapse of a few seconds to a minute for most animals (Grandin, "Euthanasia," 1359). Some researchers have given the period for calves as up to 85 seconds, and they may even experience a momentary return of awareness during a span of several minutes (Newhook and Blackmore, 295-301). Since there is no universally accepted way to judge the presence of consciousness, such figures can only be provisional.

Kosher slaughter remains illegal even today in many countries including Sweden and Switzerland. In a detailed comparison of various

---

[1] Innovations in the design of abattoirs now enable the animal to remain standing with supports after slaughter, rendering this practice obsolete (Grandin, "Euthanasia," 1358). These have been endorsed by the Rabbinical Council of America (Schochet, 284).

<132>

methods of slaughter, the American Association of Veterinary Medicine has concluded that exsanguination — death by bleeding, which includes kosher slaughter—was only recommended when combined with prior stunning or electric shock (AVMA, 265). There is no reason to suspect anti-Semitism here, but the debate is far from resolved. Medical experts, sometimes with the support of the Israeli government, have written highly sophisticated defenses of kosher slaughter (Schochet, 284-286).

It is impossible to say with certainty what method of slaughter is most humane. The judgment is ultimately a matter of empathy, of mentally putting oneself in the place of the animal. That involves our perceptions of life and death, and these are subject to wide cultural variation. There is no reason to think that animals share our contemporary notions of death, either as a gateway to Heaven and Hell or as absolute extinction. They probably have some understanding of death, but it is very difficult for us to reconstruct this in imagination. If kosher slaughtering gives them a momentary awareness of their fate, is that a blessing or a curse?

Arthur Koestler's *Darkness at Noon*, based on the Moscow trials in Stalin's Russia, is one of the many novels of totalitarianism which use imagery of the stockyard. Throughout the novel, the hero, who was accused of betraying the revolution, imagined himself placed before a firing squad for execution. In the last sentence of the novel, we learn that he was not shot but killed by being struck unexpectedly from behind. By being slaughtered like a steer, he was denied even the most basic human dignity.

The Campaign Against Kosher Slaughter

In 1855 the Royal Society for the Prevention of Cruelty to Animals sued the Jewish community in London on the ground that kosher methods of slaughter were cruel (Schochet, 283). In the latter part of the nineteenth century, kosher slaughtering rivaled vivisection as the primary concern of the animal protection movement in Germany and Switzerland (Tröhler and Maehle, 176-177). The Swiss banned kosher slaughter in 1893. Other countries including Norway, Sweden, and Italy banned it over the next few decades (Schochet, 283), as did Bavaria and several other provinces of Germany (Jentzsch, 45). Like vivisection, kosher slaughter symbolized the allegedly sinister detachment of materialistic thought. This sort of materialism, in turn, was identified with Jewish tradition. In the enormously popular anti-vivisectionist novel *Gemma oder Tugend und Laster {Gemma, or Virtue and Vice}* by Elpis Melena {a pseudonym for Marie-Espérance von Schwarz}, published in Germany in 1890, the vivisectionists turned out to be a diabolic cult that ritually tortured animals using the pretense of scientific investigation. While Melena did not mention the Jews specifically, she evoked popular images of them engaged in kosher slaughter.

<133>

The enormous symbolic significance that the Nazis attached to blood made death by bleeding seem perverse. From their point of view this was not simply a matter of being killed but also being first deprived of primeval vitality. Jews were called "bloodsuckers" and "parasites." The animals being slaughtered in a kosher manner would twitch (Grandin, "Euthanasia," 1359). This is a muscle spasm, but many people interpreted the reflex as a sign of torment. Kosher slaughter was called a form of ritualistic torture, a cult of cruelty practiced by a coarse and unfeeling people (Brumme, "Blutkult," 392). A popular story by Hans-Peter Richtel that was used as Nazi propaganda described kosher slaughter as follows:

> . . . the Jewish priest approaches the cow and slowly lifts the knife of sacrifice. The animal feels threatened with death, it lows and seeks to break free, but the Jew knows no pity. With lightning speed he thrusts the knife into its neck; the blood spurts; everything is sullied by it; the animal struggles furiously; its eyes roll back in agony . . . The merciless Jew does nothing to shorten the suffering of the bloody animal; he wallows in it; he needs blood . . . (Farbe-Vassas, 141).

The Nazi propaganda film *Der ewige Jude* included a grisly series of scenes of sheep and steers suffering horrible agonies as they are killed. Jews were then shown laughing, and the narrator proclaimed ". . . their so-called religion prevents the Jews from eating meat butchered in the ordinary way, so they let the animals bleed to death."

Professionalized Slaughter

The debate on exsanguination reflected the conflict between traditional farming and modernity. As the Nazis themselves noted, slaughter by exsanguination without prior stunning was not practiced only by the Jews (Giese and Kahler, 151). It was also practiced on independent farms, in some cases following traditions that go back to ancient times. The Nazis did indeed proclaim the superiority of rural life in their propaganda, yet they offered the actual farmers little support. Tradition was consistently sacrificed to efficiency (Schoenbaum, 176-177).

The veterinary profession in Germany began to assert a claim to authority on the subject of slaughter during the Weimar Republic. In the 1920s, "Slaughter Yard Studies" and "Meat Inspection" became official subject subjects taught at veterinary schools (Schimanski, 34). In a short time employment at slaughter yards had become a particularly lucrative and prestigious veterinary specialty (65). The veterinarians in Germany were highly nationalistic and anti-Semitic even before the Nazi seizure of power. In 1933 there were only two Jewish students of veterinary medicine

<134>

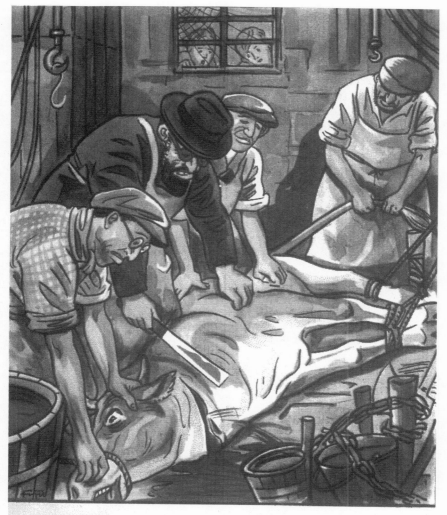

Wieder stürzt das Tier zu Boden. Langsam stirbt es. Die Juden aber stehen herum und lachen dazu.

Fig. 12. Page from an anti-Semitic German children's book published in 1935, entitled *Der Giftpilz* {*The Poisonous Mushroom*}, showing Jews engaged in kosher slaughter. The caption reads, "Again the animal falls to the ground. It is dying. The Jews, however, are standing around and laughing about it." Courtesy of the American Holocaust Memorial Museum (photo #40012).

<135>

in all of Germany (74, 113). The veterinary establishment was immediately absorbed into the power structure when the Nazis seized control of the government. By the end of summer of 1933, 75% of the faculty at the major Veterinary School in Hannover had joined the Nazi party and half of the students belonged to Nazi organizations (315). The veterinarians as a whole had the highest level of Nazi party membership of any professional group in Germany (Dominick, 113).

People in Germany had long considered veterinarians responsible not only for medical care, but for all issues relating to animals. The government called on veterinarians to formulate and interpret animal protection laws. The primary advisor of Hitler on policy involving animals was Friedrich Weber, a veterinarian who participated with Hitler in the abortive coup of 1923. An intimate companion of Hitler, Weber soon became President of the newly formed Chamber of Veterinarians which combined all German veterinarians into a monolithic bureaucracy. After the Nazis came to power the veterinary profession policed itself, eliminating dissenters and Jews without even having to be asked (Brumme, "Weg," 36). Veterinary medicine was a relatively new profession at the time, and veterinarians aspired to the status of other doctors. They were eager to cooperate with officials who held the keys to power (Bornemann and Brumme, 122). In a message to all veterinarians published on September 1, 1939, as the war began, Frederich Weber wrote in *Deutsches Tierärzteblatt*:

> German Veterinarians!
> A great hour of decision in the history of our people has struck.
> The Führer has called every German man and woman to the full
> service of Germany. He himself is our shining model, showing
> that from this time on the individual counts for nothing; only
> Germany and its future are important.
> German veterinarians will all follow his call . . . (Wernicke, 216).

With the attacks on kosher slaughter and other forms of killing by exsanguination, the veterinarians asserted their control over a sphere that had long been left to individuals.

Regulating slaughter and placing it under control of licensed veterinarians gave the state additional power over the meat industry, which was largely placed in the service of the war effort. In spite of severe shortages of food at home, the enormous stockyard in Dresden was busy as never before with killing and butchering going on around the clock to supply the needs of the troops. The activity was so intense that many prisoners from captured territories were brought in as forced laborers. Most of the animals were shipped in from occupied territories on the Eastern Front. From the Soviet region of Kursk alone, the Germans stole 280,000 cattle,

<136>

250,000 pigs and 420,000 sheep (*Vereinigte Fleisch*, 19-20). The constant traffic of cattle cars between Germany and the occupied territories provided a cover for the transportation of victims to the concentration camps.

An official commentary on the law on slaughtering of animals {passed April 21, 1933} stated that, "Almost all German veterinarians consider the ritual slaughter performed by Jews to be inhumane." It cited a questionnaire on kosher slaughter distributed to all faculty in anatomy and physiology at veterinary schools throughout Germany and Austria. This was answered by 85% of the respondents, and all described kosher slaughter with words such as "cruel," "barbaric," "horrible," "disgusting," and "inhuman" (Giese and Kahler, 152-153). The law described various methods of killing to be used with different species in great detail (164-177). An exception to the mandate for anesthesia was made for fowl, which could be decapitated with a single blow (171). The law also required that slaughter be carried out only by trained butchers. One interesting provision was that the slaughter must take place in closed rooms. Only helpers and supervisors were allowed to be present, and nobody under 14 years old (165). Perhaps these stipulations may have been intended as a safeguard against slaughter as a public ritual, something that works of Nazi propaganda such as *Der ewige Jude* erroneously suggested was being practiced by the Jews. The reason given for the provisions was to avoid coarsening of the public.

The rigidity of the Nazi laws and the vehemence of the attack on kosher butchering suggest motivations beyond humane concern. How could the authorities be so sure which way of killing was most humane or even that there was a single correct way? The perception of suffering in animals is intuitive and influenced by culture. Why were no allowances made for local custom, much less religious practice? Could it not be that some traditions, the Jewish one included, might have had ways of handling the knife or interacting with the animals which were highly humane but could not easily be copied? The debate on kosher slaughtering was a rather typical confrontation between inherited tradition, here epitomized by practicing Jews, and technocracy, represented by the veterinarians. The conflict was especially representative of the ways in which the opposing sides regarded the prospect of pain. In general, Traditional practices attempt to give meaning to pain, while modern ones seek to eliminate pain.

<137>

Both sides had legitimate arguments. The veterinarians were likely correct in their belief that slaughter with prior stunning offered a better guarantee of painless death. The traditional means of slaughter, by contrast, seemed to grant animals more respect as sentient beings.[2] The extreme vehemence of the Nazi attacks on death by exsanguination reflected an attempt to strip killing and death of the last remnants of ancient ritual, thus depriving them of any meaning beyond what the Nazis themselves might assign.

Slaughter as a Metaphor

Raul Hilberg has argued that other anti-Semitic measures taken by the Nazi government such as pogroms and expulsion had precedents, but the concentration camps were something entirely new. They would, however, not have been even imaginable without modern techniques of mass production. Hilberg was not entirely correct when he wrote that, "the killing center . . . has no prototype, no administrative ancestor" (221). Both industrial slaughterhouses and concentration camps were organized as factories that produced not conventional goods but death.[3]

Before the modern era, killing of animals by the hundreds or thousands was rare, though not unknown. Occasionally, conquering armies would vent their rage not only through slaughter of vanquished people but of their animals as well, as the Bible tells us was done by the Hebrews in the land of Canaan. Massive sacrifices of animals were sometimes made to the gods on particularly momentous occasions. According to the Bible 22,000 oxen and 120,000 sheep were sacrificed to Yahweh at the dedication of Solomon's temple (1 Kings 8:63). At the beginning of the Second Punic War, the Romans sacrificed all the animals born in that spring (Lewinsohn, 102). The Romans would later slaughter enormous numbers of animals and people as entertainment in their circuses. The capture of victims for these lurid spectacles did much to reduce the population of large animals such as the hippopotamus, elephant, and lion in North Africa. The opening of the Colosseum under the Roman Emperor Titus was followed by 100 days of celebration, and 5,000 animals were slaughtered on a single day (Attenborough, 113).

Such killing was not justified on pragmatic grounds. Most of the meat had to be wasted. There was no way in which such quantities of meat could

---

[2] Temple Grandin believes that recognizing a religious dimension in slaughter can help people perform it humanely. She designed a plant for kosher slaughter that would not involve chaining or hoisting of animals; upon seeing it in operation in 1992 she wrote, "I felt . . . as if God had touched me . . . . A good restraint chute operator has to not just like the cattle but love them." (*Thinking*, 205).

[3] For an analysis of the concentration camps as reflecting the techniques and values involved in mass production, see Bauman, 6-12.

<138>

be either consumed or transported before they would spoil. These limits were narrower in more southern lands, since the colder winters of the north made it easier to preserve meat by freezing. The historian William McNeill has suggested that the special brutality of European wars north of the Alps derived from the slaughter of cattle and pigs in winter, making bloodshed on a massive scale "a normal part" of the yearly routine. These beasts required a lot of fodder, and the lack of vegetation allowed people to keep only a small number for breeding through the spring. This could have contributed to a "remarkable readiness to shed human blood and think nothing of it" (64). The Nazis proudly proclaimed themselves the heirs of this northern culture, particularly in its rural form.

Up through the middle of the nineteenth century, meat production had remained a local or family affair. It changed radically in the 1860's, as railroads enabled animals to be transported great distances for slaughter. The meat could then be transported to distant markets for sale. This made possible a vast and highly centralized industry where animals were soon slaughtered by the hundreds of thousands every day. The industry developed a highly specialized division of labor, a characteristic architecture, and codes of behavior (Pick, 178-181). Soon after their inception, the industrial slaughter plants began to be used to symbolize abuse of human beings. In *The Jungle*, first published in 1906, Upton Sinclair used slaughterhouses to symbolize the exploitation of laborers through dehumanizing work. Abattoirs brought new ways of thinking about killing and, in consequence, about life and death.

The Psychology of Slaughter

James Serpell has described psychological mechanisms used in factory farming that resemble those of the Nazis who worked in concentration camps. Cruelty toward animals destined for slaughter is, Serpell has explained, a means of avoiding potentially distressing identification with these creatures. Pigs are sometimes placed in quarters so cramped that they are unable to either stand up or lie down properly. They are kept in filthy conditions with no amenities at all beyond what is necessary to keep them alive until the appointed time for slaughter has arrived (3-18). Sometimes they must spend their entire lives in concrete boxes of windowless metal buildings. Two hundred and fifty thousand chickens may be confined within a single structure, and the frequent deaths which result from such overcrowding are simply calculated against the money that is saved on space (Williams, 61). "Detachment and unnecessary brutality," Serpell wrote, "seem to be universal components of intensive animal husbandry, presumably because they help to distance the farmer from the mass suffering and slaughter for which he is either directly or indirectly responsible" (Serpell, 155). The slaughter of animals is also characterized

<139>

by concealment (Serpell, 158-159; Pick, 181), and abattoirs are carefully kept from public view. Industrial abattoirs have often provided metaphors for mechanized killing, whether in factories, modern wars, or even concentration camps (Pick, 178-188).

Heinrich Himmler, who founded the SS and oversaw the Nazi death camps, was initially a chicken farmer. Many of his ideas for both systematic breeding and slaughter of human beings were simply the extension of mechanized farming to people. By blurring the boundary between animals and human beings, many Nazi practices made killing of people seem like the slaughtering of animals. The Nazis forced those whom they were about to murder to get completely undressed and huddle together, something that is not normal behavior for human beings. Nakedness suggests an identity as animals; when combined with crowding, it suggests a herd of cattle or sheep. (Todorov, 160; Finkielkraut, 109). This sort of dehumanization made the victims easier to shoot or gas.

Christopher Browning, in his study of a Nazi police battalion in occupied Poland, distinguished three levels of participation. Some people became increasingly enthusiastic and sadistic killers who volunteered for firing squads and "Jew hunts." The majority performed the tasks assigned to them in a routinized manner, killing when ordered to but not seeking out special opportunities to do so. Only a small number resisted or evaded orders to murder. This matches remarkably closely the behavior that Temple Grandin observed among employees at slaughter houses. Some of them began to enjoy killing and deliberately tormented the animals. The largest number detach themselves psychologically from their tasks and kill mechanically. Some workers, often with the aid of rituals, actively attempted to alleviate the distress of the animals (Grandin, *Thinking*, 205-213).

Having grown up in Chicago, which was then considered, in the proud and famous words of Carl Sandburg, "the hog-butcher of the world," I remember how people spoke of the stockyards in hushed tones, with an attitude between revulsion and awe. Few seemed to have visited there, but the area figured prominently in the mythology of the city's mean streets, together with the Mafia of Al Capone. The meat packing industry in Chicago, rightly or wrongly, was even whispered to be an informal training ground for hit men, who would get their start by killing cattle and pigs. Those who did know the stockyards they were often admired, though with ambivalence, for their ability to negotiate that strange and terrible world.

<140>

CHAPTER 14
SACRIFICE

Noah built an altar for Yahweh, and choosing from all the clean animals and all the clean birds he offered burnt offering on the altar. Yahweh smelled the appeasing fragrance and said to himself, "Never again will I curse the earth because of man, because his heart contrives evil from his infancy. Never again will I strike down every living thing as I have done."

— Genesis (8:20-21)

HUMAN SACRIFICE IS not necessarily confined to the most "primitive" civilizations. According to sociologist Orlando Patterson, the lynching of African-Americans in the American South was a form of blood sacrifice. He pointed out that these executions reflected many common characteristics of sacrifice, whether of animals or people. There was, for example, careful attention to symbolic details such as the choice of a day and of a tree; there was the atmosphere that alternated between hushed awe and rowdiness; there was also the combination of hatred of and admiration for the victim (181-208). The mass killings perpetrated by the Nazis show a similar combination of protocol, abandon, and religiosity.

The slaughter of the Canaanites by Joshua and the Hebrews reported in the Old Testament was carried out in a systematic manner that has some resemblance to Nazi murders. Thomas Cahill pointed out that the Biblical language used in speaking of the Canaanites resembled that which was employed elsewhere in the ancient world to speak of sacrificial victims. "What we have here is human sacrifice under the guise of holy war," Cahill wrote, "compelling us to recognize how powerful a hold the need to scapegoat and shed blood has over the human heart" (171). The killing of the five kings of Canaan was clearly ritualized. They were kept locked in a cave until the slaughter of their people was complete. Then Joshua assembled all the men of Israel. The kings were brought and forced to prostrate themselves. At Joshua's command, an officer placed his foot on the neck of each. Then Joshua told the assembled people, ". . . be resolute, for this is how Yahweh shall deal with all the enemies you fight." He finally killed the kings and had their bodies hung from five trees till evening (Joshua 10:20-26).

The Scapegoat

While vehemently repudiating Christianity as a Jewish sect, Hitler constantly compared himself to Christ (Waite, 27-32). "In driving out the Jews . . . ," he once said, "I remind myself of Jesus in the temple" (27). But

<141>

Jesus was a Jew even if the Nazis sometimes absurdly tried to deny it. Many characteristics that Hitler and the Nazis attributed to Jews such as extreme egotism, destructiveness, and desire for enormous power were obvious projections of their own aspirations. So were a host of other accusations that the Nazis leveled against Jews from sexually exploiting young Aryan girls to living at public expense (Victor, 123-129). Hitler himself declared "Just as the Jews became the all-embracing world power they are today only in their dispersal, so shall we today, as the true chosen people of God, become in our dispersal the omnipresent power . . ." (Victor, 144). He was always tormented by a suspicion that he might be partly Jewish. The same is true of a great many of the leading Nazis, including Heydrich, Streicher, and Rosenberg (Victor, 146-147). The anti-Semitism of the Nazis reflected a combination of identification and self-loathing (Victor, 142-145). For them the Jews were a shadow-image on which to project forbidden wishes and secret fears.

The term "scapegoat" derives from the ritual described in the Old Testament where the sins of Israel are placed upon a goat that is then driven into the wilderness for the demon Azazel (Leviticus 16: 5-22). The practice of placing all the guilt of the community on a surrogate, either human or animal, which is then driven away or sacrificed may be found in many cultures from Babylon and Rome to medieval Japan. An example is the ancient Greek ceremony of Thargelia. The victim, known as "pharmakos," was usually a vagrant or a criminal kept at public expense. He was ritually beaten with branches to the music of flutes then finally chased away. That ceremony was strikingly similar to the ritualized violence against Jews which often accompanied Christian holy days in medieval Europe. "Scapegoat" is now commonly used to refer to any group which is compelled to bear the guilt of a society, such as the Jews in Hitler's Germany or the Kulaks in Stalin's Soviet Union. The psychological mechanism entails a sort of magical thinking even when the purposes are not expressed in overtly supernatural terms. According to René Girard all sacrifice—that is, sacramentalized killing—is a form of scapegoating, as a community tries to focus the blame for a catastrophe on a victim who is to be killed in place of themselves (*Violence*, 79-91).

The sacrificial victim is a double of the perpetrator. Girard argues that the victim is a substitute who is killed in place of the people of a community. The victim must resemble these people to a point where they can appear as one to the deity. The victim must at the same time have a separate identity. The most likely victims are those on the fringes of society. When sacrificial victims are animals, they are generally domesticated ones which share in the life of the community. When they are people, they tend to be those who were partially set apart through a special status whether as kings or slaves (*Violence*, 143-168, 269-270). The Jews in Germany during

<142>

the early twentieth century certainly had this sort of ambiguous status. Hitler himself once said that the Jew was as closely akin to the Aryan "as a blood brother" (Victor, 144). The Nazis shared with the Jews an emphasis on biological identity. Furthermore, the God of the Nazis, the "German God" who was often referred to but never depicted, had far more resemblance to Yahweh than to Jesus. Sacrificial victims are generally viewed with a special ambivalence, between contempt and glorification. They are initially treated with enormous scorn, as the sins of the entire community are placed upon them. After they have been killed, they are sacralized out of gratitude for freeing the community from the burden of sin (Girard, *Scapegoat*, 44). Had the Nazis not lost World War II, they might have eventually rehabilitated and even glorified their victims in accord with the logic of sacrifice.

Purity and Judaism

The ban on meat with blood is only one of a long series of dietary restrictions among practicing Jews. These are called "kosher," a Yiddish term which means "proper" or "appropriate." Kosher practices seem arbitrary to the nonbeliever, and even Jews who are highly learned in Hebrew tradition cannot explain them entirely. Some, such as the prohibition against pork, could possibly have had an origin in health concerns, since the flesh of pigs can carry trichinosis. Other prohibitions, however, do not even lend themselves to such speculative explanations.

Jewish dietary law permits eating only those mammals which chew grass and have split hooves such as the cow and lamb (Leviticus 11:1-8). There are prohibitions against carrion (Deuteronomy 14:21) and against the fat of sheep and oxen (Leviticus 7:23). The thigh muscle may be eaten only after the socket has been removed, a taboo which commemorates the thigh wound received by Jacob when he wrestled with a divine being (Genesis 30:25-6, 32-33). By tradition, meat and milk cannot be eaten together and must be prepared using separate vessels, since the Bible declares, "You are not to boil a kid in its mother's milk" (Deuteronomy 14:21).

Prohibited animals are considered "unclean." The distinction between clean and unclean beasts may have been taken by the Hebrews from the religion of Zoroaster, which maintained that some animals were created by Ormuzd, the god of goodness and light, and others by Ahriman, the spirit of darkness. In the Bible, unclean animals are frequently associated with demonic powers, starting with the serpent in Eden. While the category of "unclean" animals refers in practical terms primarily to dietary prohibitions, the term is generally used in clearly pejorative ways. More than anything else, it expresses revulsion. Jews are often forbidden to touch things that are unclean. Those who touch the carcass of an unclean animal

<143>

must themselves remain unclean till evening (Leviticus 11: 24-8). The division of animals into "clean" and "unclean" corresponds to the separation of humanity into the Israelites and the heathens (Meyer, 97).

This division also reflects a fundamental characteristic of societies of herders such as the Hebrews, in contrast to those of agriculturalists. Societies of herders are internally egalitarian with respect to both man and beast, but they are hostile to those outside their community; agricultural societies construct elaborate hierarchies that include both human beings and animals (Digard, 224-226). The arbitrariness of many of the Jewish prohibitions is also a sort of justification; in part because they are not entirely comprehensible to the outside world, the rules set the Jewish people apart from their neighbors. The prohibitions are a means of organizing the world. Many provisions of Jewish law seem intended to prevent a confusion of things and roles. Cattle are not to be mated with animals of another breed, nor should two kinds of grain be sown in the same field (Leviticus 19:19). An ox and a donkey should not draw a plough through the field together (Deuteronomy 22:10). A man is not to wear the clothing of a woman, nor a woman to wear that of a man (Deuteronomy 22:5). The rules not only distinguish Jew and gentile but divide creatures into distinct classes as well.

According to anthropologist Mary Douglas, the laws foster an ideal of holiness and purity which is based on division of all things into clear and distinct categories. Thus it maintains that both the sacrificial animal (Leviticus 9:2-4) and the priest who performs sacrifice must be without blemish or deformity (Leviticus 21:17). Animals are appropriate as food when they conform to a recognized category, but those which appear anomalous are rejected. Thus pork is forbidden, since pigs have cloven hoofs but are not ruminants. Eels and worms inhabit water like fish, but they lack fins and scales so their status is ambiguous, and so they too are forbidden (Douglas, 42-58). Animals that are not slaughtered according to prescribed rules are not considered to be truly food. In the words of Douglas, unclean animals are "the obscure, unclassifiable elements which do not fit the pattern of the cosmos" (96).

Purity and National Socialism

Never unique to Judaism, the ideal of spiritual cleanliness was carried over into Christianity. Its clearest expression is the ritual of baptism, a ritual cleansing performed as immersion or sprinkling with water. The ideal is also present in the Eucharist. Instead of being defilement as in Judaism, the drinking of blood becomes a means of purification. Those who refuse blood are suspected of being unclean. Over the centuries this ideal of cleanliness took ever more various forms. Early Protestants aspired to return to the pure simplicity of early Christianity. The Nazis also

<144>

emphasized an ideal of purity, and they also viewed those outside their community as unclean. They were also hostile to anomalies, whether animal or human, and insisted on "pure" {rein} races which conformed to a preestablished type.

Contemporary classifications of animals are far more detailed and sophisticated than those of the ancient world. From a modern point of view, the pig would certainly not appear to be an incomplete ruminant, nor would the eel seem like a cross between serpent and fish. But modern people are still disconcerted when animals do not seem to fit neatly into categories; they usually view the hyena, which is biologically between canine and feline, with revulsion (Glickman, *passim*). For the Nazis "purity" was not entirely different from the Old Testament concept of "cleanliness." Hitler and the Nazi movement were very intolerant of conceptual ambiguities (Weinstein, 136).

Hitler showed an obsessive concern with personal hygiene by compulsively washing his hands (Waite, 15). He very often used the imagery of dirt to describe people whom he disliked. "If Jews were alone in this world," he once remarked, "they would suffocate in dirt and filth" (Waite, 25). The term devised by Nazi scientists for their eugenic measures, "racial hygiene," reflects this preoccupation with purity and dirt. A large sign at the crematorium at Dachau read, "Here cleanliness is a duty. Don't forget to wash your hands!" The language of hygiene was even used to describe the gas chambers, as the execution was referred to as a "shower" and the victims as "bath guests" (USHMM, RG-04.019*01, 2).

From the Nazi point of view, the Jews were an anomaly and therefore impure. The Jews did not fit into received classifications, being neither nationals nor foreigners. They did not have any obviously identifiable physical or even intellectual features. One could not with any confidence recognize a Jew walking down the street (Weinstein, 140-145). As a Nazi primer for young people put it, "The Jew always attempts to disguise himself by changing his name and faith . . ." (Brennecke, 80). Other groups persecuted by the Nazis were also ambiguous. The handicapped, almost by definition, are anomalies; so are homosexuals. Douglas mentions that people often attribute uncanny powers to those who do not conform to accepted classifications. They call those who defy easy classification are called names like "sorcerers" or "witches" (95-114). Thus Jews were constantly accused of controlling international finance and of nefarious occult practices.

Douglas observed that the demand for purity — that is, for a world of sharply defined categories — inevitably leads societies to contradictions. Those who make the demand are faced with the impossible task of explaining away or eliminating anomalous elements in their conceptual frameworks (163). A corollary is that a more uncompromising insistence

<145>

on purity will inevitably lead to even greater contradictions. Once again the Nazi movement seems to fit the pattern perfectly. The gap between the humane aspirations articulated in animal protection laws and the cruelty of the Nazis toward human beings is only one example.

What is a "Holocaust"?

The very word "Holocaust," sometimes criticized but very widely used, pertains to animal sacrifice. Among people of the ancient Mediterranean the slaughter of animals was generally a festive occasion with the inedible parts, bones and gall bladder together with a little meat, left on the altar for a deity while the rest was consumed by human beings. Sometimes the Greeks and others took an ironic view of this practice. If the gods were truly greater than humankind, why should people get the better share? Hesiod declared this division a ruse by the titan Prometheus to fool the gods, and it became a standard joke in Greek comedy (Burkert, *Homo*, 7). A Holocaust was a Hebrew sacrifice in which the entire animal was given to Yahweh to be consumed by fire. The prototype was the sacrifice of the shepherd Abel to Yahweh from his flock, according to tradition made before people and animals had begun to eat meat.

The word "Holocaust" literally means "burning of the whole." The usage of the word for the Nazi murders is based an identification between the Jewish people and the sacrificed animal. The imagery parallels the way Christ is traditionally represented as the sacrificial lamb. In a strange way the term "Holocaust" equates the Nazis, as those who performed the sacrifice, with priests of ancient Israel. The term was first popularized in the 1960s by American Jews, so it cannot tell us anything directly about how the Nazis regarded their deeds. It can, however, tell us something about the way we regard the mass murders, which may have some elements in common with the Nazi perspective. The awed hush which envelops the Holocaust even today is suggestive of blood rites. While blood sacrifice often involves the vilification of the victims, this is only one stage in the process of sacralization. As Hubert and Mauss pointed out, "Sacrifice . . . effects an exaltation of the victims, which renders them divine" (79).

Our word "sacrifice" comes from the Latin "sacer," meaning "holy." Something is offered to the deities and thereby consecrated (Hubert and Mauss, 9). According to Hubert and Mauss, "Sacrifice is a religious act which, through the consecration of a victim, modified the condition of the moral person who accomplishes it or that of certain objects with which he is concerned" (13). The Nazi "final solution" certainly fits that definition, in so far as it was conceived as a purification of the German race. More precisely, it is what Hubert and Mauss called "a sacrifice of expiation" (53). The routine of killing ended in the consumption of the bodies by fire, a feature that is common in rites of purification. Though elaborately

<146>

rationalized, it was clearly not undertaken on the basis of science or even practical politics. The Nazi Holocaust differs from archaic rituals because it belonged to the industrial age and was done on a corresponding scale. As the Nazi state placed itself at the center of religious life, the divide between bureaucratic regulation and religious ritual became indistinct.

We use the term "sacrifice" for killing in many contexts that are at least not consciously religious, particularly in relation to war (Ehrenreich, 18-19). Even the killing of laboratory animals in experiments (Arluke, 98-99) and the industrialized slaughter of animals in technologically sophisticated plants (Grandin, "Behavior," 210-212) takes on a religious quality. When killing is done detachment proves difficult for almost everyone, and people are likely to sacramentalize the act through such means as prayer and ritual. Miranda Green described the purpose of ancient sacrifice, human or animal, as follows: "By being given over to the supernatural world, the sacrificial victim served to shift these Otherworld forces toward the earth and focus them on the person or persons who performed the ritual" (94). In other words, sacrifice is a means of communication between the human and divine worlds (Hubert and Mauss, 97). It has much the same importance in pagan religions as prayer does in monotheistic ones. The life force of the sacrificial victim is released, drawing the attention of the divinities. Blood sacrifice is a means to partially control the circulation of cosmic energy. In relatively secular terms, sacrifice is a way of asserting cosmic importance through an act of violence.

This logic is also consistent with the *Lebensphilosophie* of the Nazis, according to which the individual is merely a temporary embodiment of the life force. Such mythic thinking is relatively explicit in the way the Nazis spoke of their fallen heroes. Jay Baird has identified the "blood myth" as a theme which pervaded the culture of Nazi Germany. It "featured the death of the noble warrior, his resurrection, and his spiritual return to the fighting columns of brown shirts" (*To Die*, 73). But what of the spirits of those killed by the Nazis? They might, as a sacrificial substitute, have the same role.

Rites of Blood

As the war and the Holocaust continued, Heinrich Himmler increasingly practiced what he took to be ancient Germanic rites secretly in the headquarters of the SS (Goodricke-Clarke, 183-190). Some of these may very well have been directly connected with the mass killings. To an extent the Nazi death camps were consciously inspired by animal sacrifice. Both Hitler and Himmler had been impressed by the portrait of Ghenghis Khan in a popular book by Michael Prawdin. They greatly admired the way in which Ghenghis Khan ensured the loyalty of his followers through what

<147>

Hitler called "a bond of blood" {*Blutkitt*} created through common participation in killing. This did not only apply to participation in battles. Tribesmen would sacrifice a white stallion, bull, ram, and dog, and then pledge their loyalty by saying, ". . . may that happen to us which happened to these animals if we break our vow. . . ." Inspired by this example, Hitler and Himmler tried to guarantee the loyalty of subordinates through systematically involving them in the mass executions of human beings (Breitman, 39-45; Prawdin, 40).

This sort of formula is common in blood sacrifice, especially for occasions such as initiations and contracts. In Rome, for example, it had been common to consummate any covenant of the state with the sacrifice of a pig. As he killed the animal in the temple of Jupiter, the priest would say, "If the Roman people injure this pact, may Jupiter smite them, as I smite this pig with a stone" (Lewinsohn, 102). Of course, members of the SS did not need any ritual formula to remind them that, if they did not follow orders, they could be prisoners in the death camps rather than administrators or guards. The Aztecs ceremonially offered prisoners to their gods on a scale not altogether unlike that of Nazi executions (Ehrenreich, 59-67). The Aztecs made killing an occasion for public ceremony, but the mass murders were done largely in secret by the Nazis. If, however, fewer people witnessed the Nazi murders, far more participated indirectly. The entire society was involved in a network of political and economic relationships which included the death camps. Either way people were bound together by the act of killing, one of the traditional functions of blood sacrifice.

<148>

CHAPTER 15
THE HELL OF AUSCHWITZ

"Thou knowest," urges Indra, "that by the presence of a dog Heaven itself would be defiled." His mere glance deprives the sacraments of their consecration. Why, then, should one who has renounced his very family so strenuously object to giving up a dog?
— Coomaraswamy and Nivedita, *Myths of the Hindus and Buddhists*

INITIALLY DEVOTED TO reuniting humanity with the realm of animals, the Nazi regime opened a new divide between the two. The Holocaust now stands as a uniquely human phenomenon. It is not terribly hard to find analogues to most human activities among animals. From crows to chimpanzees, animals make and use tools. They not only kill but engage in communal battles both with their own kind and with other species that resemble war. Nevertheless, the detached, methodical destruction of others in the Holocaust seems at first to have no parallel among animals.

Some people credit rats with a perverted intelligence almost comparable to that of human beings. Ernst Jünger's description of the rats that haunted the trenches in World War I, used much the same sort of imagery that the Nazis would later apply to Jews. He told how hunting rats was a favorite diversion of the soldiers. "Repulsive, nauseous creatures!" Jünger's wrote, "Their rustling multitudes carry with them a penetrating effluvium, and I can never help thinking of their secret doings among the dead in the cellars of the village" (*Storm*, 38). The Nazi film *Der Ewige Jud* began by showing pictures of rats. A narrator explained, "Just as the rat is the lowest of animals, the Jew is the lowest of human beings." The film compared the spread of rats across the globe to the wandering of Jews. Awaiting sentencing by the Nuremberg tribunal, Hans Frank, the former governor of Poland, applied the image of the Pied Piper, who rids the village of Hamelin of rats and then of children, to Hitler (Victor, 218). Later, physician Hans Zinsser stated:

Man and the rat are utterly destructive. All that nature offers is taken for their own purposes, plant or beast. Gradually these two have spread across the earth, keeping pace with each other and unable to destroy each other, though continually hostile. They have wandered from East to West, driven by their physical needs, and — unlike any other species of living things — have

<149>

made war upon their own kind. The gradual, relentless, progressive extermination of the black rat by the brown has no parallel in nature so close as that of the similar extermination of one race of man by another (208-9).

But rats, like people, also have a gentler side. In Günter Grass' novel *The Rat*, a female rodent encountered the narrator as the ultimate survivor. Her kind was present on the earth long before human beings and will persist after people have become extinct. She and the other rats surveyed the whole panorama of human history in all its grandeur and its vanity.

More recently, Art Spiegelman has written a comic strip that tells the story of how his parents survived Auschwitz. The Jews were drawn as mice, while the Nazis were either cats or pigs. With a black humor that perhaps only camp survivors understand and only their progeny dare perpetuate, he used such an outrageous pun as calling the death camp "Mauschwitz."

The symbolic significance of rodents lies primarily in their capacity for survival and in their adversarial relationship with human beings. Spiegelman prefaced the second volume of *Maus* with a quotation from a newspaper in Pomerania during the middle 1930's: "Mickey Mouse is the most miserable ideal ever revealed. Healthy emotions tell. . . every honorable youth that the dirty and filth-covered vermin, the greatest bacteria carrier in the animal kingdom, cannot be the ideal type of animal. Away with the Jewish brutalization of the people! Down with Mickey Mouse! Wear the Swastika Cross!"

Cats pursuing mice often represent attempted murder or genocide. A cat will sometimes play with a cornered mouse, teasing the rodent with apparent opportunities to escape. Finally, when the mouse is terrified and exhausted, the cat will make a meal of her prey. Grass used this behavior as a metaphor for the sadism of Nazi Germany in a novella appropriately entitled *Cat and Mouse*. But it is not only cruelty that makes cats fascinating to writers. More than any other animals, cats are delicately balanced between wildness and domesticity. While comfortable in human homes, they retain the fierceness and the independence of a predatory animal in the wild. Another source of fascination is the association of cats with demonology, especially as presumed companions of witches in the Renaissance. In his detective thriller *Felidae*, the German-Turkish writer Akif Piринçci told of the rise and fall of a feline Hitler. The hero was a tom named Francis who followed a trail of murdered cats through obscure corners of the city and underground passageways to the laboratory of a crazed human scientist. There he finally apprehended the murderer, a brilliant tom named Claudandus, who had been horribly tortured by vivisectionsts. After learning to use computers, Claudandus conceived a plan to breed house cats backward and again produce their wild ancestor.

<150>

This was the agenda of the Nazis, who had wished to recreate the primal vitality of ancient Aryans through eugenic controls.

Just as the abattoir is a symbol of the horrors of Nazi Germany, so the laboratory for animal experimentation is a common metaphor for those of the Soviet Union under Stalin. In the novel *We*, which appeared in the thirties, the Russian Eugene Zamiatin used images taken from such laboratories to describe the totalitarian state. In his society of the future, most of humanity lives underneath an enormous dome. Everyone is constantly observed, monitored, and analyzed. Privacy is reduced to a few seconds in a day. Borrowing a motif from famous experiments by Robert Boyle which proved that living things require oxygen, the author has those who rebel against society placed under a glass cover where they die of suffocation.

George Orwell, in *Animal Farm*, used the industrialized farm as a symbol of modern despotism. Building on the tradition of Aesop, he created a world in which pigs control, slaughter, and market other creatures. The substitution of animals for people is a device to create psychic distance. Characters in Orwell's *Animal Farm* and Spiegelman's *Maus* are inwardly human but animal in form. When they treat one another as animals, we are not sure whether to regard it as normal, criminal, funny, or grotesque.

The Hell of Auschwitz

Traditional images of Heaven, and most especially of Hell, reflect the uneasiness people have felt about their treatment of animals. Artists generally represent hardly any identifiable animals in either place, perhaps because of doubts as to whether animals have souls. Painters generally represent angels as entirely anthropomorphic apart from their wings; they depict devils with bizarre combinations of human and animal features. Since demons generally walk upright on two legs and have human hands, they are perhaps closer to apes or monkeys than to any other animal. They frequently have long tails; they often walk on hooves rather than on feet; many of them have horns. Often a devil will have the legs of a goat like the Greek Pan. Their most dramatically bestial feature is usually a large mouth with sharp teeth like those of a predator. Satan is often represented as eternally chewing on the worst of sinners. Traditionally, the doorway to Hell is an enormous mouth where sinners are devoured, an image perhaps originally suggested by the way in which snakes swallow their prey whole.

Bestial as they are, demons do not always prefer raw meat. Very often, sinners are cooked alive before being devoured. Medieval painters often showed sinners boiling in huge pots tended by demons, a sort of diabolic stew. Monsters stir this broth, sometimes poking the sinners with pikes (Sax, *Serpent*, 47-48). Occasionally, as in the Hell from the richly imagina-

<151>

tive "Garden of Earthly Delights" by Hieronymus Bosch, a rabbit-headed demon carries the bodies of sinners who are trussed up on a pole like game. Bosch even showed in the center of his Hell a huge demon on a privy, swallowing and excreting sinners. The traditional roles of human beings and animals are reversed in Hell. Fantastic animals — that is, demons — hunt, herd, cook, and eat people, just the way people have done to animals on earth. This reversal may reflect a discomfort that people have felt about their treatment of animals. Earlier societies had used rituals and prayers to placate the spirits of animals. Lacking such rituals, people of the Christian Middle Ages imagined the spirits taking revenge on men and women. While the demons combined features of many creatures, their appearance and activities marked them as predators. It was precisely these animals, large carnivores, which were generally demonized and first hunted to near extinction in Europe and the Near East. To put it simply, Hell was the triumph of predation. The contemporary Yiddish author, Isaac Bashevis Singer, visualized Hell as "one huge slaughterhouse" (18).

The fear of being eaten is also found in fairy tales including such favorites as "Hansel and Gretel" and "The Juniper Tree" from the Brothers Grimm. The taboo against cannibalism, together with that against incest, is one of the most fundamental ways in which humanity sets itself apart from other creatures, and the violation of this prohibition {demons are also part human} in Hell signifies reversion of people to a bestial state. In the words of George Steiner, "The concentration and death camps of the twentieth century . . . are Hell made immanent" (54). The *Inferno* of Dante anticipated the death camps in its intricate, almost technocratic, organization. In popular imagery, Hitler replaced Satan as the embodiment of evil; Himmler, Goebbels, and Göring become an unholy trinity at his service. The gas chambers replaced the fires of Hell, while other Nazis variously become major and minor demons.

The Plight of Animals

The first detailed public discussion of the laws on animal protection in Nazi Germany was an essay that I wrote jointly with Dr. Arnold Arluke entitled "Understanding Nazi Animal Protection and the Holocaust" and published in the fall 1992 issue of the journal *Anthrozoös*. The resulting discussion became so passionate that nuances of our analysis were often lost as people praised or attacked us in pointlessly extravagant terms. That the Nazis might be capable of humane legislation was such a disconcerting idea that even the detached, academic style of our paper could not make it acceptable to many people. The topic of animals, like the Holocaust itself, evokes passions of great intensity and confusion. Thus, Ingrid Newkirk, a founder of the animal-rights organization PETA, said in the late eighties, "Six million died in concentration camps; six million broiler

<152>

Fig. 13. Miniature in the *Hortus deliciarum* of Herrad of Landsberg, ca 1185 CE. Showing Jews in Hell. Here, as in most medieval depictions of Hell, the usual roles of animals and people are reversed. Demons cook, fatten, herd, hang up, slaughter, and eat people, just as men and women do with livestock. Note that the demons here are slaughtering people in what appears to be a kosher manner — with a single cut to the neck.

<153>

chickens will die this year in slaughterhouses," clearly implying that the eating of fowl was at least the equivalent of the Holocaust (Sax, "Holocaust Images," 109). Opponents of animal rights sometimes deliberately bait their adversaries with flamboyant displays of cruelty such as tearing heads off of wounded birds (Lengeman, 37). The debate touches people in an extremely visceral way and at a point that often seems beyond the reach of argument. Images of mistreated animals seem to reach some reservoir of guilt and love, of which we are unaware in most of our waking lives. The plight of animals can dramatize extreme catastrophes, even those that seem to transcend our powers of imagination. What detail could more effectively dramatize the plight of those in the siege of Paris during 1871 than that citizens were forced to kill and butcher two beloved elephants, Castor and Pollux, in the *Jardin des Plants*, for food? More recently, during the early nineties, the popular American news show "60 Minutes" ran a segment on a blind man who could not afford food for his seeing-eye dog. On the same day, the show ran another segment on the plight of mothers on welfare. People sent in hundreds of checks for the blind man and his dog, while the welfare mothers received little beyond angry letters. A few years later, one of the most poignant images in the news of the siege of Sarajevo was of a bear starving in the zoo. For many weeks a soldier came daily to feed the bear from his meager rations. At last the animal died and was butchered for food. We may be criticized for caring so much for such creatures when fellow human beings are dying. The emotional power of such images of mistreated animals may, admittedly, easily be exploited or abused. It is easy to categorically dismiss these images as "sentimental," but our emotions do not follow any calculus of suffering or obligation.

The example of the Nazis should not, therefore, turn us against the cause of animal welfare. Nazi stereotypes of Jews as rigid, mechanical resemble the popular stereotypes of Nazis in media today. People sometimes regard every position taken by the Nazis as polluted in rather the same way as Nazis sometimes regarded anything associated with Jews. "Turnabout" might be "fair play," as the familiar saying goes, but it is usually not good scholarship. Abuses by Communists do not mean we should abandon egalitarian ideals, nor do Nazi crimes discredit regard for the natural world. We should admit that the Nazis, whatever their motives, were right in much of their humane legislation. They were also right to protect predators such as the wolf, though they were mistaken in claiming that predators are more intelligent and even more moral than other creatures. In many respects, the Nazis were more like the rest of us than we care to acknowledge.

The mentality that often enabled the Nazis to be kind to animals, yet cruel toward human beings, was an extreme manifestation of tendencies found throughout western culture since at least the start of the modern

<154>

period. This paradox is formulated with precision by Keith Thomas in *Man and the Natural World*:[1]

> The growth of towns had led to a new longing for the
> countryside. The progress of cultivation had fostered a taste for
> weeds, mountains and unsubdued nature. The newfound
> security from wild animals had generated an increasing concern
> to protect birds and preserve wild creatures in their natural
> state. Economic independence of animal power and urban
> isolation from animal farming had nourished emotional
> attitudes which were hard, if not impossible, to reconcile with
> the exploitation of animals by which most people lived.
> Henceforth an increasingly sentimental view of animals as pets
> and objects of contemplation would jostle uneasily alongside the
> harsh facts of a world in which the elimination of "pests" and
> the breeding of animals for slaughter grew every day more
> efficient. (301).

That combination of Romanticism and technocratic brutality was simply heightened to the point of caricature in Nazi Germany. If the Third Reich was as an expression of nihilism generated by the gap between our sensibilities and our practices, the potential for another such event is certainly with us today.

---

[1] Thomas focuses his study primarily on early modern England, but his conclusions are applicable to all of Euro-American civilization.

<155>

CHAPTER 16
THE CULT OF DEATH

Under the tree-tops
Is quiet now!
In all the woodlands
Hearest thou
Not a sound!
The little birds are asleep in the trees;
Wait! Wait! And soon like these,
Sleepest thou!

—Goethe, "Wanderer's Nightsong" (trans. H. W. Longfellow)

THERE IS A special feeling of horror about the Nazi crimes, not fully explained by the death and suffering they caused. Far more people were killed by Stalin and by Mao than by Hitler. Several historical events including black slavery and the near genocide of Native Americans may rival or exceed the suffering and destruction caused by the Nazi murders, but none inspires comparable horror. One reason is simply that the Nazi camps were documented in greater detail and publicized more widely than other terrors. There are, however, also elements here which cannot be explained by quantitative measures. One feature that adds to our revulsion at the concentration camps is that people were denied any recognition that the death and pain belonged to them. Rather than the sealing of an individual destiny, death became impersonal and anonymous.

The horror is certainly on a smaller scale, but analogous feelings may be aroused by some industrial farms for animals. What is disturbing is not that creatures should be killed or eaten. Their lives, in any case, would always have been precarious in the wild. Few animals of the woods and fields live to maturity, and almost none die of old age. A baby rabbit is very likely to be violently killed by a hawk or by disease within a day of birth. What is most disturbing in factory farms is not that animals are killed but that they are not allowed to live. They are not allowed individual stories; they cannot explore the world, nor choose their mates. Turkeys bred for supermarkets often have such enormous breasts that they cannot reach one another to reproduce except by artificial insemination. Our discomfort goes far beyond the issue of the capacity of animals to feel pain. It seems to me entirely likely that many animals in industrial farms may be so brutalized by the combination of genetic manipulation and lack of stimulation that they lose the capacity to suffer very much. If that has not already happened, it soon may. Some people in agribusinesses already talk of limbs that may one day be grown artificially from cultures. As in the

<156>

mystical technocracy of Nazi Germany, life would become detached from death so they would no longer be parts of a single cycle.

The patterns we can observe in the Nazi treatment of animals may help to illuminate their attitudes toward human beings. At least on the level of conscious intent, the mentality of the Nazis was largely technocratic. This applies to the way in which they approached the slaughter of animals; it also applies to their mass murder of human beings. The ideal of the Nazis, especially of the SS, was to kill dispassionately without either cruelty or regret. This technocratic ideal is apparent in the horrifying words of Himmler to leaders of the SS on October 4, 1943:

> What happens to a Russian, to a Czech, does not interest me in the slightest. What the nations can offer in good blood of our type we will take, if necessary by kidnaping their children and raising them with us. Whether nations live in prosperity or starve to death interests me only in so far as we need them as slaves for our culture. . . . We shall never be rough or heartless when it is not necessary; that is clear. We Germans, who are the only people in the world who have a decent attitude toward animals, will also assume a decent attitude toward these human animals. But it is a crime against our own blood to worry about them . . . (Fest, 115).

Yet to bring people to this degree of detachment, it was necessary to desensitize them and accustom them to killing. Initiations of both Hitler Youth and SS men frequently involved practicing cruelty toward both animals and human beings (Victor, 110-113). Each person involved in mass executions had to pass through a stage of cruelty to one of technocratic detachment, but the cruelty was perpetuated by the constant need for new initiates.

The brutality of the Nazis was an attempt to emulate the natural world. First of all, they viewed nature not as a source of bucolic peace but as a vast and amoral power. Secondly, the Nazis identified with the power of nature, emulating her putative dominance and cruelty. In attempting to drive entire races to extinction, the Nazis believed they were simply expediting the work of nature whose rule was "survival of the fittest." Artificial selection through death camps was simply a substitute for natural selection. Even their cult of "hardness," their determination to eliminate pity, was an emulation of the natural world. The submission they demanded of everyone from officers to inmates of concentration camps was the obedience of an organism to the force of instinct. Thirdly, they saw large predators, especially the wolf, as the major symbols of this power. Their emulation of these animals was reflected in all aspects of their culture

<157>

from scientific study to popular rhetoric. They admired the hunting of wolves, protected wolves, and filled their rhetoric with references to wolves. Finally, the Nazis conceived of the supposed enemies of nature whom they wished to dominate or else annihilate as domesticated animals such as sheep. Appealing to what seemed the natural order, they used an identification with predators as a sanction to kill with very little restraint. The fierce wolf or eagle became an archetypal image of power and domination. In the name of the natural world, the Nazis sought to extend their power almost without limit, even to direct the course of evolution itself. That aspiration led to increasingly intricate regulation of both animals and human beings.

Mircea Eliade has written that ". . . certain mythical themes still survive in modern societies, but are not readily recognizable since they have undergone a long process of laicization" (*Myth*, 28). Like the Fascists in Italy, the Nazis invoked myth not in the name of some bucolic paradise but in that of aggressive modernization. They enthusiastically embraced modernity, not for its comforts and conveniences but as a terrible apocalypse. Technology would emancipate human beings from pity and restraint, thereby creating a new barbarism. Imagery of death permeated the movement from the apocalyptic speeches of the Führer to the skulls on helmets of the SS.

Jay Baird wrote in *To Die for Germany* that, "The German cult of heroism was tied more to death than to life, more to destruction than to victory. Hitler held the memory of fallen heroes in almost religious awe, and he was much more at home among the dead than he was among the living" (xi). Fascination with death is a fundamental part of human experience, but Baird argued that it took on a special quality among the Nazis:

> Germany could serve as a model for heroic mythology based on
> national despair, which differs fundamentally from the form of
> heroism celebrated by the English, French, Russians, and
> Americans during the Great War. When an Englishman died in
> Flanders, he was protecting King and country and a national
> way of life. But, when a German soldier died at Langemarck, his
> blood took on the properties of the blood of Christ. The death
> itself was seen as redemption, washing away the sins of the
> fathers and offering the promise of national resurrection (244).

In one hymn that was usually sung when soldiers of the SS assembled, members of the Black Order dedicated themselves "to love death" (213). The Hitler Youth placed the slogan "We were born to die for Germany" above the entrances of their camps. On taking an oath of loyalty at the age

<158>

of fourteen the boys were told "What greater and more glorious vision can a boy have than to die for Germany" (Victor, 109). The complete submergence of a human being in a collective enterprise was an analogue of death since it meant the annihilation of the individual.

In the perspective of hindsight there is something ominous in the Nazi preoccupation with methods of killing animals, even if we acknowledge that many of the laws relating to this were justified on humane grounds. An unarticulated purpose of the Nazi animal protection laws was to accustom people to think of euthanasia as a positive thing. By desensitizing people, the killing of animals helped open the way for the mass murder of human beings. On a more intimate scale, some members of the SS were required to rear a German shepherd for twelve weeks then strangle the dog under the supervision of an officer (Arluke and Sax, "Understanding," 10; Victor, 110).

The historian Saul Friedländer has identified this preoccupation with death as the major feature running through the culture of Nazi Germany in everything from gas chambers to elaborately staged public funerals. In his words, "The important thing is the constant identification of Nazism and death; not real death in its everyday horror and tragic banality, but a ritualized, stylized, and aestheticized death . . ." (43). The rhetorical appeal of Nazism is the combination of kitsch and death. The two are apparently contradictory, since kitsch is a debased representation of idyllic harmony. Death, by contrast, is an experience of great solitude and terror. Nevertheless, they are frequently juxtaposed in a vulgar Romanticism that we encounter in many contexts from the bland reassurance of funeral homes to the apocalyptic spectacles in popular film (Friedländer, 25-53). Kitsch ritualistically repeats certain images and formulas in a manner that veers between celebration and exorcism.

Geoffrey Gorer has called this phenomenon "the pornography of death." He points out that as scenes of death in bed have largely disappeared from Western literature in the last hundred years or so fantasies of violent death have become particularly important in popular entertainments from Westerns to war stories. He compares this phenomenon to the pornography of sex, saying "In both types of fantasy, the emotions which are typically expected — love {with sex} and grief {with death} — are paid little or no attention, while the sensations are enhanced as much as a customary poverty of language permits" (75). "Pornography of death" is a perfect description of most art favored by the Nazis. In the words of Peter Adam, "The cult of heroic death became a major obsession in the arts. Painting, sculpture, film, and literature constantly glorified death and the deeper meaning of sacrifice" (79). The favorite theme of Nazi artists, together with idealized depictions of peasant life, was the war. They portrayed it as an epic struggle yet almost entirely without suffering (159).

<159>

One critic wrote in 1938 of the canvases by Nazi artist Franz Eichhorst: "The beauty and singularity of these frescoes is the almost total absence of blood and screams . . . {and} the . . . readiness to fight and to be sacrificed. . . ." (Adam, 162). In a similar spirit Nazi animal painters like Michael Kiefer celebrated the predations of eagles and lions (132). This impulse toward a hygienic death, divorced from sorrow or physical decay, seems to join many features of Nazi society from the animal protection laws to the gas chambers. The entire society was engaged in a perpetual homage to death.

That a society should be moved by a desire for self-destruction may seem counterintuitive. In a culture heavily influenced by Darwinism, we automatically think of survival as a universal goal. Nevertheless, this desire for annihilation has been pointed out by a great many scholars of Nazi Germany working with highly different approaches. David Schoenbaum in *Hitler's Social Revolution*, a sociological study, concluded that the Third Reich aspired to the destruction of bourgeois society, but it sought to accomplish this by using the very industries that society itself had created. A fascination with massive destruction regardless of its object runs through the speeches of Hitler, who told a Nuremberg rally in 1929 that out of a million children born in a given year the 800,000 or so who were weakest and most "unworthy" of life should be killed to strengthen the population (Waite, 392). Albert Speer reported that Hitler loved to watch scenes of mass destruction:

I recall his ordering showings in the Chancellery of the films of burning London, of the sea of flames over Warsaw, of exploding convoys, and the rapture with which he watched those films. I never saw him so worked up as toward the end of the war, when in a kind of delirium he pictured for himself and for us the destruction of New York in a hurricane of fire. He described the skyscrapers being turned into gigantic burning torches, collapsing on one another, the glow of the exploding city illuminating the dark sky (Speer, 80).

The extreme recklessness which marked his entire career from the abortive coup in Munich to the attack on Russia and the declaration of war on the United States confirms the assessment that his personality was, in the words of one German psychologist, "massively self-destructive" (Waite, 392). Unable to do anything more to Slavs, Jews, Gypsies, and the handicapped in the final weeks of his life, Hitler issued orders for the destruction of France and Germany.

<160>

Since Hitler virtually *was* the Nazi movement, it is difficult to see how people would have followed him had they not, unconsciously at least, shared this desire for annihilation. As Saul Friedländer has put it:

> ... to understand the phantasms that underlay many Germans' relationship to Hitler, the frenzy of their applause, their attachment to him until the last moment, it is necessary to take into account their perverse rapport with a chief and a system for reasons that certainly were not explicit and would not have shown in an opinion poll: The yearning for destruction and death (75).

Killing is one way to move closer to the mystery of death, and the Nazis practiced it on a prodigious scale.

That longing certainly has its analogues in many traditions, particularly those of warriors. Military epics have generally found more glory in defeat than in victory. *The Iliad* ends in uncertainty, but a shadow of doom seems to hang over the Greeks as well as the Trojans. In the medieval French *The Song of Roland*, the hero refuses to blow his horn and call for help, knowing full well that his unwillingness will bring destruction on himself and all his men. Historians call Napoleon one of the greatest military leaders in history, yet he is remembered less for his victories than for his catastrophic defeats — at Trafalgar, in Russia, and at Waterloo. Even in the United States, a country generally lacking in tragic sensibility, the American defeat at the Alamo is remembered with far more passion than the eventual American victory in the Mexican War. Similarly, Custer's "last stand" appeals to the imagination in America far more than all of the victories the European colonists achieved over the Indians put together. It is, however, the medieval *Song of the Nibelungs*, which provides an almost uncanny anticipation of the Third Reich. Told by a wise women that they would not return from the land of the Huns, the knights of Burgundy knowingly made the journey that was to end in their destruction. When their hosts tried to welcome them graciously, they provoked a war by gratuitous acts of brutality. Hagen, who led the Burgundians, without provocation killed the infant son of the king of the Huns. Finally, the guests were annihilated in an orgy of destruction, and they found far greater fulfillment in fighting till the end than ever in practicing the arts of peace.

On February 2, 1943, as the siege of Stalingrad was collapsing, Hermann Göring compared the German soldiers in Russia to the knights of Burgundy in an article in the newspaper *Völkische Beobachter*. "They as well," he wrote, "stood in a hall full of fire and blood and fought to the very end ... and even after a thousand years, every German will speak of

<161>

this battle with a shudder of holy reverence. . . ." A short time later, however, the entire German army at Stalingrad surrendered rather than face annihilation. Such comparisons were common. Hitler himself, perhaps more conscious of their implications, ordered that the tapestry in the waiting room of the Reichstag depict scenes from the Eddas rather than the *Song of the Nibelungs* (Gugenberger and Schwiedlenka, 146-147). In a fit of temper during a speech of 1943 Hitler exclaimed that in the event of a German defeat he would not find it at all regrettable if every German man, woman, and child were killed by the enemy (Breitman, 44).

This infatuation with death certainly runs through much of German culture and goes back long before the Nazi period. Reading the poetry of German Romanticism, one will find a thematic monotony. Over and over, one finds lyrics where a poet is wandering alone through a great forest and is overcome by longing for death. Such lyrics are found in the work of Goethe, Mörike, Eichendorff, and countless imitators, and they became increasingly stereotyped through the nineteenth century.

Friedländer has pointed out that, "If often . . . peoples have venerated oppressive, barbarous, and terrorist power, and sometimes exterminated one another as under Stalin, they have never {before the Nazis} at one and the same time venerated oppression and propagated apocalyptic visions" (134). Freud theorized in his late works that the longing for death was prior to aggression (*Beyond*, 48). Perhaps the theory does not have the universality which the founder of psychoanalysis claimed, yet it fits the Nazi movement very well. The late theoretical work of Freud suggests a surprisingly simple explanation of the Nazi murders. The obsession with death in German culture was so strong that its deflection required a sacrifice of comparably vast dimensions — what we know as the "Holocaust." Even this proved futile as the regime finally turned its fury inward, destroying itself. Had the United States developed the atomic bomb in time to use it on Germany, as originally planned, that might have been the fulfillment of Hitler's fondest dream.

What made the longing for death take on such an extreme form in the Nazi period? Through their inability to tolerate ambiguities, Hitler and the Nazis made demands on the world which could never be satisfied. More concretely, the demand for a racially pure society could never be anything but a phantom in a world where peoples and cultures had been blending since time immemorial. By the standards which the Nazis upheld, as vague as they were absolute, there could only be pollution and filth so their entire civilization had to be destroyed (Victor, 130-131).

The gas chambers of the Nazi concentration camps were initially designed for the stated purpose of "euthanasia." The death by gas was first intended for handicapped infants but gradually extended to others. The babies were followed by older children, then by insane and retarded adults.

<162>

Finally, the killing was extended to Jews, Gypsies, alcoholics, Jehovah's Witnesses, homosexuals, and others. Being placed in the gas chamber was referred to as "Gnadentod," meaning "mercy death" (Proctor, *Racial Hygiene*, 177-222). The very word resonates with a sort of Wagnerian Romanticism. It recalls the term "Liebestod" or "love-death" in Wagner's opera *Tristan and Isolde*.

An archaic image frequently suggested by Nazi rhetoric was the great wolf Fenris, sired by the Germanic god of fire. Fenris eventually grew so huge and fierce that the gods themselves were terrified. To bind him they ordered a chain made of the breath of fish, the beards of women, the roots of mountains, and the footfall of a cat, things subtle and elusive as the restraints of civilization. It appeared thin and delicate as a cord of silk, yet it had supernatural strength. Oracles predicted that as the final battle of the gods approached Fenris would break the chain. Though the Nazis at times invoked the gods, they were clearly on the side of the wolf.

<163>

Fig.14. "Ochsenstall" by Max Beckmann (1933).

APPENDIX 1
NAZI TOTEMISM

The Nazi combination of brutality towards human beings and solicitude towards animals had been frequently observed at least since the beginning of their reign. In November of 1933, just after they had come to power, the Nazis passed a detailed law on animal protection, which seriously limited the use of animals in medical experimentation, while giving numerous protections to livestock, farm animals, and pets. These protections were further strengthened in the next decade by a more detailed law passed in 1938, as well a long series of additional laws on such subjects as slaughter, hunting, and transportation of animals.

For decades immediately after the fall of Nazi Germany, the contrast between the Nazi treatment of animals and people was generally presented as a grotesque irony, as well as perhaps a measure of their irrationality and dehumanization. As Diane Ackerman put it in *The Zookeeper's Wife*, "Although Mengele's subjects could be operated on without any painkillers at all, a remarkable example of Nazi zoophilia is that a leading biologist was once punished for not giving worms enough anesthesia during an experiment" (86). The irony may be entirely appropriate, but it does not explain anything. Elsewhere in this book, I observed that the Nazi treatment of animals and people seemed to follow at least a fairly consistent pattern. First of all, both in their rhetoric and practice, the Nazis constantly

<164>

blurred traditional divisions between animals and human beings. This involved, for example, branding, herding, systematically breeding, and industrially slaughtering men and women, while providing animals with many protections of the sort traditionally accorded to people:

> Loyalty to race replaced loyalty to species — that is, to humanity — in the morality of the Nazi movement. They organized their cosmos less around humankind than around the Germanic nation, not as it existed but as they imagined it ought to be. The Germanic nation, in turn, might include certain animals and exclude many citizens. As an article in a major German veterinary journal of 1937 stated, "Through the National Socialist laws on animals, any creature, just like a human being, enjoys appropriate protection on account of its belonging to the national (völkische) community." (107).

The Nazi regime was extremely ethnocentric, but, since it accorded very little or no intrinsic value to human life, it was not anthropocentric.[1]

This finding has been confirmed by subsequent research. As Stefan Dirscherl has put it in his recent, highly detailed study of the Nazi laws for protection of animals and nature:

> The ethnic (*völkisch*) affiliation became the central feature, which, in a grotesque application of a racist ideology, gave animals a legal standing, while denying that to Jews, Slavs, Gypsies, that is, all "non-Aryans" . . . . The animal was viewed part of the ethnic German community, and whoever attacked an animal was seen as attacking that community (159, my translation).

This policy was brutal, but it was by no means incoherent. It defined kinship in terms of membership in an ecosystem rather than the fellowship of humankind.[2]

Many Nazis were also entirely conscious of rejecting anthropocentrism. An official preamble to the original Nazi animal protection law of

---

[1] There has always been a tension between anthropocentrism and ethnocentrism. At the extremes, they are probably incompatible. For a discussion of this, see: Tim Ingold, "Humanity and Animality," *Companion Encyclopedia to Anthropology*, ed. Tim Ingold (New York: Routledge, 1994) 71-73.

[2] For a good summary of animal protection in Nazi Germany, in particular the priority given to membership in a biological community over membership in a species, see: Daniel Jütte, "Tierschutz und Nationalsozialismus: Eine Unheilvolle Verbindung," *Frankfurter Allgemeine Zeitung* Dec. 12 2001.

<165>

1933 proclaimed a breakthrough from an "anthropocentric-aesthetic concern" for animals to a "pathocentric-ethical" one, in which animals would not be protected simply on account of human sensibilities but for their own sakes (Dirscherl 48). The influential Nazi educator Ferdinand Rossner went considerably further. He described the Nazi doctrine of blood and race as the "Third Copernican Deed," which would finally put an end to anthropocentrism. The first such deed had, of course, been the astronomy of Copernicus, which had removed the earth from the center of the cosmos, and the second had been the Theory of Evolution, which did the same for the human species. Nazism would complete the work of these ideas by depriving "human personality" of its special status (see p. 42; also, Rossner 367-68). But an odd ambiguity runs through the account of Rossner, which I believe is typical not only of the Nazis also of many subsequent attempts to move beyond anthropocentrism. He presents the de-centering of humankind in Nazi ideology as the culmination of a triumphalist narrative, of the sort traditionally associated with a belief in human progress. This shows, as I will elaborate shortly, that the Nazi attempt to cast aside anthropocentrism was very tentative and incomplete.

When I first noticed this pattern in Nazism, I had not found an analytic framework that would enable me to place this pattern into any larger social, historical, or anthropological context. It seemed too clear and consistent to constitute simply a bizarre anomaly, yet I did not have any label to place on it. Furthermore, my investigations were impeded by the extreme sensitivity that surrounded, and partly still surrounds, the study of Nazi Germany. Though this was rarely stated explicitly, any philosophy, practice, or intellectual category associated with it was automatically assumed to be discredited. For that reason, the entire subject of Nazi animal protection laws remained, apart from fragmentary anecdotes, taboo until at least the 1980s (Dirscherl 20).

On discovering, in the early 1990s, through primary materials, that the Nazis had an extensive program of animal protection and anticipated many later ideas about animal rights, I sent my preliminary findings to the editor of an academic journal. He expressed interest as well as perplexity, but, though there was nothing incendiary about my manuscript, warned me to expect "a firestorm of protest." There is now a fairly substantial body of academic literature focused on the treatment of animals in Nazi Germany, but there are, so far as I am aware, no theories that are very effective in making sense of it (Dirscherl 205). We have, however, probably obtained sufficient distance from the subject to be able to discuss it relatively freely, comparing Nazi institutions with those of other societies without necessarily denigrating the latter. Accordingly, I will argue that the society which the Nazis were endeavoring to create approaches the

<166>

pattern of other non-Western societies known to some anthropologists as "totemism."

Nazi Culture and the Holocaust

The destructiveness of the Nazis, though enormous, was, unfortunately, not by any means unprecedented or unique in human history.[3] An attempt to compare the atrocities of the past on a systematic basis is *The Great Big Book of Horrible Things* by Matthew White, a study which is a product of extensive and meticulous scholarship. Since our records of the past are very incomplete, almost all of the statistics on which the book is based are disputed by some respected historians. Nevertheless, White always conscientiously notes alternative estimates of deaths, tries to explain discrepancies, and gives reasons for his selection among these estimates. The book, its sub-title to the contrary, cannot possibly come close to being "definitive," but it does give a rough idea of how the carnages of history might be weighed, bringing some order to the study of comparative genocide.

Instances of mass killing vary so greatly in their dynamics that moral comparisons are difficult, and in part contingent on highly personal values, as even a quick summary of some findings will illustrate. The event with greatest number killed, to nobody's great surprise, is the Second World War, whose total of 66 million killed includes military and civilian casualties on all sides. Tied for second and third place are Mao Zedong and Genghis Khan, with 40 million killed each, but the fourth event may startle people — famines in British India, which caused a total of 27 million deaths (529). White's statistics do not support the idea, argued by Daniel Goldhagen in *Hitler's Willing Executioners*, that the Holocaust can be traced primarily to singular attributes of German national character. According to White, the Germans have participated in 11 multicides in their history, which is a very substantial number, but the same as the Americans and fewer than the French, Chinese, British, and Russians (553).

---

[3] Nevertheless, some feel that the Holocaust has an existential terror that sets it apart from other multicides. For some contrasting perspectives on this perception, see Alan S. Rosenbaum, ed., *Is the Holocaust Unique: Perspectives on Comparative Genocide* (New York: Westview Press, 1996). This is a legitimate debate, but all parties should recognize that, like many questions in the humanities, it cannot be resolved objectively.

<167>

White's most important observation is the lack of any very obvious pattern in the atrocities (532). That conclusion might at first sound a bit bland, but it is necessary to counter the many highly oversimplified assertions, which place the blame on a single cause such as, for example, backwardness, modernity, religion, atheism, Judeo-Christian tradition, capitalism, Communism, Islam, nature, and so on. Atrocities can occur under a vast range of governments, and can be rationalized by many ideologies. Given this variation, it seems naïve to expect a simple explanation for the people's frequent inhumanity to one another, or to draw a direct line of cause and effect between any one cultural feature that prevailed in Nazi Germany and the concentration camps. Rather, explanations must be sought in complex matrixes of causes and effects, and any lessons are likely to be nuanced, complex, and perhaps not easy to apply today.

The Four Ontologies

Scholars of have often sensed that the society of Nazi Germany was not simply more brutal but, in fundamental ways, profoundly different from our own. In my opinion, research has been hampered by the lack of a theoretical apparatus that could be used to describe the difference. This is perhaps why so much discussion of the Nazi period has centered on concepts that, elsewhere, would have seemed anachronistic such as "civilization" and "barbarism" or "reaction" and "modernity."

More current conceptual tools are, I believe, provided by the French anthropologist Philippe Descola, who has identified what he believes are the four basic ontologies that exist across human cultures: "animism," "naturalism," "totemism," and "analogism." The chart on the following page is a highly simplified version of a chart that he uses to describe the differences.

<168>

Animism	Totemism
"Nature" derives its specifications from "culture" ("projection").	"Nature" and "culture" are continuous ("participation") but internally segmented by properties that nonhumans embody (correspondences between differential gaps).
Anthropological label: **Anthropogenism**	Anthropological label: **Cosmosgenism**
Naturalism	Analogism
"Culture" derives its specifications from its differences from "nature."	"Nature" and "culture" are continuous within a cosmos organized as a society (a sociocosmic order).
Anthropological label: **Anthropocentrism**	Anthropological label: **Cosmocentrism**

These schemata are not types of cultures so much as patterns by which people organize their experience, particularly with respect to the construction of a collective identity (Descola, *Beyond Nature and Culture* 247-80). While a single ontology may predominate in a given culture, others will probably also be present. Modern Occidental culture, for example, is, for the most part, naturalistic, but analogism survives, among other places, in occult, New Age, and neo-pagan communities. No ontology entirely defines a culture, but only sets broad limits to its range of possible forms.

According to Descola, animism, in which beings are physically different but internally the same, generally prevails among indigenous peoples in most of Africa, the Americas, and Siberia. In analogism, all beings are profoundly different, both physically and internally, and are only understood through complex patterns and analogies. It is characteristic of Chinese culture, as well as that of the Renaissance in the West, and there have been enclaves of it in Mexico, west-central Africa, and northern Siberia. In totemism, all beings from humans to insects or trees are fundamentally the same, both physically and internally. They form geographically-based collectives in which individual identity is tenuous

<169>

and membership transcends lines of species. This ontology predominates primarily among the aboriginal peoples of Australia, though it is also found in the cultures of the Algonquin Indians. Naturalism, in which there is a sharp division between humankind and other entities, is now the dominant model of the West. It divides society into "cultures," which are the product of human autonomy, while holding that the natural world is regulated by cosmic law.

The vast scope of Descola's vision is more characteristic of the nineteenth through early twentieth centuries than of the more circumspect academia of today. Descola admits that his ideas may appear naïve or oversimplified to specialists in particular civilizations (*Beyond Nature and Culture* 402-06), and the scrutiny of his ontologies by academics across the disciplines has barely begun. For my purposes here, however, absolute precision is by no means necessary. The extreme simplicity of his ontologies makes them particularly useful at a time when, with the information overload, any attempt at a coherent of analysis of a society threatens to be overwhelmed by the sheer mass of factual material.

Is Descola's theory of the four ontologies "scientific"? I would answer mostly in the affirmative, but that is not fully clear. It is hard to say just how the theory could be definitively confirmed or disproved by empirical investigations. Furthermore, since it is in part about scientific methodologies, it cannot be entirely subject to them. Perhaps, then, it might be better characterized as "applied philosophy" than as "science." But, whichever label we prefer, I find the theory very useful. Its application is primarily descriptive, and I believe the theory has helped me to make sense of phenomena that once seemed almost impervious to analysis.

Nazi Totemism

The culture that the Nazis aspired to, and partially created, in Germany corresponds to Descola's description of totemism down to many details. It is, as we have seen, a collective based largely on territory, in which inclusion was shared by a vast range of living things, but the possession of human form did not necessarily confer kinship or status. Furthermore, there is the absolute subordination of the individual to a communal identity. As the Nazis sometimes put it, "You are nothing, the Volk is everything" (Dirscherl 16).[4] The German word "Volk," as used here, is only very imperfectly translated with the English "people." It refers not to a collection of individuals but to an almost mystical sort of unity of human beings, based on language, culture and, by extension, all the

---

[4] Accordingly, the Nazi law tended to center around collective rather than individual interests, rights, and concerns Frank Uekoetter, *The Green and the Brown: A History of Conservation in Nazi Germany* (New York: Cambridge University Press, 2006) 65-66.

<170>

features of their ancestral lands (Blanning, 108-09). The Nazis also shared with totemic societies a constant preoccupation with their mythic origins, usually traced to the alleged practices of a vaguely remembered "Aryan" race and civilization.[5]

The moieties of the Australian continent had, in the words of Descola, totems that constitute "a kind of ontological prototype of which totemic species constitutes the emblematic expression, not the concrete archetype, from which . . . qualities (of its members) are derived" (*Beyond Nature and Culture* 158-59). The Nazis, though not divided into moieties, had such a totem in the wolf. Hitler used the code name "little wolf," and often referred to himself as a "wolf." Many institutions in Nazi Germany, especially those of the military, had names that included the word "wolf," and the wolf was constantly invoked in Nazi propaganda. Most significantly, the Nazis tried to structure their society to an appreciable extent on what they saw as the model of a wolf pack, characterized by "loyalty, fierceness, courage, obedience, and sometimes even cruelty" (see pp. 74-77).

There is a bit of totemism in the ideal of the nation state, which emerged largely in the latter eighteenth and nineteenth centuries. It involves personal identification with a territory and, by extension, its landscapes, flora, and fauna. Nations, like totemic moieties or tribes, are often symbolized by animals, for example the British bulldog, the Russian bear, the Canadian beaver, or the American eagle. Furthermore, countries generally mythologize their origins by stylizing, and often falsifying, events of their foundation, and making their heroes larger than life. Historical episodes such as the American Revolution, the Irish rebellion of 1798, or the Battle of Teutoburg Forest become myths of origin, which are constantly reenacted, not entirely different from the Dreamtime of Native Australians. But, for most people, the nation state has seldom been more than one bond among many, a partially totemic enclave in a generally anthropocentric culture. In carrying nationalism, with its totemic associations, to an unprecedented extreme, the Nazis altered the foundation of their society.

The precise intentions of the Nazis count for little here, because the ontologies described by Descola are generally beneath the threshold of consciousness (Descola *Beyond Nature and Culture* 92, 101-11). Furthermore, Nazi policies probably served more to reflect than create a change in ontology. After being in power for little more than one turbulent decade,

---

[5] For more on totemism, see Philippe Descola, *Beyond Nature and Culture*, trans. Janet Lloyd (Chicago: University of Chicago Press, 2013) 144-71. For more on these stories of Aryan origin before, during, and after the Nazi period, see: Joscelyn Godwin, *Arktos: The Myth of the Pole in Science, Symbolism, and Nazi Survival* (Kempton, IL: Adventures Unlimited Press, 1996), Nicholas Goodrick-Clarke, *Black Sun: Aryan Cults, Esoteric Nazism, and the Politics of Identity* (New York: New York University Press, 2003)

<171>

the Nazi regime did not have any time to consolidate any major changes in the patterns of daily life. One cannot study it by examining an established body of tradition, but only relatively fragmentary initiatives. Explanations such as "politics" or "propaganda" might partially explain details of this process, but not the overarching patterns. Although I cannot definitively prove this, my sense is that the record shows the contours of a totemic culture that was beginning to emerge, at the same time as the Nazis came to power, though not necessarily because of them.

The Nazis were certainly not deliberately aspiring to be like the native Australians or other totemic cultures. There is no reason to believe that they were even remotely aware of this structural similarity between aboriginal societies and their own, so the resemblance must certainly be due to convergence. This further indicates that Nazi totemism was not a case of atavism so much as of ongoing cultural evolution. Finally, it suggests that totemism, with its intense intimacy between human beings and other forms of life, may have an enduring appeal for people in many cultures.

The Nazis were not, however, entirely totemic, or at most only in aspiration. Many of the fundamental features of Nazi society such as the inclination to violence, the intensely hierarchic structure, the xenophobia, and the obsession with sacrifice[6] are not characteristic of totemic societies. Furthermore, the totemic aspirations in Nazi ideology were almost invariably rationalized by naturalistic philosophy and science. In this respect, the Nazis were perhaps analogous to advocates of "creation science" today, who endeavor to explain fossils by invoking the Biblical account of Noah's Flood. The result is a sort of hybrid creation that is neither truly science nor religion.

One also need not idealize the aboriginal peoples of Australia as "noble savages" or anything of the sort in order to observe that they are relatively peaceful. They have not been continually at war with one another and, so far as anyone is aware, have never been involved in any mass slaughter of human beings.[7] Out of the several hundred instances of systematic mass killing identified and discussed by White, not a single one involves the aboriginal peoples of Australia.

This will not seem paradoxical if we remember that the human exceptionalism that has accompanied naturalism has, in practice, given humankind far more status than protection. Anthropocentrism has produced impressive cultural accomplishments, including the noble

---

[6] Sacrifice is very rare in totemic cultures, but was an incessant preoccupation of the Nazis: see pp. 139-58; see also Descola, *Beyond Nature and Culture*, 228-30.
[7] For a history of the indigenous peoples of Australia since their initial contact with Europeans, as well as a discussion of their beliefs, see: Jane Lydon, *Fantastic Dreaming: The Archaeology of an Aboriginal Mission* (New York: Altamira Press, 2009).

<172>

sentiments in the American *Declaration of Independence* and the French *Declaration of the Rights of Man*. But the rise of naturalism was accompanied by a massive expansion of slavery by Europeans. Anthropocentrism failed to prevent the near genocide of Native Americans, the Napoleonic Wars, two World Wars, the GULAG, and several other instances of mass killing. We cannot, therefore, make a simple connection between the Nazis' abandonment of anthropocentrism and their inhumanity.

The Nazis combined many of the relationships that prevail in totemism with the systematic ruthlessness that is characteristic of naturalism. Descola distinguishes between "predatory" relationships, often found in animistic societies based on hunting, in which people seek to incorporate others into their collective and personal identities, and the drive toward the annihilation of others. Accordingly, "Naturalism is thus destructive rather than predatory in its behavior toward certain categories of both humans and non-humans." This results from an inability, often in spite of intense longing, to establish reciprocity with agents outside the perceived boundaries of humankind (Descola *Beyond Nature and Culture* 399-400). In effect, the Nazis promoted their totemic collective, which included landscapes and animals, with the sort of militancy that, in modern times, had previously been reserved mostly for the confrontation with agents beyond the confines of "civilization."

Esoteric Nazism

As already noted, there are many elements of Nazi culture and ideology that do not at all fit the totemic model, including the obsession with rank, the elaborate ceremonies, and occult practices, but these as well are not necessarily anthropocentric. Among the Nazi leaders, this side of their movement is most closely identified not with Hitler but with Heinrich Himmler. It is also apparent in the writing of Savitri Devi, born Maximiani Portas of Greek-English heritage, who converted to Hinduism and moved to India after World War II. She was an important influence on George Lincoln Rockwell, Collin Jordan, and most other important neo-Nazis, as well as a founding member of the American National Socialist Party. She fused Nazism with Hinduism, and believed that Hitler had been an avatar of the god Vishnu. In her view, the caste system in India was the sort of racial hierarchy that Hitler has sought to establish in Europe. Savitri Devi is often considered the founder of "esoteric Nazism," an element within neo-Nazi culture, which is now focused on extremely speculative histories, forgotten kingdoms, mystical practices, and animal rights.[8]

---

[8] For a detailed discussion of Savitri Devi, her neo-Nazism, and her impact, see: Nicholas Goodrick-Clarke, *Hitler's Priestess: Savitri Devi, the Hindu-Aryan Myth, and Neo-Nazism* (New York: New York University Press, 1998).

<173>

According to Savatri Devi, Nazism was a doctrine of universal love, exemplified above all in the concern of Hitler, whom she considered the greatest man in Western history, and his followers for the suffering of animals. As to the Holocaust, she did not deny but, rather, mythologized it. Hitler was, in her view, a force of nature and, thereby, exempt from blame, while the Holocaust was a sort of Hell for those who had foisted anthropocentrism and egalitarianism on Aryan culture.

She wrote in the preface to her book *The Impeachment of Man*, written at the end of World War II but first published in 1959, about the accounts of atrocities that she had been told of in a deNazification camp:

> Those tales, intended to shatter the world, failed, however, to impress *me* — at least in the sense that the "reeducators" desired. They failed to change my attitude towards National Socialism.... I had heard or seen too much of all forms of exploitation of animals by man — from the daily brutalities one witnesses in the streets of Southern Europe, not to speak of the Orient, to the appalling deeds perpetrated in the secrecy of vivisection chambers, but fully described in certain scientific publications — not to feel more than indifferent to the fate of human beings, save in the rare cases these happen to be my own brothers in faith (ix-x).

As Savitri Devi constantly emphasized, Hitler and many of his close followers aspired to vegetarianism, both in their own lives in their vision of a future society (Dirscherl 81-82). For Savitri Devi, nature was a state without ambiguities, but humanity in its degenerate condition had disrupted the natural order. Human beings were intrinsically superior to other animals, yet they had forfeited that status. Using some highly inaccurate zoology, she argued that all animals were naturally either herbivorous or carnivorous, but it was perverted to be both. By returning to a vegetarian diet, humanity would also return to the natural order, in which people, at least some of them, were destined for supremacy.

<174>

In Savitri Devi's view, there is only a very fluid boundary between human beings and animals, but the sharp division between humankind and nature has been replaced as an organizing principle by a cosmic order in which every being has a rank. The underlying ontology here seems to be neither naturalism nor totemism but, rather, analogism, which is often characterized by elaborate hierarchies.

The End of Anthropocentrism

For historians, the schemata articulated by Descola will be most useful in describing events that take place on the special and temporal boundaries of regions in which different ontologies prevail. Common sense would suggest that these would be areas of intense misunderstanding, and, though this has not been studied intensely, experience seems to bear that out. The early modern period, which Descola sees as a transition in the West from analogism to naturalism, was characterized by extremely violent wars of religion and persecutions during the fifteenth and sixteenth centuries. If, as seems likely, the period dominated by naturalism is starting to fade,[9] that may possibly explain the violence of the twentieth century, which produced two World Wars and the Cold War. It may be, for example, that we tend to exaggerate the homogeneity, as well as the universality, of what is known as the "West," thus obscuring very fundamental cultural differences that lay behind the conflict between Communism and capitalism.

There is no reason to suppose that naturalism, with its inherent anthropocentrism, is destined to remain dominant forever, and that paradigm is now again being questioned intensely. Over the past several decades there has been a convergence of thought in several subjects including environmentalism, history, philosophy, biology, artificial intelligence, and literature, in which anthropocentrism — and, by association, naturalism — is rejected as destructive to ecosystems, animals, and even human beings. [10]

In spite of the intense criticism, however, little is said about what might eventually replace anthropocentrism. Perhaps that silence is appropriate, since, in spite of the growing reservations, naturalism remains the foundation of almost all of our philosophies, even those that criticize it. The three major candidates to replace anthropocentrism are ecocentrism, biocentrism, and Gaiacentrism, which are popularly equated with one

[9] Philippe Descola, "Constructing Natures: Symbolic Ecology and Social Practice," *Nature and Society: Anthropological Perspectives*, eds. Philippe Descola and Gísli Pálsson (New York: Routledge, 1996) 103-26, cited 19-20.
[10] For some perspectives on the increasing rejection of anthropocentrism, see: Rod Boddice, ed., *A History of Attitudes and Behaviors toward Animals in Eighteenth- and Nineteenth Century Britain* (Lewiston, UK: Edwin Mellen Press, 2008).

<175>

another, though very important differences among them will probably emerge in the years to come. Though unsure just how far the analogies can be taken, I would say that these correspond roughly to the ontologies, apart from naturalism, that have been proposed by Descola; ecocentrism to totemism; biocentrism to animism, and Gaiacentrism to analogism.

The Nazis have often, and rightly, been called "a warning from history." In this case, the cautionary note applies to the abrupt and violent way in which they have subverted naturalism and partially adopted totemism, not to totemism itself. After a few centuries in which the dominant culture had postulated a vast gap between human beings and animals, and without fully internalizing alternative values and behaviors, the Nazis abruptly not only blurred but often almost completely effaced this division. This canceled the restraints of custom and morality, and one result was that it became relatively easy to kill vast numbers of human beings.

In popular rhetoric, overcoming anthropocentrism is now often glibly presented as almost a panacea, and there is often little or no appreciation of the depth of cultural changes that would involve. They are not simply a matter of embracing some new abstract philosophy, but would involve eventually subverting many unconscious assumptions. We would need to re-imagine the fundamental categories with which we divide up the world. What it required is not de-emphasizing the individual, which is essentially what the Nazis did, but reevaluating what it means to be an "individual." Not only the difference between human beings and animals must be called into question but also, and simultaneously, other equally basic differences such as that between animals and plants as well as between living things and inanimate objects.

The Environmental Movement

For many decades, some of the most passionate and persistent calls for overcoming anthropocentric perspective have come from the environmental movement. It is hard, however, to know whether, or to what extent, these constitute a break with anthropocentrism, since a reader is not always sure what is intended as metaphoric. When Aldo Leopold recommends "Thinking Like a Mountain" (129-32), should we understand that in a relatively direct way? If so, Leopold is very close to totemism or to animism. If not, this injunction is probably a poetic elaboration based on our familiar Western paradigm. Leopold's essay itself does not definitively answer the question, and I suspect the author himself was not entirely sure. At any rate, there is a strong undertone of neo-pagan and totemic imagery running through the work of Leopold and his followers in the environmental movement.

<176>

In 1935, not long after Hitler's ascent to power, Leopold visited Germany to learn about methods of forestry, and came back profoundly impressed, especially by the German reintroduction of raptors and predators to their woods. Shortly after his visit, he founded The Wilderness Society, and began a series of writings that eventually laid the foundation for the environmental movement in the United States and beyond [see pp. 79-80]. Since that time, a sort of totemism has pervaded the environmental movement.[11] When Green political parties came to influence in Europe during the 1980s, many feared they could lead to a revival of Nazism,[12] but that did not happen. Though they may have neglected the perspectives of people of color, these parties have been notably free of racism and xenophobia (Dominick III 111-12).

My own position is that the totemism of the environmental movement may indeed be in part a heritage of Nazi Germany, but that is no reason to reject it. We generally think of history too simply in terms of extraordinary individuals, vanguards, or movements, which proposed innovations that, in spite of initial resistance, gradually gained a wider following and eventually full acceptance. Actually, history is far messier than that linear paradigm suggests. There are plenty of false starts and lots of backtracking, with no guarantees that right will triumph in the end. We may find it relatively easy to accept the fact that good people can have bad ideas, but we resist the knowledge that bad people can have good ones. But history transcends our agendas, quite regardless of whether we are smart or dumb, good or bad, and right or wrong. Our ideas constantly lead to developments very different from what we anticipate. The question of how sincere the Nazis were in their concern for animals and the environment seems to me not only ultimately unanswerable, like most questions of human motivation, but also of comparatively minor importance, since the impact of movements always goes far beyond anybody's conscious intent. Our major focus, therefore, should be not so much on where ideas come from but on where they seem to be leading us at present.

---

[11] Boria Sax, "The Cosmic Spider and Her World-Wide Web: Sacred and Symbolic Animals in the Age of Change," *A Cultural History of Animals in the Modern Age*, ed. Randy Malamud (New York: Berg, 2007) 38-40.
[12] For a thorough study of the historical links between Nazism and contemporary green movements, see Uekoetter, *The Green and the Brown: A History of Conservation in Nazi Germany*.

<177>

Finally, if the Nazis were indeed, as I argue here, strongly influenced by a new intellectual paradigm, which was starting to emerge but had not yet been well articulated, this opens questions as to whether not only military but also intellectual resistance against the regime could have been more effective. The head of the Nazi regime was probably insane,[13] but a dialogue with some of the intellectual and academic leaders might have helped to at least limit its destructiveness. If scholars in the international community had succeeded in recognizing the emerging paradigm, articulating it more clearly, and stripping it of political rhetoric, perhaps they could have prevented, or at least limited, its exploitation by the Nazi party. Intellectual leaders of the Nazi regime such as Walter Scheidt and Konrad Z. Lorenz [14](who, after the fall of Nazism, became a scientific celebrity) may have been often deluded but were probably not unreachable.

---

[13] For a detailed psychological profile of Hitler, see George Victor, *Hitler: The Pathology of Evil* (Washington, DC: Brassey's, 1998).

[14] Walter Scheidt was the founder of Kulturbiology, a discipline remarkably similar to Sociobiology in its foundations. For a discussion of Scheidt and some of his colleagues see Boria Sax and Peter Klopfer, "Jacob Von Uexküll and the Anticipation of Sociobiology," *Semiotica* 134-135 (2001). For a discussion of Lorenz during the Nazi era, see pp 89- 91, 124-36 of this book.

<178>

APPENDIX 2
LAW ON ANIMAL PROTECTION

The government has resolved on the following law, which is hereby made known:

Section I
Cruelty to Animals
#1

(1) It is forbidden to unnecessarily torment or roughly mishandle an animal.

(2) One torments an animal when one repeatedly or continuously causes appreciable pain or suffering; the torment is unnecessary in so far as it does not serve any rational, justifiable purpose. One mishandles an animal when one causes it appreciable pain; mishandling is rough when it corresponds to an unfeeling state of mind.

Section II
Measures for the Protection of Animals
#2

It is forbidden:

1. to so neglect an animal in one's ownership, care or accommodation that it thereby experiences appreciable pain or appreciable damage;

2. to use an animal unnecessarily for what clearly exceeds its powers or causes it appreciable pain, or which it — in consequence of its condition — is obviously not capable of;

3. to use an animal for demonstrations, film-making, spectacles, or other public events to the extent that these events cause the animal appreciable pain or appreciable damage to health;

4. to use a fragile, ill, overworked or old animal for which further life is a torment for any other purpose than to cause or procure a rapid, painless death;

5. to put out one's own domestic animal for the purpose of getting rid of it;

6. to set or test the power of dogs on cats, foxes, and other animals;

7. to shorten the ears or the tail of a dog over two weeks old. This is allowed if it is done with anaesthesia;

8. to shorten the tail of a horse. This is allowed if it is to remedy a defect or illness of the tail and is done by a veterinarian and under anesthesia;

<179>

9. to perform a painful operation on an animal in an unprofessional manner or without anesthesia. Castration is regarded as a painful operation with horses, with cattle over nine months old, with pigs over six months old, and with sexually mature sheep and goats. Anesthesia is not necessary in so far as the pain connected with the operation is only minute, if a similar or comparable operation on human beings is not normally accompanied by anesthesia, or if anesthesia in a particular case is impossible according to veterinary standards;

10. to kill an animal on a farm for fur otherwise than with anesthesia or in a way that is, in any case, painless;

11. to force-feed fowl;

12. to tear out or separate the thighs of living frogs.

#3

The importation of horses with shortened tails is forbidden. The Minister of the Interior can make exceptions if special circumstances warrant it.

#4

The temporary use of hoofed animals as carriers in the mines is only permitted with the permission of the responsible local authorities.

Section III
Experiments on Living Animals
#5

It is forbidden to operate on or handle living animals in ways that may cause appreciable pain or damage for the purpose of experiments, to the extent the provisions of #6 through #8 do not mandate otherwise.

#6

(1) The Minister of the Interior can at the proposal of the responsible governmental or local authorities confer permission on certain scientifically led institutes or laboratories to undertake scientific experiments on living animals, when the director of the experiment has sufficient professional education and reliability, sufficient facilities for the undertaking of animal experiments are available, and a guarantee for the care and maintenance of the animals for experiment has been made.

(2) The Minister of the Interior can delegate the granting of permission to others among the highest officials of the government.

(3) Permission may be withdrawn without compensation at any time.

#7

<180>

In carrying out experiments on animals (#5), the following provisions are to be observed:

1. The experiments may only be carried out under the complete authority of the scientific director or of a representative that has been specifically appointed by the scientific director.

2. The experiments may only be carried out by someone who has previously received scientific education or under the direction of such a person, and when every pain is avoided in so far as that is compatible with the goal of the experiment.

3. Experiments for research may only be undertaken when a specific result is expected that has not been previously confirmed by science or if the experiments help to answer previously unsolved problems.

4. The experiments are only to be undertaken under anesthesia, provided the judgement of the scientific director does not categorically exclude this or if the pain connected with the operation is outweighed by the damage to the condition of the experimental animals as a result of anesthesia.

Nothing more severe than a difficult operation or painful but unbloody experiment may be carried out on such an unanesthetized animal.

Animals that suffer appreciable pain after the completion of such a difficult experiment, especially involving an operation, are, in so far as this is, in the judgement of the scientific director, compatible with the goal of the experiment, immediately to be put to death.

5. Experiments on horses, dogs, cats, and apes can only be carried out when the intended goal may not be achieved through experiments on other animals.

6. No more animals may be used than are necessary to resolve the associated question.

7. Animal experiments for pedagogical purposes are only permitted when other educational tools such as pictures, models, taxonomy, and film are not sufficient.

8. Records are to be kept of the sort of animal used, the purpose, the procedure, and the result of the experiment.

#8

Experiments on animals for judicial purposes as well as inoculations and taking of blood from living animals for the purpose of diagnosing illness of people or animals, or for obtainment of serums or inoculations according to procedures that have already been tried or are recognized by the state, are not subject to provisions #5 through #7. These animals, however, are also to be killed painlessly if they suffer appreciable pain and if it is compatible with the goals of the experiment.

<181>

Section IV
Provisions for Punishment
#9

(1) Whoever unnecessarily torments or roughly mishandles an animal will be punished by up to two years in prison, with a fine, or with both these penalties.

(2) Whoever, apart from the case in (1), undertakes an experiment on living animals (# 5) without the required permission will be punished by imprisonment of up to six months, with a fine, or with both of these penalties.

(3) A fine of up to five hundred thousand marks or imprisonment will, apart from the punishment mandated in (1) and (2), be the punishment for whomever intentionally or through negligence

1. violates prohibition #2 though #4;

2. acts against regulation #7;

3. violates guidelines enacted by the Ministry of the Interior or by a provincial government according to #14;

4. neglects to prevent children or other persons that are under his/her supervision or belong to his/her household from violating the provisions of this law.

#10

(1) In addition to the punishments in #9 for an intentional violation of the law, an animal belonging to the condemned may be confiscated or killed. Instead of confiscation it may be ordered that the animal be sheltered and fed for up to nine months at the cost of the guilty party.

(2) If no specific person can be identified or condemned, the confiscation or killing of an animal may be undertaken in any case when the other prerequisites are present.

#11

(1) If someone is repeatedly guilty of intentionally violating the provisions that are punishable according to #9 the local authorities that are responsible can prohibit that person from keeping certain animals or from business involving them either for a specified period or permanently.

(2) After a year has passed since the imposition of the punishment the responsible local authorities may rescind their decision.

(3) An animal subject to appreciable negligence in provision, care, or shelter may be taken away from the owner by the responsible local authority and accommodated elsewhere until there is a guarantee that the animal will be cared for in a manner above reproach. The cost of this accommodation shall be paid by the guilty party.

<182>

#12

If in a judicial process it appears doubtful whether an act violates a prohibition of #1, (1) or (2), a veterinarian shall be summoned as early in the process as possible and, in so far as it concerns a farm, an agricultural official of the government shall be heard.

Section V
Conclusion
#13

Anesthesia as it is understood in this law means all procedures that lead to general painlessness or eliminate localized pain.

#14

The Minister of the Interior can issue judicial and administrative decrees for the completion and enforcement of this law. In so far as the Minister of the Interior does not make use of this power local governments can make the necessary decree for implementation.

#15

This law becomes binding on February 1, 1934 with the exception of #2, (8) and #3, (11), for which the Minister of the Interior must set the time of implementation in consultation with the Minister of Food and Agriculture.

The laws #145b and #360, (13) of the law of May 30, 1908 (RGBL* 314) remain unchanged.

Berlin, November 24, 1933

Signed:

Adolf Hitler
Chancellor

Frick
Minister of the Interior

Minister of Justice
Dr. Gürntner

<183>

APPENDIX 2
BRIEF CHRONOLOGY OF LEGISLATION ON ANIMALS AND NATURE IN THE THIRD REICH

April 21, 1933   Law on the Slaughter of Animals (RGBL #1, 203)

April 21, 1933   Order on the Slaughter of Animals (RGBL #1, 212)

April 24, 1933   Order of the Prussian Ministry of the Interior on the Slaughter of Cold-Blooded Animals

May 9, 1933   Decree of the Prussian Ministry of the Interior on Vivisection

Nov. 24, 1933   Law on Animal Protection (RGBL #1, 987)

Jan. 18, 1934   Prussian Law on Hunting

Feb 23, 1934   Decree of the Prussian Ministry of Commerce and Employment on Education at Primary, Secondary and College Levels on the Law for Animal Protection.

June 20, 1934   First Order on the Enforcement of the Animal Protection Law (RGBL #1, 516)

July 3, 1934   Law on Hunting (RGBL #1, 549)

Nov. 15, 1934   Decree of the Minister of Science, Education and National Culture on Schools and Animal Protection

June 26, 1935   Law on the Protection of Nature (RGBL #1, 821)

March 27, 1936   Order on the Slaughter and Holding of Living Fish and Other Cold-Blooded Animals (RGBL #1, 13)

March 17, 1936   Law on the Promotion of Animal Breeding (RGBL #1, 175)

<184>

March 18, 1936	Order on Plants Growing in the Wild and on Protected Animals in the Wild (RGBL #1, 181)
April 20, 1936	Decree of the Imperial Forest Master on Feral Cats
March 17, 1937	Decree of the Ministry of the Interior on Guidelines for the Loading and Transportation of Animals
Sept. 9, 1937	Order on the Importing of Birds for Scientific Purposes (RGBL #1, 331)
Jan. 19, 1938	Order on the Lighting and Ventilation of Stalls in Agricultural Businesses (RGBL #1, 37)
Feb. 16, 1938	On the Certification of Veterinarians
May 23, 1938	Expanded Version of the Animal Protection Law (RGBL # 1, 98)
June 9, 1938	Decree of the Minister of the Interior on Wandering Animal Shows and Menageries
Sept. 8, 1938	Law on Animal Protection During Transport by Railroad (RGBL #2, 663)
Sept. 24, 1938	Decree of the Imperial Forest Master on Organizations Devoted to Protection of Nature
Nov. 11, 1938	Decree of the Ministry of the Interior on Guidelines on the Loading and Transportation of Animals in Motor Vehicles
Feb. 13, 1939	On the Implementation of Measures for Animal Protection in Ostmark
July 24, 1939	On the Implementation of Measures for Animal Protection in the Sudentenland
Aug. 29, 1940	Order on the Introduction of Animal Diseases and the Implementation of Measures for Animal Protection in the Incorporated Eastern Lands
Oct. 29, 1940	Law on the Inspection of Meat (RGBL #1, 1463)

<185>

Dec. 31, 1940   Law on the Shoeing of Horses (RGBL 1941, #1, 2)

April 10, 1941   Order of the Civil Government in Alsace on
                 the Slaughter of Animals

Aug. 5, 1941   Order of the Civil Government in Alsace on the
                 Implementation of Measures for Animal Protection

Feb. 15, 1942   Decree Prohibiting Jews from Keeping of Pets

<186>

BIBLIOGRAPHY

Archival Sources

NA — National Archives, College Park, MD.

RA — Rockefeller Archives, Tarrytown, NY.

USHMM — United States Holocaust Memorial Museum, Washington, DC

Books and Articles

Ackerman, Diane. *The Zookeeper's Wife: A War Story*. New York: W. W. Norton, 2007.

Adam, Peter. *Art of the Third Reich*. New York: Harry N. Abrams, 1995.

Arendt, Hannah. *Origins of Totalitarianism*. London: Allen and Unwin, 1962.

Arluke, Arnold. "Sacrificial Symbolism in Animal Experimentation: Object or Pet?" *Anthrozoös*, vol. 2, #2 (Fall 1988): 98-117.

_____ and Boria Sax. "The Nazi Treatment of Animals and People." *Reinventing Biology*. Ed. Lynde Birke and Ruth Hubbard. Bloomington: Indiana UP, 1995: 228-260.

_____ and Boria Sax. "Understanding Nazi Animal Protection and the Holocaust." *Anthrozoös*, Vol. 5, #1 (Fall 1992): 6-31.

Attenborough, David. *The First Eden: The Mediterranean World and Man*. Boston: Little, Brown and Company, 1987.

AVMA {American Veterinary Medicine Association}. "1986 Report of the AVMA Panel on Euthanasia." *Journal of the American Veterinary Medicine Association*, vol. 188, #3 (Feb. 1): 252-268.

Aycoberry, Pierre. *The Nazi Question: An Essay on the Interpretations of National Socialism (1922-1975)*. Trans. Robert Hurley. New York: Pantheon, 1981.

Bach, H. L. *The German Jew: A Synthesis of Judaism and Western Civilization, 1730-1930*. New York: Oxford UP, 1984.

Baird, Jay W. *To Die for Germany: Heroes in the Nazi Pantheon*. Bloomington: Indiana UP, 1990.

_____. "Julius Streicher — Der Berufsantisemit." *Die Braune Elite II: 21 weitere biographische Skizzen*. Ed. Ronald Smelser, Enrico

<187>

Syring, and Rainer Zitelmann. Darmstadt: Wissenschaftliche Buchgesellschaft, 1993: 231-242.

Barber, Lynn. *The Heyday of Natural History*. Garden City, NY: Doubleday, 1980.

Bauer, Yehuda. *The Holocaust in Historical Perspective*. Seattle: University of Washington Press, 1980.

Bäumer, Änne, ed. *NS-Biologie*. Stuttgart: S. Hirzel, 1990.

_____. See: Bäumer-Schleinkofer, Änne.

Bäumler-Scheinkofer, Änne. "Biologie unter dem Hackenkreuz: Biologie und Schule im Dritten Reich." *Universitas*, vol. 47, #547 (January 1992): 48-61.

_____. See: Bäumer, Änne.

Bauman, Zygmunt. *Modernity and the Holocaust*. Ithaca: New York UP, 1993.

Berenbaum, Michael and Abraham J. Peck, eds. *The Holocaust and History: The Known, the Unknown, the Disputed and the Reexamined*. Bloomington: Indiana UP, 1998.

Berman, Charles. *Orion's Legacy: A Cultural History of Man as Hunter*. New York: Penguin; Books, 1996.

Bertalanffy, Ludwig von. "Die organismische Affassung und ihre Auswirkung." *Der Biologe*, (a) starting in vol. 10, #7/8 (1940): 247-258; (b) continued in #9/10, (1941): 337-345.

Bernstein, Irwin S. "Dominance: The Baby and the Bathwater," with comments by various scholars. *The Behavioral and Brain Sciences*, #4 (1981): 419-45.

Bidermann, Gottlob Herbert. . . .*und litt an meiner Seite*. Reutlingen: Steinach Verlag, 1995.

Birke, Linda and Mike Michael. "The Heart of the Matter: Animal Bodies, Ethics, and Species Boundaries." *Society and Animals*, vol. 6, #3 (1998): 245-261.

Blanning, Tim. *The Romantic Revolution*. New York: Modern Library, 2012.

Blount, Margaret. *Animal Land: The Creatures of Children's Fiction*. New York: Avon, 1974.

Blunt, Wilfred. *The Ark in the Park: The Zoo in the Nineteenth Century*. London: Hamish Hamilton, 1976.

Boddice, Rod, ed. *A History of Attitudes and Behaviors toward Animals in Eighteenth- and Nineteenth Century Britain*. Lewiston, UK: Edwon Mellen Press, 2008.

Bookchin, Murray and Dave Foreman. *Defending the Earth: A Dialogue Between Murray Bookchin and Dave Foreman*. Ed. Steve Case. Boston: South End Press, 1991.

<188>

Bornemann, Regina and Martin Fritz Brumme. "Symbole ständischen Denkens. Das Beispiel der "Reichstierärteburg Hoheneck." *Veterinärmedizin im Dritten Reich*. Ed. Johann Schäffer. Giessen: Deutsche Veterinärmedizinische Gesellschaft, 1998: 91-128.

Bramwell, Anna. *Blood and Soil: Richard Walter Darré and Hitler's 'Green Party'*. Abbotsbrook, England: Kensal, 1985.

Breitman, Richard. *The Architect of Genocide: Himmler and the Final Solution*. New York: Knopf, 1991.

Brennecke, Fritz. *The Nazi Primer: Official Handbook for Schooling the Hitler Youth*. Trans. Harwood L. Childs. New York: Harper, 1966 (reprint of the 1938 edition).

Brettschneider, Hubert. *Der Streit um die Vivisektion im 19. Jahrhundert* (2 vols.). Stuttgart: Gustav Fischer, 1962.

Browning, Christopher R. *Ordinary Men: Reserve Police Battalion 101 and the Final Solution in Poland*. New York: HarperCollins, 1992.

Brumme, Martin Fritz. "'Mit dem Blutkult der Juden ist endgültig in Deutschland Schluss zu machnen': Anmerkungen zur Entwicklung der Anti-Schächt Bewegung." *Medizingeschichte und Gesellschaftskritik: Festschrift zum 65. Geburtstag von Gerhard Baader*. Ed. Michael Humbenstorf et al., Frankfurt am Main: Verlag Deutscher medizinische Gesellschaft, 1994: 391-417.

_____. "Tierarzt und Tierschutz in Deutschland in der ersten Hälfte des 20. Jahrhunderts. Eine Skizze zur Historisierung einer aktuellen Diskussion." *Argos: Bulletin van het veterinair Historisch Genootschap*, Summer 91: 29-39.

_____. "Tierschutz als Zivilizationskritik: Zur Politischen Qualität einer ethisch motivierten Bewegung." *Tagung der Fachgruppe: "Tierschutzrecht und gerichtliche Veterinärmedizin."* Ed. K. Löffler. Stuttgart-Hohenheim: Deutsche Veterinäramedizinische Gesellschaft, 1993: 31-47.

_____. "Der Weg zur Machergreifung und Gleichschaltung. Tierärztlicher Beruf im Umbruch?" *Veterinärmedizin im Dritten Reich*. Ed. Johann Schäffer. Giessen: Deutsche Veterinärmedizinische Gesellschaft, 1998: 25-43.

Buchner, Alex. *Kampf im Gebirge: Erfahrungen und Bekenntnisse des Gebirges*. Munich-Lohnhausen: Schild, 1957.

Buchner, Leander. "Zur Bedeutung des Pferdes in der Wehrmacht." *Veterinärmedizin im Dritten Reich — Hochschule, Militär, Verwaltung, Praxis: Fünfte Tagung der DVG Fachgruppe "Geschichte der Veterinärmedizin."* Ed. Johann Schäffer. Hannover: DVG, 1997: 26-27.

_____. "Zur Bedeutung des Pferdes in der Wehrmacht."
Veterinärmedizin im Dritten Reich. Ed.Johann Schäffer. Giessen:
Deutsche Veterinärmedizinische Gesellschaft, 1998: 135-144.

Burkert, Walter. *Creation of the Sacred: Tracks of Biology in Early Religions*.
Cambridge: Harvard UP, 1996.

_____. *HOMO NECANS: The Anthropology of Ancient Greek
Sacrificial Ritual and Myth*. Trans. Peter Bing. Berkeley: U. of
California Press, 1983.

Cahill, Thomas. *The Gift of the Jews: How a Tribe of Desert Nomads
Changed the Way Everyone Thinks and Feels*. New York: Doubleday,
1998.

Canetti, Elias. *Crowds and Power*. Trans. Carol Stewart. New York:
Seabury, 1978.

Caplan, Arthur L., ed. *When Medicine Went Mad: Bioethics and the
Holocaust*. Totowa, NJ: Humana Press, 1992.

Carras, Roger A. *A Perfect Harmony: The Intertwining Lives of Animals and
Humans throughout History*. New York: Simon and Schuster, 1996.

Chamberlain, Houston Stewart. *Foundations of the Nineteenth Century*
(two vols.). Trans. John Lees. New York: Howard Fertig, 1968.

Chaucer, Geoffrey. *The Canterbury Tales*. New York: Bantam Books, 1981.

Clark, David. " 'The Last Kantian in Nazi Germany': Dwelling with
Animals after Levinas." *Animal Acts: Configuring the Human in
Western History*. Ed. Jennifer Ham and Matthew Senior. New York:
Routledge, 1997: 165-198.

Cockburn, Andrew. "A Short, Meat-Oriented History of the World From
Eden to the Mattole." *New Left Review*, April-May 1996: 16-42.

Comfort, David. *The First Pet History of the World*. New York: Fireside,
1994.

Corbey, Raymond and Bert Theunissen. *Ape, Man and Apeman:
Changing Views since 1900*. Leiden: Leiden UP, 1995.

Corbey, Richard and Peter Mason. "Limited Company." *Anthrozoös*, vol.
7, #2 (1994), 90-102.

Crosby. Alfred W. *Ecological Imperialism: The Biological Expansion of
Europe, 900-1900*. New York: Cambridge UP, 1986.

Darré, Richar Walter. *Das Bauerntum als Lebensquelle der nordischen Rasse*.
Berlin: J. F. Lehmanns Verlag, 1942.

_____. "Das Schwein als Kriterium für nordische Völker und
Semiten." *Volk und Rasse*, vol. 2, #3 (1927): 138-151.

_____. *Der Schweinemord*. Munich: Verlag der NSDP, 1937.

Darwin, Charles. *The Descent of Man and His Selection in Relation to Sex*.
New York: Oxford UP, 1987.

<190>

Daszkiewicz, Piotr, and Jean Aikhenbaum. "Aurochs, retour d'un animal préhistorique . . . ou manipulation scientifique?" *Le Courrier de l'environnement*. #33 (April 1998): 73-79.

Davis, Belinda. *Home Fires Burning: Everyday Politics and Political Culture in World War I Berlin*. Unpublished Manuscript. Rutgers, NJ: 1997.

Defonesca, Misha. *Misha: A Mémoire of the Holocaust Years*. Bluebell, Pennsylvania: Mt. Ivy Press, 1997.

Deichmann, Ute. *Biologists under Hitler*. Trans. T. Dunlap. Cambridge, Mass.: Harvard UP, 1996.

Delort, Robert. *Les animaux ont une histoire*. Paris: Editions du Seuil, 1984.

Derr, Mark. "The Politics of Dogs." *The Atlantic Monthly*. March 1990: 49-72.

Descola, Philippe. *Beyond Nature and Culture*. Trans. Lloyd, Janet. Chicago: University of Chicago Press, 2013.

_____. "Constructing Natures: Symbolic Ecology and Social Practice." *Nature and Society: Anthropological Perspectives*. Eds. Descola, Philippe and Gísli Pálsson. New York: Routledge, 1996. 103-26.

Devi, Savitri. *Impeachment of Man*. Caluctta: Privately Published, 1959.

Digard, Jean-Pierre. *L'homme et les animaux domestiques:Anthropologie d'une passion*. Paris: Fayard, 1989.

Dirscherl, Stefan. *Tier- und Naturschutz im Nationalsozialismus: Gesetzgebung, Ideologie und Praxis*. Göttingen: Deutsche Nationalbibliothek, 2012.

Dittrich, Werner. "Wehrgeistige Erziehung im lebenskundlichen Unterricht." *Der Biologe*, vol. 9, # 1-2 (1940): 53-56.

Dominick III, Raymond H. *The Environmental Movement in Germany: Prophets and Pioneers, 1871-1971*. Bloomington: Indiana UP, 1992.

Douglas, Mary. *Purity and Danger: An analysis of the concepts of pollution and taboo*. New York: Routledge, 1994.

Dower, John W. *War Without Mercy: Race and Power in the Pacific War*. New York: Pantheon, 1986.

Effertz, J. "Bericht über die Jahrestagung." In *Deutsche Zeitschrift für Tierpsychologie*, vol. 1 (1937): 189-191.

Ehrenreich, Barbara. *Blood Rites: Origins and History of the Passions of War*. New York: Henry Holt, 1997.

Eliade, Mircea. *From the Stone Age to the Eleusian Mysteries* (Vol. 1 of *A History of Religious Ideas*). Chicago: U. of Chicago Press, 1978.

_____. *Myths, Dreams and Mysteries*. New York: Harper Torchbooks, 1967.

_____. *Myths, Dreams and Mysteries*. New York: Harper Torchbooks, 1967.

<191>

Ellis, John. *Cavalry: The History of Mounted Warfare*. Edinburgh: Westbridge Books, 1978.

Engelmann, Bernt. *In Hitler's Germany: Daily Life in the Third Reich*. Trans. Krishna Winston. New York: Pantheon, 1986.

Evans, E. P. *The Criminal Prosecution and Capital Punishment of Animals: The Lost History of Europe's Animal Trials*. Boston: Faber and Faber, 1987.

Etz, Ekkard and Andrea Sohn, eds. *Europameistershaft der Springreiter* (program of a European riding competition). Mannheim: J. Ph. Walter Druckerei, 1997.

Fantel, Max. "I once Admired Hitler." *The New York Times*. Sunday, April 30, 1995: E15.

Farbe-Vassas, Claudine. *The Singular Beast: Jews, Christians and the Pig*. Trans. Carol Volk. New York: Columbia UP, 1997.

Farnsworth, Wells E. "Reject Nazi Data?" *The Scientist*, vol. 3, #1 (Jan. 9, 1989): 10.

Ferry, Luc. "Les animaux ont-ils des droits?" *Le Point*, April 1, 1995 (#1176): 50-56.

_____. *The New Ecological Order*. Trans. Carol Volk. Chicago: U. of Chicago Press, 1995.

Fest, Joachim. *The Face of the Third Reich: Portraits of the Nazi Leadership*. Trans. Michael Bullock. New York: Pantheon, 1970.

Fink, Ida. *A Scrap of Time and Other Stories*. Trans. Madeline Levine and Francine Prose. New York: Pantheon, 1987.

Fischel, Werner. "Probleme der tierpsychologischen Grundlagenforschung." *Der Biologe*, vol. 13, #5-6 (1944): 65-75.

Fischer, Eugen."Die Rassenmerkmale des Menschen als Domestikationserscheinungen." In: *Zeitschrift für Morphologie und Anthropologie*, vol. 18 (1914): 479-524.

Fischer, H. " 'Draussen vom Walde. . .' Die Einstellung zum Walde im Wandel der Geschichte." *Mensch und Tier*, vol. 11 (1993-4): 119-136.

Fischer, Klaus P. *Nazi Germany: A New History*. New York: Continuum, 1995.

Fleischner, Eva, ed. *Auschwitz: Beginning of a New Era? Reflections on the Holocaust*. New York: Cathedral Church of St. John the Divine, 1977.

Fleming, Gerald. *Hitler and the Final Solution*. Berkeley: U. of California Press, 1982.

Foucault, Michel. *The History of Sexuality*, Vol. 1. Trans. Robert Hurley. New York: Penguin, 1978.

Frank, Anne. *The Diary of a Young Girl*. Ed. Otto H. Frank and Mirjam Pressler. Trans. Susan Massotty. New York: Bantam Books, 1995.

<192>

Freud, Sigmund. *Beyond the Pleasure Principle*. Trans. James Strachey. New York: Norton, 1961.

Friedlander, Henry. *The Origins of Nazi Genocide: From Euthanasia to the Final Solution*. Chapel Hill: U. of North Carolina Press, 1996.

_____. *Civilization and its Discontents*. Trans. James Strachey. New York: Norton, 1962.

Friedländer, Saul. *Reflections of Nazism: An Essay on Kitsch and Death*. New York: Harper and Row 1954.

Frisch, Karl von. *Erinnerungen eines Biologen*. Berlin: Springer, 1957.

Fromm, Bella. *Blood and Banquets: A Berlin Social Diary*. London: Geoffrey Bless, 1944.

Garbe, Heinrich. "Der Ganzheitsgedanke als Grundforderung der Rassenkundlichen Unterweisung." *Der Biologe*, vol. 7, #5 (1938): 145-152.

Gärtner, K. "Warum bin ich krank?: Bemerkungen zur evolutionsbiologischen Dimension des Krankseins." *Mensch und Tier*, vol.11 (1993-94): 169-186.

Gasman, Daniel. *The Scientific Origins of National Socialism*. New York: American Elservier, 1971.

Gay, Peter. *Weimar Culture: The Outsider as Insider*. New York: Harper and Row, 1968.

Giese. "Die Deutsche Tierschutzgesetzgebung." *Zeitschrift für Tierpsychologie*. vol. 1 (1937): 187-188.

Giese and Kahler. *Das deutsche Tierschutzrecht: Bestimmungen zum Schutz der Tiere*. Berlin: Duncker and Humbolt, 1944.

Giese, Christian and Beate Jung. "Zur Klinik der Hundekrankheiten in den 1930/40er Jahren." *Veterinärmedizin im Dritten Reich*. Ed. Johann Schäffer. Giessen: Deutsche Veterinärmedizinische Gesellschaft, 1998: 276-292.

Gilbert, Martin. *The Holocaust: A History of the Jews of Europe during the Second World War*. New York: Henry Holt, 1985.

Girard, René. *The Scapegoat*. Trans. Yvonne Freccero. Baltimore: Johns Hopkins UP, 1986.

_____. *Violence and the Sacred*. Trans. Patrick Gregory. Baltimore: Johns Hopkins UP, 1977.

Glaser, Hermann. *Spiesser-Ideologie: Von der Zerstörung des deutschen Geistes im 19. und 20. Jahrhundert*. Freiburg: Rombach, 1964.

Glickman, Stephen. "The Spotted Hyena From Aristotle to the Lion King: Reputation is Everything." *Social Research*, vol. 62, #3 (Fall 1995): 501-539.

Godwin, Joscelyn. *Arktos: The Myth of the Pole in Science, Symbolism, and Nazi Survival*. Kempton, IL: Adventures Unlimited Press, 1996.

<193>

Goldhagen, Daniel. *Hitler's Willing Executioners: Ordinary Germans and the Holocaust*. New York: Vintage, 1997.

Goldsmith, Oliver. *History of Animated Nature* (2 vols.). London: Smith and Elder/ T. Tegg and Son, 1838.

Goodrick-Clarke, Nicholas. *Black Sun: Aryan Cults, Esoteric Nazism, and the Politics of Identity*. New York: New York University Press, 2003.

_____. *Hitler's Priestess: Savitri Devi, the Hindu-Aryan Myth, and Neo-Nazism*. New York: New York University Press, 1998.

_____. *The Occult Roots of Nazism: Secret Aryan Cults and their Influence on Nazi Ideology*. New York: New York UP, 1992.

Gorer, Geoffrey. "The Pornography of Death." *Death: Current Perspectives*. Ed. Edwin S. Schneidman. Palo Alto, Ca: Mayfield, 1976: 71-76.

Göring, Hermann. *The Political Testament of Hermann Göring*. Trans. H. W. Blood Hermann. London: John Lang, 1939.

Gorny, Hein, Wolf Baudissin and D. Wilhelm Braun. *Ein Pferdebuch*. Munich: F. Bruckmann, 1938.

Gosse, Philip Henry. *The Romance of Natural History*. London: James Nisbet, 1860.

Grandin, Temple. "Euthanasia and Slaughter of Livestock." *Journal of the American Veterinary Medicine Association*," May 1, 1994 (Vol. 204, #9): 1354-1360.

_____. "Behavior of Slaughter Plant and Auction Employees Toward the Animals." *Anthrozoös*, Vol. 1, #4 (1988): 205-213.

_____. *Thinking in Pictures: And Other Reports from My Life with Autism*. New York: Vintage, 1995.

Grass, Günter. *Cat and Mouse*. Trans. Ralph Manheim. New York: Harcourt, Brace and World, 1961.

_____. *Dog Years*. Trans. Ralph Manheim. London: Secker and Warburg, 1965.

_____. *The Rat*. Trans. Ralph Manheim. New York: Harcourt, Brace and Janovich, 1987.

Green, Miranda. *Animals in Celtic Life and Myth*. London: Routledge, 1992.

Greit, Walter. "Aufbau und Aufgaben des Reichsbundes für Biologie." *Der Biologe*, vol. 8, #7-8 (1939): 233-241.

Grimm, Jacob and Wilhelm. *The Complete Fairy Tales of the Brothers Grimm*. Trans. Margaret Hunt and James Stern. New York: Pantheon, 1972.

Gröning, Gerd. See: Wolschke-Buhlman, Joachim and Gert Gröning.

Gruhier, Fabien. "Les Français en sont fous." *Le Nouvel Observateur*, January 16-22, 1997 (#1608): 4-9.

<194>

Gugenberger, Eduard and Roman Schwiedlenka. *Die Fäden der Nornen: Zur Mach der Mythen im politischen Bewegungen*. Vienna: Verlag für Gesellschaftskritik, 1993.

Günter, Hans F. K. *Rassenkunde des jüdischen Volkes*. Munich: J. F. Lehmann, 1930.

Haeckel, Ernst. *The Evolution of Man: A Popular Exposition of the Principal Points of Human Ontogeny and Phylogeny* (2 vols.). No translator given. Arkron: Werner, 1900.

_____. *The Riddle of the Universe at the Close of the Nineteenth Century*. Trans. Joseph McCabe. New York: MacMillan, 1900.

Ham, Jennifer and Matthew Senior, eds. *Animal Acts: Configuring the Human in Western History*. New York: Routledge, 1997.

Hampton, Bruce. *The Great American Wolf*. New York: Henry Holt, 1997.

Händel, Ursula. *Tierschutz*. Frankfurt am Main: Fischer, 1984.

Haraway, Donna. *Primate Visions: Gender, Race and Nature in the World of Modern Science*. New York: Routledge, 1989.

Finkielkraut, Alain. *The Wisdom of Love*. Trans. Kevin O'Neil and David Suchoff. Lincoln, NB: U. of Nebraska Press, 1997.

Haugwitz, Dietrich von. Personal letter to Boria Sax, in possession of the author. Jan. 23, 1995.

Heine, Heinrich. *The Poetry of Heinrich Heine*. Trans. Aaron Kramer. New York: Citadel, 1969.

Heinroth, Katharina. *Mit Faltern begann's: Mein Leben mit Tieren in Breslau, München und Berlin*. Munich: Kindler, 1979.

Herf, Jeffrey. *Reactionary Modernism: Technology, culture, and politics in Weimar and the Third Reich*. New York: Cambridge UP, 1993.

Hermand, Jost. *Grüne Utopien in Deutschland: Zur Geschichte der ökologischen Bewusstseins*. Frankfurt am Main: Fischer Taschenbuch, 1991.

_____. *A Hitler Youth in Poland: The Nazis' Program for Evacuating Children during World War II*. Trans. Margot Bettauer Dembo. Evanston, Il: Northwestern UP, 1997.

_____. *Old Dreams of a New Reich: Volkish Utopias and National Socialism*. Trans. Paul Levesque and Stefan Soldovieri. Bloomington: Indiana UP, 1992.

Herwig, Holger H. *The First World War: Germany and Austria-Hungary*. 1914-1918. New York: Arnold, 1997.

Herzog, Harold. "Human Morality and Animal Research: Confessions and Quandaries." In *The American Scholar*, vol. 62, #3 (1993): 337-349.

Hesse, Hermann. "Der Wolf." *Der Tierkreis: Das Tier in der Dichtung aller Völker und Zeiten*. Ed. Karl Soffel and Klabund. Berlin: Erich Reiss, 1919: 316-318.

<195>

Hilberg, Raul. *The Destruction of the European Jews*. New York: Holmes and Meier, 1985.

Hippler, Fritz, director. *Der ewige Jud*. Video. Chicago: International Historic Films, 1988 (released as film, 1941).

Hoelscher, Heinz. *Tierschutz und Strafrecht: Eine historische und rechtliche Studie unter Berücktsichtigung der ausländischen Gesetzgebung*. Heidelberg, unpublished dissertation, 1949.

Hoof, Jan A.R.A.M. and Joep A.B. Wensing. "Dominance and its behavioral measures in a captive wolf pack."*Man and Wolf: Advances, Issues, and Problems in Captive Wolf Research*. Ed. Harry Frank. Boston: Dr. W. Junk, 1987: 219-252.

Hubert, Henri and Marcel Mauss. *Sacrifice: Its Nature and Functions*. Trans. W. D. Halls. Chicago: U. of Chicago Press, 1964.

Ingold, Tim. "Humanity and Animality." *Companion Encyclopedia to Anthropology*. Ed. Ingold, Tim. New York: Routledge, 1994. 54-77.

Jaensch, E. R. "Der Hühnerhof als Forschungs- und Aufklärungsmittel in menschlichen Rassenfragen." *Zeitschrift für Tierpsychologie. Der Biologe*, vol. 2, # 1 (1939): 223-258.

Jentzsch, Rupert. "Der Weg zur Machtergreifung und Gleichschaltung. Tierärzlicher Beruf im Umbruch." Schäffer, Johann, ed. *Veterinärmedizin im Dritten Reich — Hochschule, Militär, Verwaltung, Praxis: Fünfte Tagung der DVG Fachgruppe "Geschichte der Veterinärmedizin"* (Summaries of lectures presented on November 14-15, 1997 at the Veterinary School in Hannover). Hannover: DVG, 1997: 24-43.

Jerusalem Bible. Ed. Alexander Jones. Garden City, NY, 1968.

Jünger, Ernst. *Auf den Marmorklippe*. Zurich: Eugen, ca. 1947.

_____. *The Storm of Steel: From the Diary of a German Storm Trooper on the Western Front*. Trans. Basil Creighton. New York: Howard Fertig, 1975.

Jütte, Daniel. "Tierschutz Und Nationalsozialismus: Eine Unheilvolle Verbindung." *Frankfurter Allgeimeine Zeitung* Dec. 12 2001: 3.

Kalikow, Theodora J. "Die ethologische Theorie von Konrad Lorenz: Erklärung und Ideologie, 1938 bis 1943." *Naturwissenschaft Technik und NS Ideologie: Beiträge zur Wissenschaft des Dritten Reichs*. Ed. Herbert Mehrtens and Steffen Richter. Frankfurt am Main: Suhrkamp, 1980.

Kamenetsky, Christa. *Children's Literature in Hitler's Germany: The Cultural Policy of National Socialism*. Athens, Ohio: Ohio UP, 1984.

Kaplan, Jerrrey. "Savitri Devi and the National Socialist Religion of Nature." *The Pomengranate*. #7 (February 1999): 4-12.

Kaschnitz, Marie Luise. *Der alte Garten: Ein Märchen*. Düsseldorf: Suhrkamp, 1975.

<196>

Kaye, Howard L. *The Social Meaning of Modern Biology: From Social Darwinism to Sociobiology*. New Haven: Yale UP, 1986.

Keen, Sam. *Faces of the Enemy: Reflections of the Hostile Imagination*. New York: Harper and Row, 1991.

Kellert, Stephen R. and Edward O. Wilson, eds. *The Biophilia Hypothesis*. Washington, D. C.: Island Press, 1993.

Kete, Kathleen. *The Beast in the Boudoir: Petkeeping in Nineteenth Century Paris*. Berkeley: U. of California Press, 1994.

Kipling, Rudyard. *The Two Jungle Books*. Garden City, NY: The Sun Dial Press, 1895.

Kisch, Guido. *Jews in Medieval Germany*. Chicago: U. Of Chicago Press, 1949.

Kittel, Gerhard. *Die historische Voraussetzung der jüdischen Rassenmischung*. Hamburg: Hanseatische Verlagsanstalt (Schriften des Reichsinstituts für Geschichte des neuen Deutschlands), 1939.

Klemperer, Victor. *I Will Bear Witness: A Diary of the Nazi Years, 1942-1945*. Trans. Martin Chalmers. New York: Random House, 2000.
_____. *LTI*. Leipzig: Reclam, 1975.

Klopfer, Peter. *An Introduction to Animal Behavior: Ethology's First Century*. Englewood Cliffs, NJ: Prentice-Hall, 1974.
_____."Konrad Lorenz and the National Socialists: On the Politics of Ethology." *International Journal of Comparative Psychology*, vol. 7, # 4 (1994): 202-208.

Koehler, Otto. *Die Aufgabe der Tierpsychologie (Schriften der Königsberger gelehrten Gesellschaft*, vol 18, # 6). Halle/Salle: Max Niemeyer Verlag, 1943.
_____. Review of *Der Geistige Aufsteig der Menschheit* by H. Weinert. *Der Biologe*, vol. 11, #1/2 (1942): 51.

Koenig, Otto, ed. *Wozu aber hat das Vieh diesen Schnabel? Briefe von Oscar Heinroth und Konrad Lorenz*. Munich: Piper, 1988.

Koonz, Claudia. *Mothers in the Fatherland: Women, the Family and Nazi Politics*. New York: St. Martin's Press, 1987.

Krogh, Christian von. "Immer Wieder: Abstammung oder Schöpfung." *Der Biologe*, vol. 9, #12 (1940): 414-417.

Kühl Stefan. "The Cooperation of German Racial Hygienists and American Eugenicists." *The Holocaust and History: The Known, the Unknown, the Disputed and the Reexamined*. Ed. Michael Berenbaum and Abraham J. Peck. Bloomington: Indiana UP, 1998: 134-152.

Kuhn, Thomas. *The Structure of Scientific Revolutions*. Chicago: U. of Chicago Press, 1970.

Kuhnert, Max. *Will We See Tomorrow? A German Cavalryman at War, 1939-1942*. London: Leo Cooper, 1993.

<197>

Langer, Lawrence L. *Preempting the Holocaust*. New Haven: Yale UP, 1999.

Laqueur, Walter. *The Terrible Secret: Suppression of the Truth about Hitler's "Final Solution*. Boston: Little, Brown, 1980.

Lehrner, Richard M. *Final Solutions: Biology, Prejudice and Genocide*. University Park, PA: Pennsylvania U. Press, 1992.

Lengeman, William. "The Great Pigeon Shoot." *Terra Nova*, vol. 2, #1 (1970): 27-39.

Leopold, Aldo. "The Conservation Ethic." Journal of Forestry, #3, (1933): 634-643.

_____. *A Sand County Almanac and Sketches Here and There*. (1949) New York: Oxford UP, 1968.

Lerner, Richard M. *Final Solutions: Biology, Prejudice and Genocide*. University Park, PA: Pennsylvania UP, 1992.

Levinas, Emmanuel. *Difficult Freedom: Essays on Judaism*. Trans. Seán Hand. London: Athlone, 1990.

Lewinsohn, Richard. *Animals, Men and Myths: An Informative and Entertaining History of Man and the Animals Around Him*. New York: Harper and Brothers, 1954.

Levi-Strauss, Claude. *The Savage Mind*. Trans. George Weidenfelt et al. New Haven: Yale UP, 1967.

Lockwood, Randal. "Dominance in Wolves: Useful Construct or Bad Habit?" *The Behavior and Ecology of Wolves*. Ed. E. Klinghammer. New York: Garland, 1979: 225-244.

_____ and Guy R. Hodge. "The Tangled Web of Animal Abuse: The Links between Cruelty to Animals and Human Violence." *Humane Society News*, Summer 1986: 1-6 (Reprinted by the Humane Society of the United States).

Löns, Hermann. *Im Walde und auf der Heide: Ein Buch vom deutschen Wald und deutschen Wild*. Berlin: Safari Verlag, ca. 1933.

_____. *Isengrins Irrgang: Tier und Jagdgeschichten herausgegeben für den Schulgebrauch*. Cologne: Hermann Schaffstein Verlag, ca. 1920.

Lopez, Barry Holstun. *Of Wolves and Men*. New York: Scribner's, 1978.

Lorenz, Konrad Z. *King Solomon's Ring: New Light on Animal Ways*. Trans. Marjorie Kerr. Wilson. New York: Thomas Y. Crowell, 1952.

_____. . "Die angeborener Formen möglicher Erfahrung." *Zeitschrift für Tierpsychologie* vol. 5, #2 (1942): 235-409.

_____. "Biologische Fragestellung in der Tierpsychologie." *Zeitschrift für Tierpsychologie*, vol. 1 (1937): 24-32.

_____. "Durch Domestikation verursachte Störungen arteigenen Verhaltens." *Zeitschrift für angewandte Psychologie und Charakterkunde*, 1940: 2-81.

<198>

_____. *Man Meets Dog*. Trans. Marjorie Kerr Wilson. Cambridge: The Riverside Press, 1955.

_____. "Nochmals: Systematik und Entwicklungsgedanke im Unterricht." *Der Biologe*, vol. 1, #2 (1940): 24-36.

_____. *On Aggression*. Trans. Marjorie Kerr Wilson. New York: Harvest, 1974.

_____. "Oskar Heinroth 70 Jahre." *Der Biologe*, vol. 2/3, #10 (1941): 45-47.

_____. *The Waning of Humaneness*. Trans. Robert Warren Kickert. Boston: Little, Brown, 1983.

_____ and Nikolaus Tinbergen. "Taxis und Instincthandlung in der Eirollbewegung der Graugans." Zeitschift der Tierpsychologie, vol. 2, (1938): 1-29.

Lotter, Konrad. "Nationale Ästhetik in Deutschland." *Widerspruch*, vol. 14, #26, (1955): 9-24.

Lydon, Jane. *Fantastic Dreaming: The Archaeology of an Aboriginal Mission*. New York: Altamira Press, 2009.

Mann, Thomas. "A Man and His Dog." In *Essays of Three Decades*. Trans. H. T. Lowe-Porter. New York: Modern Library, 1936: 438-499.

McNeil, William H. *The Pursuit of Power: Technology, Armed Force and Society since A. D. 1000*. Chicago: U. of Chicago Press, 1982.

Mech, David L. *The Wolf: The Ecology and Behavior of an Endangered Species*. Garden City, NY: American Museum of Natural History, 1970.

Maier, Charles. *The Unmasterable Past: History, Holocaust, and German National Identity*. Cambridge, Mass.: Harvard UP, 1988.

Meine, Curt. *Aldo Leopold: His Life and Work*. Madison: University of Wisconsin Press, 1987.

Melena, Elpis (pseud. Marie-Espérance von Schwarz). *Gemma oder Tugend und Laster*. Franz: Munich, 1890.

Menache, Sophie. "Dogs: God's Worst Enemy." *Society and Animals*, vol. 5, #1 (1997): 23-44.

Menninger, Karl A. "Totemic Aspects of Contemporary Attitudes toward Animals." *Psychoanalysis and Culture*. Ed. G. B. Wilbur and W. Muensterberger. New York: John Wiley and Sons, 1951: 42-74.

Meyer, Heinz. *Der Mensch und das Tier: Anthopologische und kultursoziologische Aspekte*. Munich: Heinz Moos, 1975.

Meyer, Helmut. "Response to Arluke and Sax." *Anthrozoös*, vol. VI, #2 (1993): 88-90.

Montagu, Ashley. *Man's Most Dangerous Myth: The Fallacy of Race*. Fourth Edition. New York: World Publishing, 1964.

Montaigne, Michel de. *The Essays of Montaigne*. Trans. E. J. Trechmann. New York: Oxford UP, circa 1960.

<199>

Moran, Greg. "Dispensing with 'the Fashionable Fallacy of Dispensing with Description in the Study of Wolf Social Relationships."*Man and Wolf: Advances, Issues, and Problems in Captive Wolf Research*. Ed. Harry Frank. Boston: Dr. W. Junk, 1987: 205-218.

Mosse, George L. *The Crisis of German Ideology: Intellectual Origins of the Third Reich*. New York: Grosset and Dunlap, 1964.

_____. *Toward the Final Solution: A History of European Racism*. New York: Howard Fertig, 1978.

Mowat Farley. *Never Cry Wolf*. Boston: Little, Brown, 1963.

Müller, Inge. *Wenn ich schon sterben muss*. Berlin (East): Aufbau, 1985.

Murphy, G. Ronald. *The Saxon Savior: The Germanic Transformation of the Gospel in the Ninth-Century Heliand*. New York: Oxford UP, 1989.

Newhook, J. C. and D. K. Blackmore. "Electoencephalic studies of stunning and slaughter of sheep and calves." *Meat Science*, #6: 221-233, 295-301.

Newman, Stuart A. "Carnal Boundaries: The Comingling of Flesh in Theory and Practice." *Reinventing Biology*. Lynde Birke and Ruth Hubbard, eds. Bloomington: Indiana UP, 1995: 191-227.

Nietzsche, Friedrich. *The Birth of Tragedy and The Genealogy of Morals*. Trans. Francis Golffing. New York: Doubleday, 1956.

_____. *The Will to Power*. Trans. Walter Kaufmann and R. J. Hollingdale. New York: Vintage, 1968.

Nolte, Ernst, et al. *Forever in the Shadow of Hitler: Original Documents of the "Historikersteit."* Trans. James Knowlton and Truett Gates. Atlantic Highlands, NJ: Humanities Press, 1993.

Norman, Hippolyt, ed. *Kriegeskomerad Pferd*. Berlin: Wilhelm Limpert, 1938.

Noske, Barbara. *Humans and Other Animals: Beyond the Boundaries of Anthropology*. London: Pluto Press, 1989.

Novick, Peter. *The Holocaust in American Life*. Boston: Houghton Mifflin, 1999.

Otten, Paul. "Wie behandle ich die Lebensgemeinsschaft 'Der Wald' in meinem lebenskundlichen Unterricht." *Der Biologe*, vol. 12, #3 (1943): 73-7.

Paley, William. *Natural Theology*. New York: American Tract Society, circa 1830.

Parker, John. *The Killing Factory: The Top Secret Worlds of Germ and Chemical Warfare*. London: Smith Gryphon Publishers, 1996.

Patterson, Orlando. *Rituals of Blood: Consequences of Slavery in Two American Centuries*. Washington, D.C.: Civitas Counterpoint, 1998.

Petitjean, Gérard. "Les Français entre chiens et loups" (interview with Jean-François Terassse). *Le Nouvel Observateur*, January 16-22, 1997 (#1608): 12-13.

<200>

Peukert, Detlev J. K. *Inside Nazi Germany: Conformity, Opposition, and Racism in Everyday Life*. Trans. Richard Deveson. New Haven: Yale UP, 1987.

Pick, Daniel. *War Machine: The Rationalization of Slaughter in the Modern Age*. New Haven: Yale UP, 1991.

Piekalkiewicz, Janusz. *The Calvary of World War II*. London: Orbis Publishing, 1979.

Pirinçc, Akif. *Felidae*. No translator given. New York: Villard, 1993.

Pliny the Elder. *Natural History: A Selection*. Trans. John F. Healy. New York: Penguin, 1991.

Plochmann, Richard. "Mensch und Wald." *Rettet den Wald*. Ed. Horst Stein. Bonn: Kindler, circa 1975: 157-197.

Prawdin, Michael (pseud. Michael Charol). *Tschingis-Chan und seine Erbe*. Stuttgart: Deutsche Verlags-Anstalt, 1957.

Proctor, Robert N. *The Nazi War on Cancer*. Princeton: Princeton UP, 1999

_____. *Racial Hygiene: Medicine Under the Nazis*. Cambridge: Harvard UP, 1988.

Rammner, Walter. *Das Tier in der Landschaft: Die deutsche Tierwelt in ihren Lebensräumen*. Leipzig: Bibliographisches Institut, 1936.

Reche, Otto. "Natur- und Kulturgeschichten des Menschen in ihren gegenseitigen Beziehungen." *Volk und Rasse*, vol. 3, # 2 (1928), 65-81.

Regan, Tom. *The Case for Animal Rights*. Berkeley: University of California Press, 1983.

Remak, Joachim, ed. *The Nazi Years: A Documentary History*. Englewood Cliffs, NJ: Prentice Hall, 1969.

Riefenstahl, Leni. *Triumph of the Will*. Video. Los Angeles: Janus Productions: 1986 (released as film, 1934).

Ritvo, Harriet. *The Animal Estate: The English and Other Creatures in the Victorian Age*. Cambridge, Mass.: Harvard UP, 1987.

Rosenbaum, Alan S., ed. *Is the Holocaust Unique? Perspectives on Comparative Genocide*. Boulder: Westview Press, 1996.

Rossner, Ferdinand. "Systematik Und Entwicklungsgedanke Im Unterricht." *Der Biologe* 8.2 (1940): 366-72.

Rosenfeld, Alvin. *Imagining Hitler*. Bloomington: Indiana U P, 1985.

Rosenberg, Alfred. *Der Mythos des 20. Jahrhunderts*. Munich: Hoheneichen Verlag, 1935.

Rossner, Ferdinand. "Systematik und Entwicklungsgedanke im Unterricht." *Der Biologe*, vol. 8, #2, (1940): 366-372.

Russell III, Edmund P. "Speaking of annihilation': Mobilizing for war against human and insect enemies." *The Journal of American History*, vol. 82, #4: 1505-1524.

<201>

Sachs, Hans. *Hans Sachsens Ausgewählte Werke* (2 vols.). Leipzig: Insel Verlag, 1945.

Salisbury, Joyce E. *The Beast Within: Animals in the Middle Ages.* New York: Routledge, 1994.

Salten, Felix. *Bambi: A Life in the Woods.* Trans. Whittaker Chambers. New York: Simon and Schuster, 1928.

Sauerbruch, Ferdinand. *Das War Mein Leben.* Bad Wörishofen: Kindler and Schiermeyer, 1951.

Sax, Boria. "Are there Predators in Paradise?" *Terra Nova*, vol. 2, #1 (1997): 59-68.

_____. "The Cosmic Spider and Her World-Wide Web: Sacred and Symbolic Animals in the Age of Change." *A Cultural History of Animals in the Modern Age.* Ed. Malamud, Randy. New York: Berg, 2007. 27-48.

_____. *The Frog King: On Legends, Fables, Fairy Tales and Anecdotes of Animals.* New York: Pace UP, 1990.

_____. "The Holocaust as Blood Sacrifice." *Anthrozoös*, vol. 13, #1 (2000)

_____. "Holocaust Images and Other Powerful Ambiguities in the Debates on Animal Experimentation." *Anthrozoös*, vol. 6, #2 (1993): 6-31.

_____. *The Parliament of Animals: Anecdotes and Legends from Books of Natural History, 1775-1900.* New York: Pace UP, 1992.

_____. *The Serpent and the Swan: Animal Brides in Literature and Folkore.* Dorrence, Ohio: McDonald and Woodward, 1998.

Sax, Boria, and Peter Klopfer. "Jacob Von Uexküll and the Anticipation of Sociobiology." *Semiotica* 134-135 (2001): 767-78.

Schäffer, Johann, ed. *Veterinärmedizin im Dritten Reich — Hochschule, Militär, Verwaltung, Praxis: Fünfte Tagung der DVG Fachgruppe "Geschichte der Veterinärmedizin"* (Summaries of lectures presented on November 14-15, 1997 at the Veterinary School in Hannover). Hannover: DVG, 1997.

_____. *Veterinärmedizin im Dritten Reich.* Giessen: DVG, 1998.

Schama, Simon. *Landscape and Memory.* New York: Knopf, 1995

Schejelderup-Ebbe, Thorleif. "Beiträge zur Sozialpsychologie des Haushuhns." *Zeitschrift für Psychologie*, #88 (1922): 225-252.

Schenkel, Rudolf. *Ausdrucks-Studien an Wölfen: Gefangenschafts-Beobachtungen.* Leiden: E. J. Brill, 1947.

_____. "Submission: Its Features and Function in the Wolf and Dog." *The American Zoologist*, #7 (1967): 319-329.

Schimanski, Michael. *Die Tierärztliche Hochschule Hannover im Nationalsozialismus* (doctoral dissertation). Hannover: Tierärztliche Hochschule Hannover, 1997.

<202>

Schochet, Elijah Judah. *Animal Life in Jewish Tradition: Attitudes and Relationships*. New York: Ktav, 1984.

Schoenbaum, David. *Hitler's Social Revolution: Class and Status in Nazi Germany 1933-1939*. New York: W. W. Norton, 1980.

Schoenfeld, Gabriel. "Death Camps as Kitsch." *The New York Times*, March 18, 1999, A25.

Schoenichen, Walter. *Biologie der Landschaft*. Berlin: J. Neumann, 1939.

Schotmeijer, Marian. *Animal Victims in Modern Fiction*. Toronto: University of Toronto Press, 1993.

Schwiechow, Walter von. "Schweinemast auf landeigener Futtergrundlage: Ein Beitrag zur Frage der Ernährungsselbstversorgung." *Deutsche Agrarpolitik*. July 1932: 52-56.

Serpell, James. *In the Company of Animals*. New York: Basil Blackwell, 1986.

Seton-Thompson, Ernest. "Lobo, the King of Currumpaw." *Wild Animals I Have Known*. New York: Charles Scribners, 1900: 15-56.

Shakespeare, William. *The Merchant of Venice*. Ed. Barbara A. Mowat and Paul Westine. The New Folger Library. New York: Washington Square Press, 1992.

Shell, Marc. *The Children of the Earth: Literature, Politics and Nationhood*. New York: Oxford UP, 1993.

Shirer, William L. *Berlin Diary: The Journal of a Foreign Correspondent 1934-41*. New York: Knopf, 1941.

Sinclair, Upton. *The Jungle*. New York: Penguin, 1985.

Singer, Isaac Bashevis. *Love and Exile: An Autobiographical Trilogy*. New York: Farrar, Straus and Giroux, 1997.

Singer, Peter, ed. *In Defense of Animals*. New York: Basil Blackwell, 1985.

Sklar, Dusty. *The Nazis and the Occult*. New York: Dorset Press, 1977.

Smellie, William. *The Philosophy of Natural History*. Ed. John Ware. Boston: Hilliard, Gray, 1836.

Smelser, Ronald, Enrico Syring and Rainer Zitelmann, eds. *Die Braune Elite II: 21 weitere biographische Skizzen*. Darmstadt: Wissenschaftliche Buchgesellschaft, 1993: 231-242.

Speer, Albert. *Spandau: The Secret Diaries*. Trans. Richard and Clara Winston. New York: Macmillan, 1976.

Spengler, Oswald. *Man and Technics: A Contribution to a Philosophy of Life*. Trans. Charles Francis Atkinson. New York: Knopf, 1963

Spiegelman, Art. *Maus: A Survivor's Tale* (2 vols.). New York: Pantheon, 1991.

Steiner, George. *In Bluebeard's Castle*. New Haven: Yale UP, 1971.

Steinhart, Peter. 1995. *The Company of Wolves*. New York: Knopf, 1995.

<203>

Stephanitz, Max von. *The German Shepherd Dog in Word and Picture*. Trans. and revised J. Schwabacher. Jena: Anton Kämpfe, 1923.

Stern, Fritz. *The Politics of Cultural Despair: a study in the rise of the German Ideology*. Berkeley: University of California Press, 1974.

Stevens, Phillip. "Satanism: Where are the Folklorists?" *New York Folklore*, vol. 15, #1-2 (1989): 1-22.

Streicher, Julius, ed. "Jüdischer Mordplan: gegen die nichtjüdische Menschheit aufgedeckt." Special issue of *Der Stürmer*, May 1934.

Tacitus. *The Agricola and the Germania*. Trans. H. Mattingly and S. A. Handford. New York: Penguin, 1986.

Todorov, Tzvetan. *Facing the Extreme: Moral Life in the Concentration Camps*. Trans. Arthur Denner and Abigail Pollak. New York: Henry Holt, 1996.

Thomas, Keith. *Man and the Natural World: A History of the Modern Sensibility*. New York: Pantheon, 1983.

Tinbergen, Niko. "Die Überspringbewegung." *Zeitschrift für Tierpsychologie*, vol. 4, #1 (1940-1941): 1-140.

_____, *Klieuw*. Leiden: Boucher, 1948.

_____, B. J. D. Meeuse, L. K. Boerema and W. W. Varossieau. "Die Balz des Samtfalters, Eumenis (=Satyrus) semele (L.)." *Zeitschrift für Tierpsychologie*, vol. 5 (1943): 182-226.

Scheidt, Walter. *Kulturbiolobie: Vorlesungen für Studierende aller Wissensgebiete*. Jena: Verlag von Gustav Fischer, 1930.

Schreckenberg, Heinz. *The Jews in Christian Art: An Illustrated History*. New York: Continuum, 1996.

Shandley, Robert, ed. *Unwilling Germans?* St. Paul: University of Minnesota Press, 1998.

Sicher, Efraim. "The Burden of Memory: The Writings of the Post-Holocaust Generation." *Breaking Crystal: Writing and Memory after Auschwitz*. Ed. Efraim Sicher. Chicago: University of Illinois Press, 1998: 19-90.

Stengel (Lothar Stengel-von Rutkowski). "Sittliche Entartung und Geburtenschwund." *Der Biologe*, vol. 7, # 5, (1938): 164-5.

Thurston, Mary Elizabeth. *The Lost History of the Canine Race: Our 15,000-Year Love Affair with Dogs*. New York: Avon Books, 1996.

Tröhler, Ulrich and Andreas-Holger Maehle. "Anti-Vivisection in Nineteenth-century Germany and Switzerland: Motives and Methods." *Vivisection in Historical Perspective*. Ed. Nicolaas Rupke. New York: Croom Helm, 1987: 149-187.

Tuan, Yi-Fu. *Dominance and Affection: The Making of Pets*. New Haven: Yale UP, 1984.

Uekoetter, Frank. *The Green and the Brown: A History of Conservation in Nazi Germany*. New York: Cambridge University Press, 2006.

<204>

Vereinigte Fleisch und Wurstwerke Dresden. *50 Jahre Fleisch und Wurstwerke Dresden*. Dresden: Landesdruckerei Dresden, 1966.

Victor, George. *Hitler: The Pathology of Evil*. Washington, D.C.: Brassey's. 1998.

Wade, Nicholas. "Doctors Question Use of Nazis' Medical Atlas." *The New York Times*, Nov. 26, 1996: C1 and C10.

Wagner, Richard. "Heldentun und Christenheit." *Gesammelte Schriften und Dichtungen* von Richard Wagner. Second edition, vol. 10. Leipzig: C. W. Fritsch, 1888: 276-285.

_____. "Offenes Schreiben an Herrn Ernst von Weber." *Gesammelte Schriften und Dichtungen* von Richard Wagner. Second edition. Vol. 10. Leipzig: C. W. Fritsch, 1888: 194-210.

Waite, Robert G. L. *The Psychopathic God Adolf Hitler*. New York: Basic Books, 1977.

Warnbrunn, Werner. *The Dutch under German Occupation 1940-45*. Stanford, CA: Stanford UP, 1963.

Weber, Hermann. "Organismus und Umwelt." *Der Biologe*, vol. 11, #3/4, (1940): 57-68.

_____. "Der Umweltbegriff der Biologie und seine Anwendung." *Der Biologe*, vol. 8, #7/8, (1939): 245-61.

Weil, Jiri. *Life With a Star*. New York: Farrar, Straus and Giroux, 1989.

Weinreich, Max. *Hitler's Professors: The Part of Scholarship in Germany's Crimes Against the Jewish People*. New York: Yiddish Scientific Institute, 1946.

Weinstein, Fred. *The Dynamics of Nazism: Leadership, Ideology and the Holocaust*. New York: Academic Press, 1980.

Wiesel, Elie. *From the Kingdom of Memory : Reminiscences*. New York: Schocken Books, 1990.

Welfeld, Irving. *Why Kosher? An Anthology of Answers*. Northvale, NJ: Jason Aronson, 1996.

Wernicke, Rudolf K. H. "Die Formierung des Veterinärwesens im besetzten Polen 1939 bis 1945." *Veterinärmedizin im Dritten Reich*. Ed. Johann Schäffer. Giessen: Deutsche Veterinärmedizinische Gesellschaft, 1998: 214-261.

White, Lynn Jr. *Machina Ex Deo: Essays in the Dynamism of Western Culture*. Cambridge: MIT Press, 1968.

White, Matthew. *The Great Big Book of Horrible Things: The Definitive Account of History's 100 Worst Atrocities*. New York: W. W. Norton, 2012.

Williams, Joy. "The Inhumanity of the Animal People: Do Creatures have the Same Rights that We Do?" *Harper's*. August 1997 (vol. 295, #1767): 60-67.

<205>

Wilson, Edward O. "Biophilia and the Conservation Ethic." *The Biophilia Hypothesis*. Ed. Stephen R. Kellert and Edward O. Wilson. Washington, DC: Island Press, 1993.

Wipperman, Wolfgang. "Der Hund als Propaganda und Terrorinstrument im Nationalsozialismus." *Veterinärmedizin im Dritten Reich*. Ed. Johann Schäffer. Giessen: DVG, 1998: 193-206.

Wolfschmidt, Mattias. "Der Einfluss tierzücherischer Gedanken auf die Entwicklung der Eugenik — Ein Werkstattbericht." *Veterinärmedizin im Dritten Reich — Hochschule, Militär, Verwaltung, Praxis: Fünfte Tagung der DVG Fachgruppe "Geschichte der Veterinärmedizin."* Ed. Johann Schäffer. Hannover: DVG, 1997: 17-18.

Wolschke-Buhlman, Joachim. "The Wild Garden and the 'Nature Garden' — aspects of the garden ideology of William Robinson and Willy Lange." *Journal of Garden History*, Vol. 12, #3 (1992): 182-206.

Wolschke-Buhlman, Joachim and Gert Gröning. "From Open-Miindedness to Naturalism: Garden Design and Ideology in Germany During the Early 20th Century." *Plant-People Relationships: Setting Research Priorities*. Ed. Joel Flager. New York: Food Products Press, 1994: 133-51.

Worster, Donald. *Nature's Economy: A History of Ecological Ideas*. Second Edition. New York: Cambridge UP, 1995.

Wüst, W. "Die Arbeit des Ahnenerbes." *Der Biologe*, vol. 8, #7-8 (1939): 241-245.

Zamiatin, Eugene. *We*. Trans. G. Zilboorg. New York: E. P. Dutton, 1952.

Zinsser, Hans. *Rats, Lice and History*. New York: Macmillan, 1963.

<206>

INDEX

<207>

<208>

<209>

<210>

<211>

tradition 9, 18, 20, 26; in
romanticism 27-29; Nazi
perspective on 11, 23, 30, 31-
33, 64, 66, 94, 96, 99, 105-
107, 109, 157
Never Cry Wolf (Mowat) 70
Newkirk, Ingrid 152-153
Nietzsche, Friedrich 19-21, 22, 83,
116
Noah (biblical) 37, 129, 141
Noske, Barbara 8

O

On Aggression (Lorenz) 80
ontologies 168-170; see also
analogism, animism,
naturalism, totemism,
The Origin of Species (Darwin) 28,
38, 40; see also Darwin
Orwell, George 151
oxen 138, 143

P

Padua, Paul Mathias 53
Paganism 15-21, 26-28, 30, 59,
147; compared to Judeo-
-Christian tradition 16-21,
26-28; Nazi revival of 30, 59
Paley, William 18, 96,
Patterson, Orlando 141
Peiner, Werner 83, 86
Pernkopf, Eduard 92-93
Pets 8, 11, 54, 72, 74, 87, 101, 103,
108-110, 111, 155, 171
Peukert, Detlev 112
pigs 9, 54-61, 73, 137, 140, 143-
145, 148, 150, 151, 165;
Jewish attitudes toward 54-
56, 143-144; Christian
attitudes toward 54-55, 57;
Darre's theory about 56-61
Pirincci, Akif 150
Pliny the Elder 8, 26

Prawdin, Michael 147-148
Predators xiii, 11, 15-24, 62, 64-
70, 72, 83, 99, 118, 125, 129,
150, 151, 152, 157, 158; in
Christianity 17-19;
demonization of 18-19;
glorification of 17, 19-23; in
Judaism 15-16; in paganism
16-21; Nazi preference for
23-24, 64-67, 70, 72, 83, 99,
118
Proctor, Robert 23, 92

R

rabbits 23, 75, 103, 107, 152, 156
Rammner, Walter 114
The Rat (Grass) 150
rats 6, 9, 22, 23, 149-150;
compared to Jews 149;
compared to humanity 149-
150
Rathenau, Walter 59, 61
Rauschning, Hermann 22
The Riddle of the Universe
(Haeckel) 40
Riefenstahl, Leni 91
Rockwell, George Lincoln 173
Röhm, Ernst 76
Romanticism 27-32, 155, 159, 162,
163; in Germany 27; Nazism
and 29-32, 155, 159, 162; in
the nineteenth century 27,
162, 163
Roosevelt, Theodore 19, 106 ,
Rosenberg, Alfred 74, 142
Rosenfeld, Alvin 5
Rossner, Ferdinand 31
Russell, Bertrand 92

<212>

S

sacrifice 26, 46, 47, 51, 53, 54, 129, 141-150, 159, 160, 162-163; Holocaust as 145-148, 162-163; defined 141-143
Saint Paul 131
Saint Peter 46
Santeria 132
Sauerbruch, Ferdinand 78
Sax, Boria xiii-xiv, xvii, 18, 23, 37, 38, 39, 151, 154, 159
Scapegoat 9, 141-143
Scheidt, Walter 42
Schemm, Hans 95
Schenkel, Rudolph 67-68, 80-81
Schoenbaum, David 58, 59, 134, 160
Schoenichen, Walter 69, 98, 105
Schrader, Gerhard 103
Der Sweinemord (Darré) 59-60
science xiii, xiv, 27, 28, 40, 41-42, 62, 91, 92, 93, 94, 95, 97, 115, 116, 121, 122, 124, 147; in Nazi Germany xiv, 91, 92, 93, 94, 95, 97, 115, 116, 166; objectivity of 91-92, 93; see also evolution
Seifert, Alwin 99
Serpell, James 100, 108, 139
Seton, Ernest Thompson 64
Shakespeare, William 71
sheep 7, 46-47, 48, 55, 57, 66, 67, 77, 78, 129, 134, 137, 138, 140, 143, 158, 165; see also lamb
Shirer, William 100
shochets 131
Sinclair, Upton 139
Singer, Isaac Bashevis 3, 130, 152
slaughter viv, 10, 27, 46, 48, 54, 55-57, 58, 59-61, 98, 105, 107, 108, 129-140, 141, 147-148, 151, 152, 153, 154; in

antiquity 155, 157; kosher 48, 49, 50-51, 52, 59, 108, 131-132, 144, 146; Nazi laws on 100, 104, 108, 169, 171
slavery 9, 48, 156
Smellie, William 18
Society for Bird Protection 108
Solomon (biblical) 138
Song of the Nibelungs 161
Speer, Albert 161
Spengler, Oswald 21-22, 43, 117
Spiegelman, Art 160
SS (Schutzstaffel) 10, 23, 43, 66, 67, 76, 77, 84, 92, 107, 110, 111, 121, 147, 157, 158, 159
stag 84
Stalin, Joseph xiv, 32, 97, 133, 142, 151, 156, 162
Steiner, George 152
Stephanitz, Max von 73-74, 79
The Storm of Steel (Jünger) 29
Streicher, Julius 49-53, 119, 142
Stuck, Franz von 52-53
Der Stürmer 52-53
"Submission: Its Features in Wolf and Dog" (Schenkel) 81

T

Tacitus 26
Talmud 37, 50, 52, 65
"Thinking like a Mountain" (Leopold)
Thomas, Keith 9, 155
Thorak, Josef 84, 85
Das Tier in der Landschaft (Rammner) 114
The Tin Drum (Grass) 6
totemism 164-172, 175, 177
Tinbergen, Nikolaus 114-115, 121-122, 124
transportation of animals, law on 104-105, 137, 170

<213>

<214>

ABOUT THIS BOOK

The body text of this book is set in Aldine type, a face inspired by the designs of the great humanist printer and publisher Aldus Manutius.

Headlines are set in Futura, a Bauhaus-influenced type that came to be one of the most popular sans-serif faces of the 20th century. Its geometric emphasis and even width of stroke takes its form from classic Greek column lettering, but looks completely modern because of its strict use of geometric forms (circles and isosceles triangles). The hot metal face was designed in 1927 for the Bauer foundry in Germany.

<215>

Made in the USA
San Bernardino, CA
23 March 2014